PINA BAUSCH'S DANCE THEATRE

Edinburgh Critical Studies in Modernism, Drama and Performance

Edinburgh Critical Studies in Modernism, Drama and Performance addresses the somewhat neglected areas of drama and performance within Modernist Studies, and is in many ways conceived of in response to a number of intellectual and institutional shifts that have taken place over the past 10 to 15 years. On the one hand, Modernist Studies has moved considerably from the strictly literary approaches, to encompass engagements with the everyday, the body, the political, while also extending its geopolitical reach. On the other hand, Performance Studies itself could be seen as acquiring a distinct epistemology and methodology within Modernism. Indeed, the autonomy of Performance as a distinct aesthetic trope is sometimes located at the exciting intersections between genres and media; intersections that this series sets out to explore within the more general modernist concerns about the relationships between textuality, visuality and embodiment. This series locates the theoretical, methodological and pedagogical contours of Performance Studies within the formal, aesthetic and political concerns of Modernism. It claims that the 'linguistic turn' within Modernism is always shadowed and accompanied by an equally formative 'performance / performative turn'. It aims to highlight the significance of performance for the general study of modernism by bringing together two fields of scholarly research which have traditionally remained quite distinct – performance / theatre studies and Modernism. In turn this emphasis will inflect and help to re-conceptualise our understanding of both performance studies and modernist studies. And in doing so, the series will initiate new conversations between scholars, theatre and performance artists and students.

www.edinburghuniversitypress.com/series/ecsmdp

PINA BAUSCH'S DANCE THEATRE
Tracing the Evolution of *Tanztheater*

Lucy Weir

EDINBURGH
University Press

Edinburgh University Press is one of the leading university presses in the UK. We publish academic books and journals in our selected subject areas across the humanities and social sciences, combining cutting-edge scholarship with high editorial and production values to produce academic works of lasting importance. For more information visit our website: edinburghuniversitypress.com

© Lucy Weir, 2018

Edinburgh University Press Ltd
The Tun – Holyrood Road
12(2f) Jackson's Entry
Edinburgh EH8 8PJ

Typeset in Sabon and Gill Sans by
Servis Filmsetting Ltd, Stockport, Cheshire,
and printed and bound in Great Britain.

A CIP record for this book is available from the British Library

ISBN 978 1 4744 3683 0 (hardback)
ISBN 978 1 4744 3685 4 (webready PDF)
ISBN 978 1 4744 3686 1 (epub)

The right of Lucy Weir to be identified as the author of this work has been asserted in accordance with the Copyright, Designs and Patents Act 1988, and the Copyright and Related Rights Regulations 2003 (SI No. 2498).

CONTENTS

LIST OF ILLUSTRATIONS

CHRONOLOGY OF CHOREOGRAPHIES

1980 (1980)
Bandoneon (1981)
Walzer [Waltzes] (1982)
Nelken [Carnations] (1982)
Auf dem Gebirge hat man ein Geschrei Gehört [On the Mountain a Cry Was Heard] (1984)
Two Cigarettes in the Dark (1985)
Viktor (1986) Coproduction with Teatro Argentina, Rome
Ahnen [Ancestors] (1987)
Palermo Palermo (1989) Coproduction with Teatro Biondo, Palermo and Andres Neumann International
Die Klage der Kaiserin [The Lament of the Empress] (1990) A film by Pina Bausch
Tanzabend II [Dance Party II] (1991) Coproduction with Festival de Otoño, Madrid
Das Stück mit dem Schiff [The Piece with the Ship] (1993)
Ein Trauerspiel [A Tragedy] (1994) Coproduction with the Wiener Festwochen
Danzón (1995)
Nur Du [Only You] (1996) Coproduction with the University of California, Los Angeles; Arizona State University; University of California, Berkeley; University of Texas at Austin; Darlene Neel Presentations; Rena Shagan Associates; The Music Center
Der Fensterputzer [The Window Cleaner] (1997) Coproduction with the Hong Kong Arts Festival Society and the Goethe-Institut Hong Kong
Masurca Fogo [Fiery Mazurka] (1998) Coproduction with EXPO 98 Lisbon and the Goethe-Institut Lisbon
O Dido (1999) Coproduction with Teatro Argentina, Rome and Andres Neumann International
Kontakthof [with ladies and gentlemen over 65] (2000)
Wiesenland [Meadowland] (2000) Coproduction with the Goethe-Institut Budapest and Théâtre de la Ville, Paris
Água [Water] (2001) Coproduction with the Goethe-Institut São Paolo and Emilio Kalil
Für die Kinder von Gestern, Heute und Morgen [For the Children of Yesterday, Today and Tomorrow] (2002)
Nefés [Breath] (2003) Coproduction with the International Istanbul Theatre Festival and the Istanbul Foundation of Culture and Arts
Ten Chi [Heaven and Earth] (2004) Coproduction with Saitama Prefecture, Saitama Arts Foundation, Japan, and Nippon Cultural Center
Rough Cut (2005) Coproduction with LG Arts Center and the Goethe-Institut Seoul
Vollmond [Full Moon] (2006)

Bamboo Blues (2007) Coproduction with the Goethe-Institut India
'*Sweet Mambo*' (2008)
Kontakthof [with teenagers aged over 14] (2008)
'... *como el musguito en la piedra, ay si, si, si* ...' [Like moss on a stone]
    (2009) Coproduction with the Festival Internacional de Teatro Santiago a
    Mil and the Goethe-Institut Chile

ACKNOWLEDGEMENTS

This volume takes as its starting point research initially conducted during my doctoral studies at the University of Glasgow, under the expert supervision of Deborah Lewer and Anselm Heinrich. I owe them my deepest gratitude for their guidance, advice and unwavering support throughout my PhD and beyond – they have been my *Doktorvater* and *Doktormutter* in the truest sense.

I have been extremely fortunate in the institutional support I received from the University of Glasgow and the Institute for the Advanced Studies in the Humanities (IASH) at the University of Edinburgh. The first version of this manuscript was drafted at IASH under the mentorship of Professor Olga Taxidou. My time here was invaluable, as Dr Peta Freestone and Donald Ferguson, along with my wonderful colleagues, made the place feel like a second home, and provided a supportive environment in which to explore the widening boundaries of this project. My colleagues and students in History of Art at the University of Edinburgh also played an important role in the final stages of compiling this monograph, which benefitted greatly from discussions within and outside the classroom. I am particularly grateful for the combined efforts of Ersev Ersoy, Jackie Jones and Kirsty Woods at Edinburgh University Press for their generosity of time, assistance and advice, and for Olga Taxidou's support and belief in seeing this project through from the very beginning.

My archival research in Germany and the USA was made possible by funding from the Deutscher Akademischer Austausch Dienst and the College of Arts at the University of Glasgow. I must acknowledge the staff members of the Akademie der Künste (Berlin), the Deutsches Tanzarchiv (Cologne), the Jerome Robbins Performing Arts Division of the New York Public Library, and, in particular, Gabriele Ruiz at the Leipzig Tanzarchiv, for their assistance and efficiency in aiding my search for primary source material. I am especially grateful to Robert Sturm for his generosity in granting me access to the video archive of Tanztheater Wuppertal Pina Bausch, as well as for proving such a welcoming and kind host in Wuppertal.

For their assistance with translation matters, I am greatly indebted to Gerry Campbell and Emmanuelle Guibé, though I must extend particular thanks to

Sarah Stier, who responded to my enquiries on esoteric subject matter with good humour and, on numerous occasions, managed to turn the translation process into an enjoyable experience. Moral support (often in the form of red wine) and proofreading throughout the writing process was generously provided by Jessica Jane Howard, Allan Madden and Samantha Sherry.

The heart of this project lies not in academic territory but in dance, and accordingly I wish to thank my dance teachers and mentors – in particular, David Chase, Natasha Gerson and Ruth Mills – for sharing with me their wisdom as performers and technical experts, and instilling in me a deep love and eternal admiration for the practice.

Finally, special gratitude is reserved for Michael Rodgers, whose seemingly endless patience, support and love have sustained me throughout the writing process.

This volume is dedicated to my parents, Philip and Mary-Rose Weir,
for a lifetime of encouragement and love.
Without them, none of this would have been possible.

INTRODUCTION

Modern dance is a palimpsest. Its continual evolution is determined by a cyclical revision of established and institutionalised techniques and aesthetics: early avant-gardists such as Isadora Duncan and Rudolf Laban broke from the rigid, academic structure of classical ballet, Mary Wigman and Martha Graham moved away from 'free' dance and improvisation by codifying modern dance vocabularies, while postmodernists such as the artists of the Judson Dance Theatre rejected outright the formalism of rigorous technique. Yet few choreographers have made so decisive an impact on the choreographic landscape as Pina Bausch. Throughout the course of a life that bore witness to the postwar reconstruction of Europe and the division and subsequent reunification of Germany, Bausch revolutionised the language of dance, evolving a creative methodology that departed from prevailing standards and aesthetics. She ultimately rejected the formalism of existing dance styles in favour of a panchronic theatrical spectacle and, despite facing heavy criticism in the first years of her directorship of the Tanztheater Wuppertal, is now recognised as one of the most radical innovators of dance in the twentieth century.

Bausch's *Tanztheater* (dance theatre) cannot be neatly categorised. It is a composite art form that occupies a liminal space. However, this volume offers a new perspective on the evolution of Bausch's hybridised approach by orienting it within an international legacy of performance practice. In doing so, I will demonstrate that Bausch's *Tanztheater* did not evolve in isolation. My analysis thus considers not only the influence of German expressive dance and American neoclassical and modern dance on Bausch's work, but, crucially, interrogates parallels with modernist and postdramatic theatre, the influence of which has been largely neglected in existing studies of her *Tanztheater*. I elucidate these connections through a chronologically structured examination of Bausch's *oeuvre*, identifying definitive phases in the evolution of her technique, and providing a comprehensive explanation of her distinctive choreographic technique. Accordingly, I propose a new methodological lens for understanding Bausch's *Tanztheater* and navigating the thorny issue of classification.

My background as an art historian informs my interdisciplinary methodological approach throughout this discussion, in which I locate her work at the intersection of dance and theatre to interrogate individual case study choreographies. In the existing literature on Bausch's repertoire, allusions are frequently made to parallels between her work and that of figures such as Antonin Artaud, Samuel Beckett, Jerzy Grotowski and Robert Wilson, yet these evident connections are rarely discussed in detail and, to date, comparative analysis with her productions does not exist. As such, I have selected examples that recur as common reference points and allow for comprehensive comparison between theatre and dance practice. This structure also reflects current trends in performance scholarship: there has been a perceptible increase in interdisciplinary writing on dance, and, in particular, modernist parallels between dance and the creative arts. Susan Jones' 2013 volume, *Literature, Modernism, and Dance* initiated an important discussion of the interrelationships between writing and movement, yet the relationship between modernist theatre and dance has, to date, not received the attention it deserves. This underscores the necessity for comparable research on Bausch's relationship with theatrical practice, in order to better understand the significant role she occupies in the history of avant-garde performance.

Hans-Thies Lehmann's conception of postdramatic theatre (2006) marks an important precedent for my methodology, a categorisation of theatre practice that has emerged since the 1960s in which all convention – plot, text, the role of the audience – is destabilised. Erika Fischer-Lichte's 2008 study, *The Transformative Power of Performance*, puts forward a similar idea, centring on the 'performative turn' from the 1960s onwards, where spectacle supersedes mimesis and the audience adopts an increasingly active role in the event.[1] This is not to say that labelling Bausch's work as postdramatic solves the issue of definition, however, or that I am homogenously classifying her work as postdramatic. Rather Lehmann's model provides us with a useful working paradigm in order to understand Bausch's *oeuvre* more effectively as a hybrid of dance and theatre – something that aligns with his notions of destabilisation and breaking with dramatic theatre convention. Like the work of Samuel Beckett (who I present as a vital parallel in this study), I argue that Bausch's *Tanztheater* can be described as both modernist and postdramatic simultaneously. Although these terms may seem anachronistic, even contradictory, in drawing upon two ostensibly different frameworks, her work resides in a marginal territory. It is precisely this 'in-betweenness' that is conveyed through the compound noun of *Tanztheater*. Thus I suggest that her *oeuvre* is, like its label, liminal and simultaneous. It sits on the cusp of modernism and the postdramatic, just as it draws upon the vocabularies of dance and theatre.

My analysis opens with a discussion of the dual influences of German and American modern dance on Bausch in the early years of her career. Beginning with her dance training in Germany and the USA, Chapter 1 locates Bausch's *Tanztheater* as emerging from an international modernist heritage. The second chapter details the materialisation of what I term her *Stichworte* method (a collagist process of questioning her dancers), and contextualises Bausch's radical break from narrative-led dance as a form of post-Brechtian theatre. The third chapter examines the relationship between Beckett's absurdist drama and what has come to be known as the 'golden' or 'vintage' era of Bausch's *Tanztheater*, while Chapter 4 analyses themes of trauma and Artaudian cruelty in her work of the mid-1980s. Here, I highlight the significance of the geopolitical context of Bausch's work, relating the dark thematic content of these pieces to the landscape of postwar Germany. Chapter 5 centres on Bausch's international co-productions (a series of works devised through residencies held in different locations), and elucidates important parallels with the postdramatic theatre of Robert Wilson. The final chapter examines issues of legacy and the aesthetics of Bausch's late choreographic style, where I suggest that her final works demonstrate a return to the aesthetics of 'pure' dance that characterised the earliest phase of her career.

Despite significant challenges and public resistance to her early pieces, Bausch produced a rich and broad *oeuvre* in a career lasting almost forty years. By the time of her death, her work had garnered major international awards and worldwide acclaim. A cameo role in Pedro Almodóvar's *Hable con ella* (*Talk to Her*, 2002), and Wim Wenders' posthumous tribute *Pina* (2011) helped bring her *Tanztheater* to a global audience, with numerous new biographies and catalogues of Bausch's work emerging in recent years. Particularly notable are the writings of Royd Climenhaga and Norbert Servos, the latter having conducted extensive work with Bausch and her company dancers across a span of three decades. Climenhaga and Servos' texts – *Pina Bausch* (2009) and *Pina Bausch: Dance Theatre* (2007) respectively – provide key contextual and descriptive detail of Bausch's working method and choreographic endeavours and form the cornerstones of *Tanztheater* research. Yet there has been little interrogation of the theatrical origins of her unique choreographic method and recurrent thematic motifs. With this study, I have sought to address this major lacuna by documenting and analysing the evolution of Bausch's method. The case studies selected represent the full breadth of her career, beginning with some of the earliest works performed by Tanztheater Wuppertal, and concluding with her last complete pieces. As a result, this volume represents a comprehensive assessment of Bausch's choreographic style and influences, from the beginning of her artistic directorship to its abrupt end.

There are myriad challenges inherent in the practice of writing about dance. Performance is a transient entity, and the researcher is left only with fragments to formulate their narrative. As the eminent dance scholar Susan Manning has observed:

> The dance scholar has no choice except to pursue the elusive and uncertain text of performance. An event bound in space and time, a performance can be read only through its traces – on the page, in memory, on film, in the archive.[2]

The importance of Bausch's contribution to the performing arts cannot be underestimated, and it is vital that the broader connections between her *Tanztheater* and international theatre practice be awarded appropriate and detailed attention. Yet it is unavoidable that as time passes, the transient remnants of her process will become further atomised. With this in mind, I hope that the following volume serves as a suitable tribute to an extraordinary artist, acknowledging her revolutionary contribution to, and impact upon, contemporary performance culture.

NOTES

1. Fischer-Lichte, *The Transformative Power of Performance*, p. 18.
2. Manning, *Ecstasy and the Demon*, p. 12.

I

A BILINGUAL DANCER

The whole time I only wanted to dance. I had to dance, simply had to dance. That was the language with which I was able to express myself'.[1]

Philippine 'Pina' Bausch was born in the midst of the Second World War on 27 July 1940 in Solingen, a city in the Bergisches Land region of Nordrhein-Westphalia. The youngest member of her family, Bausch was a somewhat introverted child. Her parents ran a modest tavern, and the demands of keeping operations afloat did not allow for much hands-on childrearing. Accordingly, she spent a significant proportion of time in their bar, sitting underneath tables and quietly observing patterns of human behaviour. Independence was fostered at an early age – when her father fell ill, she was left in sole charge of the business for two weeks, an impressive (if daunting) undertaking for a twelve year old. Bausch's youthful energy aided in overcoming her inherent shyness; she recalled performing handstands against the walls of the tavern and dancing in the guest rooms above. Her activities drew the attention of members of the local theatre troupe (regular patrons of the Bausch family bar) and, at their suggestion, she was taken to dance classes at the age of five.

The teachers in Bausch's local ballet school were immediately impressed by her extreme flexibility, which became apparent in the gymnastics-style exercises students were asked to undertake – lying supine, she was able to touch her toes to the back of her head with ease, leading one teacher to label her as a 'contortionist'. Bausch herself had little understanding of why she was twisting her body into such unnatural positions, but it was apparent that she possessed an innate physical aptitude for dance. She enrolled in regular ballet classes and began to perform small roles in local productions from the age of six. She rapidly came to the conclusion that, 'one thing was always clear for me; I didn't want to do anything other than be involved in the theatre. Nothing else but dance.'[2]

At fourteen, Bausch was accepted to study at the Folkwangschule für Musik, Tanz und Sprechen (Folkwang School for Music, Dance and Speech) in Essen, a major centre of progressive arts education in Germany. Bausch's primary area of study was classical rather than modern dance, echoing a widespread preference for ballet throughout Germany in the postwar period.[3] However, the structure of the Folkwang operated rather differently to other performing arts institutions. Established in 1927, the school's founding principles reflected a desire to synthesise study of the arts, melding music, drama, visual art and dance. Students were not strictly segregated by specialism, and cross-disciplinary collaboration was strongly encouraged. Such formative exposure to intermedia practice is a crucial indicator of the path Bausch would follow throughout her career; from her first step into professional training, she was immersed in the notion that art forms are neither fixed nor separate. It is this mentality that would later become the founding principle of her own creative methodology.

Bausch's principal teacher was Kurt Jooss, a highly regarded dancer, choreographer and ballet master who, alongside the opera director Rudolf Schulz-Dornburg and stage designer Hein Heckroth, had founded the Folkwang School. Jooss' pedagogical approach furthered the sense of innovation that characterised Bausch's interactions with students and staff. He regularly invited guest teachers from abroad, particularly from the United States, thus exposing his young dancers to a fresh array of choreographic languages and techniques. In this regard, the Folkwang departed from the classical dance school model, as students were not indoctrinated in a singular movement style, but actively encouraged to diversify their training. Indeed, Bausch claimed that, from a very early stage, Jooss expected his students to develop a sense of independence and ownership over their practice. Beyond what she called a 'broad base' of technical training, students were given space to identify their own weaknesses, but perhaps most importantly, to work out precisely what they wanted their choreography to convey.[4] Jooss' open-ended questions and desire to shift responsibility back to the dancer not only contravened the traditional hierarchy of the dance studio, but laid the groundwork for what would become Bausch's radical method.

However, Jooss also represents a key figure in the history of modern dance in Germany and, for Bausch, his impressive curriculum vitae would connect her to a historic lineage. His choreographic approach, which he labelled

Tanztheater, rejected the emerging trend for plotless dance and sought to address weightier questions around morality and society than was afforded by 'opera-house ballet', or *Theatertanz* in Jooss' phrasing.[5] At the same time, Jooss was a vocal advocate for the benefits afforded by classical technique. His *Tanztheater* was a marriage of two languages, drawing together the rigor and precision of ballet with the freedom and expressivity of modern dance. *Ausdruckstanz* (expressive dance) had become the dominant style of non-classical dance in Germany, having been increasingly standardised and institutionalised throughout the 1930s and 1940s.[6] Its centrality to German arts education forms an important baseline for understanding the radical nature of the dance theatre Bausch would later devise, but also provides us with an insight into one of the multiplicity of movement vocabularies her early work draws upon.

Defining Dance Theatre

The origins of the term *Tanztheater* can be traced back to the Weimar Republic. The expression was coined around 1927 by Rudolf von Laban, a pioneer of modern dance practice, and a point of origin for the avant-garde dynasty Bausch would inherit through her studies with Jooss. Born in Pozsony (now Bratislava) in 1879, Laban's military upbringing introduced him to physical culture at an early age. He participated in gymnastics classes, but also developed an interest in the diverse folk dances indigenous to Central Europe. Laban moved to Paris in 1900 to study art, the only outlet for his creative desires deemed acceptable by his family. By 1910, however, he had founded a dance company in Ascona, Switzerland, despite lacking any professional or formalised dance training. Laban's system emphasised the need for improvisation in the daily dance schedule, and stressed the importance of outdoor group exercise and the freedom of the body. Here, he experimented with his concept of the *Bewegungschor* (movement choir), a form of group dance designed to involve both amateur and professional performers in harmonic mass movement. His pioneering style paved the way for widespread innovation in non-classical dance throughout Europe and the United States, influencing generations of dancers and choreographers at home and abroad, and represented a dramatic departure from the prevailing ballet culture.

Mary Wigman, an early pioneer of expressive dance and Laban's most celebrated student, came to dance in her early twenties, a relatively late age to begin intensive training. After observing a demonstration of Émile-Jaques Dalcroze's Eurhythmics method, Wigman enrolled at his school at Hellerau to study rhythmic gymnastics, where she was introduced to the music of Igor Stravinsky and Arnold Schoenberg, and the work of Expressionist artists such as Oskar Kokoschka.[7] However, Dalcroze's technique clearly did not espouse the freedom of movement Wigman had hoped for. In the summer of 1913, she followed her friend Emil Nolde's advice and sought out Laban at Monte Verità; that she referred to this event as 'the first pilgrimage' indicates the quasi-religious atmosphere Laban was already cultivating at his remote school.[8] She and Laban conducted extensive investigations into spatial mapping and independence from musical accompaniment, a rejection of Dalcroze's increasingly dominant technique. Their vision of *Ausdruckstanz* represented an alternative artistic format to ballet, with classical ballet standing for the 'establishment' from which the avant-garde was trying to break free. In March 1915, Laban and Wigman opened their Schule der Bewegungskunst (School of Movement Art) in Zurich, where Laban began teaching the fundamental principles of his own dance technique. In 1920, he moved to Stuttgart in order to establish the Tanzbühne Laban, a school that attracted numerous notable students, chief among them Kurt Jooss.

Wigman would develop a dance vocabulary of her own which was, like Laban's, a distinctly anti-balletic tradition. In addition to performing barefoot and placing particular emphasis on improvised movement, she experimented with dances performed to spoken word accompaniment, percussion or, more radically, silence. Without a natural ballet dancer's physique, Wigman had to evolve both a movement vocabulary and a method of imparting it to her students that was adaptable to a range of body types. Instead of the traditional, regulated exercises of the ballet studio performed at the barre, with the assistance of a pianist, Wigman focused more on structured forms of improvisation, giving her students space and encouragement to develop individual movement styles, usually to the accompaniment of percussion instruments.[9] There is a strong sense of ritualism in her early work and, like Laban before her, non-Western cultures played an important role in informing Wigman's creative process. Her choreographic approach has been labelled 'absolute dance' for its emphasis on the centrality of an inner impulse and the subordination of design and music in favour of movement. For Wigman, it was the possibility of dance itself as an independent mode of expression that was of greatest value.

In the years leading up to the Second World War, both Wigman and Laban had garnered international fame and exported a revolutionary modern dance technique across Europe and to the United States, with the New York Mary Wigman School opening in 1931. The expansion of *Ausdruckstanz* also exerted considerable influence on the development of modern dance in Japan in the early twentieth century. European modern dance was a cultural export passed on by such influential figures as Baku Ishii, Takaya Eguchi and the composer Kosaku Yamada who, having studied in Germany, introduced Dalcroze's Eurhythmics method and the 'free dance' of Isadora Duncan to Ishii.[10] Butoh, a revolutionary dance theatre format that emerged in the wake of the Second World War, also owes a significant debt to *Ausdruckstanz*: Kazuo Ohno, one of the originators of Butoh, undertook instruction from Eguchi, who had in turn been a pupil of Wigman in Dresden before the outbreak of the Second World War. In 1933, Ohno studied with Ishii, and the following year, attended performances in Japan by the German dancer Harald Kreutzberg.[11] Ohno's collaborator Tatsumi Hijikata claimed to have seen Ishii perform while he was still a schoolboy, and, aged eighteen, entered the studio of Katsuko Masumura, a dancer who had also studied under Eguchi.[12] Thus, the collective influence of Laban and Wigman and their *Ausdruckstanz* movement reached much further than Germany's borders, impacting upon the evolution of radical dance on a global scale.

Under Jooss' mentorship, Bausch was initiated into this vital, expansive lineage in German modern dance and, with it, the shifting forms that the term *Tanztheater* would adopt. The German term is now most readily associated with the work of Bausch and her postwar contemporaries, particularly Gerhard Bohner, Reinhild Hoffmann and Susanne Linke. These choreographers emerged from a shared background in *Ausdruckstanz*, with Bohner studying at the Wigman School in Berlin and Bausch, Hoffmann and Linke training under Jooss in Essen.[13] The history of German modern dance, which would become a significant cultural export, is intimately centred around a select group of artists. This dynastic framework forms a crucial part of Bausch's training, yet it represents only one half of the bilingual movement vocabulary she would devise.

LEARNING A NEW LANGUAGE: BAUSCH IN THE USA

Following the completion of her studies at Essen in 1959, Bausch was awarded a fellowship from the Deutscher Akademischer Austauschdienst (German Academic Exchange Service) to study at the Juilliard School in New York for a year. Here on the other side of the Atlantic, Martha Graham's highly expressive revision of classical dance had taken root, and the American dance scene began to emerge as serious competition for the increasingly directionless face of postwar German dance. Graham's aesthetic garnered considerable critical acclaim throughout the 1930s and 1940s, and in the decades following the Second World War, her reputation as one of the most significant innovators of American modern dance was widely acknowledged. Meanwhile, New York City itself became a leading centre for modern dance in the interwar years and, by the 1960s, was firmly established as the American capital of dance training. Julliard's staff at the time encompassed a range of renowned pedagogues, including José Limón, Margaret Craske, Alfredo Corvino and Mary Hinkson of the Martha Graham Company. Studying at Julliard allowed Bausch to experience a range of technical approaches to dance that contrasted with the inward-looking nature of dance training in her homeland – in particular, Graham's ballet-inflected movement language.

Taking the principles and basic structure of classical ballet, Graham technique departs from convention in acknowledging the power of gravity. While classes in Graham technique are codified and set in a similar manner to ballet training, instead of beginning at the barre, the dancer commences class seated on the floor. Warm-ups usually begin with small bounces, proceeding to exercises that include breathing techniques, spiralling around the back, 'deep stretches' (also known as 'percussives') and the contraction and release of the spine. Other features of the technique include extensive floor work performed by the dancer in a seated position, on their knees, or lying on their back. Travelling sequences, in which the dancer moves across the floor, use more variations of classical exercises – the arrow-straight *jetés* (jumps) of traditional ballet are transformed into the powerful bison leap, with the back curved and arms and legs drawn up to a bent position in mid-air, and falls, where the dancer is able to rebound off the floor in direct opposition to the upright, illusionistic nature of classical dance

The ritualistic qualities of Graham's choreographies derive from her desire to explore psychology through movement and a deep belief in the innate honesty of movement as opposed to the vagaries of language. Contemporary artistic practice also had a profound impact on her dance work; her accompanist and longstanding mentor, the musician Louis Horst, introduced Graham to European modernist visual art following a visit to Vienna in 1926.[14] The impression this left on the young dancer was particularly evident in early choreographies such as *Revolt* (1927) and *Immigrant: Steerage, Strike* (1928) in that their stark, monochrome appearance and sharply angular body positions demonstrate arresting parallels with the aesthetics of German Expressionism. Even elements of Graham technique, particularly in her early choreographies, demonstrated aesthetic links to German dance. For instance, Graham's principle of contraction and release represented complex ideas that conceive of a central line running through the body that can be manipulated through creating rippling or twisted movement. As Karl Toepfer has highlighted, Wigman expressed a comparable style of movement:

> [She] liked to bend and coil the body and seems to have appreciated curvature as much as angularity, but she avoided the balletic tendency to straighten out or elongate the body. Her dancers shifted abruptly from small, stalking steps to lunging strides and glides.[15]

Graham's rigorous technique and highly expressive choreography was intended to provide a new method that evoked a distinctly American form of dance. Nevertheless, strong similarities can be detected between Wigman's movement style and that of the new generation of American modern dancers. Manning has suggested that, 'modern dance originated in Germany and America from the double impulse to not only establish movement as a self-sufficient means for expression but also to subvert and perhaps transform dominant social values'.[16] Yvonne Hardt has also challenged what she terms the 'exceptionalist narrative' of American modern dance history.[17] Wigman's three tours of the United States introduced her individual movement vocabulary to a country eager for innovative and avant-garde modern dance. Wigman would have been well aware of Graham's increasingly acclaimed technique, and, equally, Graham must have been conscious of the mounting American interest in *Ausdruckstanz*. It is significant that, in her biography of Graham's mentor Louis Horst, Janet Mansfield Soares claims that Graham had observed the renowned *Ausdruckstänzer* Harald Kreutzberg rehearsing in New York City in 1928, while Louis Horst was acting as his accompanist.[18]

During a 1985 interview, Bausch stated that, while she 'never saw Mary Wigman nor Harald Kreutzberg [perform, I] certainly saw Martha Graham, and I studied Graham technique'.[19] In the Germany that Bausch had left behind, Wigman's brand of *Ausdruckstanz* was seen as increasingly passé, but its influence had nonetheless followed her to the New World. Many of Bausch's teachers and collaborators in New York had trained in Graham technique or worked in her company, including Corvino, Hinkson, Paul Sansardo, Paul Taylor and Horst, Graham's most significant mentor. It is thus hardly surprising that, in Bausch's early works, there are strong links with elements of Graham's style.

Bausch's American training did not centre on Graham technique alone, however. In dance, her first language lay in classical ballet, and during her time in New York her primary teacher was the English-born choreographer Antony Tudor. Tudor sought to go beyond the romanticism and staid technicality of ballet, creating works that formed a bridge between classical and modern dance. He developed an intense rivalry with his contemporary, Frederick Ashton, though their individual visions of ballet were quite distinct, with Ashton generally favouring a pure classicism as opposed to Tudor's less conventional approach. Tudor studied ballet under Marie Rambert, and through her teaching, belonged to a modernist dance legacy that extended from Dalcroze's fusion of music and movement to Vaslav Nijinsky's dramatic avant-gardism. However, Tudor had also trained in the fundamentals of *Ausdruckstanz*, developed a strong interest in Jooss' dance theatre, and even experimented with Javanese dance. Equally, his artistic influences were not derived from dance alone. Tudor was a lifelong consumer of theatre, something that almost certainly informed his cerebral, allusive approach to making dance. As is also the case with Bausch, however, this aspect of Tudor's practice is rarely discussed in dance literature, and certainly deserves greater scholarly attention.[20]

Jardin aux lilas (*The Lilac Garden*, 1936) was Tudor's first major ballet, a challenging work that explored themes of memory, nostalgia and unconscious desire. In an attempt to draw the audience deeper into the setting, Tudor apparently sprayed lilac perfume into the theatre, a curious foreshadowing of Bausch's transgressive approach to stage design.[21] His fascination with psychology and social behaviours impacted strongly on his young student – in her durational, collagist works, Bausch would explore similar leitmotifs of longing, unrequited desire and the rituals of social behaviour. Tudor's choreographic process was lengthy and complex, utilising a wide variety of material in each rehearsal, but often abandoning it all the following day to try something else instead. One of his dancers recalled that, 'Tudor was very insistent that each ballet should be different, that it should have its clear "personal" style'.[22] Bausch's own approach to composition would adopt a similar form, often only selecting a single phrase or movement from an hour's worth of rehearsal time. Her curiosity regarding human behaviour and psychology is, it seems, indebted to the deeply psychoanalytic and probing approaches of Tudor and Graham.

After completing her studies at Juilliard, Tudor hired Bausch as a dancer for the Metropolitan Opera Ballet Company where he was in residence as artistic director. Working for an opera company exposed Bausch to classical music and operatic singing, instilling in her an appreciation of the form that would profoundly impact upon her own choreography. Over the course of this residence in New York, Bausch also danced on a regular basis for Paul Taylor's New American Ballet. Her professional training thus spanned both the realms of classical and contemporary techniques and the Atlantic-European gap in modern dance. It was a period of creative ferment and upheaval in artistic development. Yet when Bausch received a phone call from her former mentor Jooss, the conclusion she reached was that more inviting opportunities awaited her in her native land.

HOMECOMING

On returning to Germany in 1962, Bausch joined Jooss' recently established Folkwang Ballett as a soloist and began choreographing dances alongside her performing work. *Fragmente* (1968) was her first complete piece, accompanied by the music of Béla Bartók and danced by the rest of the company. It was followed a year later by *Im Wind der Zeit* (*In the Wind of Time*), which was, according to Hans Züllig, 'very abstract, very dancerly, very graphic', and was awarded first prize at the second International Choreography Competition in Cologne.[23] Following Jooss' retirement in 1969, Bausch succeeded her mentor as artistic director of the Folkwang Ballett, a post she retained for four years. Her choreographic work throughout this period became increasingly avant-garde. *Nachnull* (*After Zero*, 1970) – its title most likely a reference to the *Stunde Null* (zero hour) following the capitulation of the Nazi government in 1945 – featured only five dancers performing contorted, grotesque movements. It was described by Hedwig Müller as, 'a vision of the end of the world following an atomic catastrophe'.[24] In 1971, Bausch created *Aktionen für*

Tänzer (*Actions for Dancers*) at the request of the opera house and playhouse management company, the Wuppertaler Bühnen. Danced by the Folkwang company, the piece effectively formed a parody of classical ballet. A year later, she reprised the connection with the Wuppertaler Bühnen when she choreographed the Bacchanale for Wagner's *Tannhäuser*, with Susanne Linke dancing the principal role.[25]

In this period, Bausch continued to perform as a dancer at home and abroad. Reviews of her performances in this period provide evidence of her emerging bilingual movement language. Judy Kahn's analysis of Bausch's technique while performing for the Sansardo Company in 1972 recalls the serpentine quality inherent in Wigman's and Graham's respective aesthetics, and highlights the cerebral and analytical qualities that derive from Bausch's training under Tudor and Jooss. Perhaps most interesting, however, is Kahn's underscoring of a peculiar and almost grotesque quality in her movement. While Bausch's creative method is never described as a 'technique', her treatment of the arms and upper body becomes a unique choreographic signature, as is evident in the 'pure dance' works she would go on to create a few years later:

> Her body designs contort in snake-pulling movements, travelling from large patterns to their smaller, more intricate extensions, structurally similar to Emery Hermens, but choreographically unlike anything seen in this country. In her solo, she releases her back in a knee-bent 'S' and flexes her foot hard, peering at the audience with a poignant sense of humor and foreboding. Her creaturesque humanoid forms hover in an abstract yet basic realm of human experience, devoid of direct intellectual association, functioning on a paradoxically distant yet intimate level, communicating in images tucked away in the subconscious, in private dreams and public mythologies. With looming pliés, elbow-led arms, chicken-claw hands, her body tensions employ opposition and each move follows from a natural gravitational path often motivated internally by breath impulses.[26]

Bausch's reputation as a choreographer continued to grow and, in 1973, she was offered the opportunity to lead the Wuppertal Opera Ballet by its incumbent director, Arno Wüstenhöfer. She renamed the company 'Tanztheater Wuppertal', an indication of the stark change in artistic direction that she would oversee. As Jochen Schmidt has observed, it is highly significant that Bausch's assuming the directorship of Tanztheater Wuppertal coincided with the deaths of Wigman and John Cranko, respectively the unofficial representatives of *Ausdruckstanz* and contemporary ballet in Germany.[27] Despite a considerable resurgence of interest in ballet in the country throughout the 1960s, Bausch forged ahead with determination in order to explore the truly avant-garde potential of dance based on her varied experiences at home and abroad. However, her first piece with Tanztheater Wuppertal, *Fritz* (1974) dismayed audience members, some of whom stormed out of the theatre during its premiere. It is one of the few works in the repertoire never to have been restaged or revisited in any form; Bausch herself apparently remained deeply unsatisfied with it and, to date, even archival access to the piece has been restricted. *Fritz* was an abstracted, highly theatrical production that explored images of childhood fears. The title role was performed by a female dancer, and little recognisable dance took place on its stage. While this piece usually forms only a fleeting reference point in many accounts of Bausch's career, in its surrealism and disjointed structure we might read the first seeds of what would evolve into her individual creative approach. *Fritz* drew more upon a theatrical than a choreographic framework, abandoned narrative plot in favour of a dreamlike structure, and challenged audience expectation by switching the gender of its titular protagonist. While such experimentation was not particularly well received at the beginning of Bausch's directorship, she would nonetheless revisit these same tendencies in greater depth a few years later.

However, *Fritz* garnered Bausch accusations of 'mental striptease' and 'dogged humourlessness'.[28] This notoriety was enduring; in his obituary for Bausch, Luke Jennings claims that it was, 'surreally bleak even by the standards she herself would later set'.[29] Some critics were slightly more forgiving. The commentary of Horst Koegler, for example, is often left out of discussion of Bausch's early work, perhaps because it contradicts what is usually described as a universally negative reception. Koegler described *Fritz* as 'a strange phantasmagoria of a child growing up in a typical bourgeois family', claiming that the evening's programme 'enjoyed a well deserved success'.[30] Similarly, several of the dancers apparently felt quite differently about the piece; Dominique Mercy observed that, 'for the first time I had the feeling that I, Dominique, was on stage and that I was giving and saying something of myself'.[31] According to Anne Cattaneo, *Fritz* was simply, 'an homage to Jooss about childhood'.[32] Certainly, the spectre of Jooss loomed over the evening's programme, a three-part dance evening that included his ballet, *Der grüne Tisch* (*Green Table*, 1932) and Agnes de Mille's *Rodeo* (1942). It was a conspicuous choice of works to accompany Bausch's debut, and a direct reference to her bilingual training in German and American dance techniques.[33]

Indeed, in the early years of Tanztheater Wuppertal, Bausch was something of a choreographic magpie, selecting dancers with whom she felt a particular connection, rather than auditioning them on technique alone. Jan Minarik (sometimes credited in early programmes as 'Jean Mindo') was one of the few dancers to survive the transition between the Wuppertal Opera Ballet and the founding of Tanztheater Wuppertal. Mercy and his wife Marie-Louise 'Malou' Airaudo had met Bausch at Saratoga in 1970, and came to Wuppertal at her request. Bausch encountered the Australian dancer Jo Ann Endicott at a studio in London shortly after she had left the Australian Ballet, and she recruited Lutz Förster, another Solingen native, to dance in *Sacre* – three years later, he became a full-time member of the company.[34] Thus, from its earliest inception, Bausch's Tanztheater Wuppertal drew upon the talents of an increasingly multicultural assemblage of performers.

Bausch's new company structure was completely non-hierarchical, and has remained so even in the years following her death. There are no strata of dancers as in a traditional dance company, nor are there specific principal roles. Her often-repeated statement, 'I pick my dancers as people', reflects this alternative approach to dance-making. Bausch was consistently more interested in personal narratives than creating a company of 'stars'. Technique became less central to her creative process as she delved deeper into making collaborative *Tanztheater* works, seeking instead to examine the psyche and the human condition through memory and gesture. However, while she did not select dancers purely on the basis of their dance training, and pointe shoes almost never feature in her works, it should be noted that the majority of her dancers were classically trained, and even now, ballet class remains an integral part of the daily rehearsal schedule. Unlike Wigman and Graham, Bausch never sought to fully erase ballet from her own dance format, and classical technique is reflected in several of her early choreographic successes.

Transnational Modernism: *Orpheus und Eurydike*

Bausch remained unsatisfied with her early dance theatre works, and following the *Fritz* programme, produced three pieces in rapid succession that demonstrate another complete revision of her movement vocabulary and evidence the pervasive influence of her bilingual training. The early stage of Bausch's leadership of Tanztheater Wuppertal can be divided into two distinct phases. In the first, her choreographic endeavours were still firmly rooted in dance – along with *Iphigenie auf Tauris* (*Iphigenia in Tauris*, 1974), *Orpheus und Eurydike* and *Le Sacre du printemps* (both premiered in 1975) were the only pieces in her *oeuvre* that were choreographed as pure dance throughout. In both *Orpheus* and *Sacre*, Bausch reverted to a more traditional form of choreography. There is a sense that, with these pieces, she was attempting to test a variety of more conventional, balletic approaches gleaned from her training in Europe and in the United States, using classical scores and recognisable narratives to structure each work. This also signified the only point in Bausch's career where she created straightforward or 'pure' dance pieces, before abandoning this kind of choreography for a new collagist method over the coming years.

First performed on 23 May 1975 at the Wuppertal Opera House, *Orpheus* represents a high point in Bausch's early choreographic style, referencing a variety of influences from her respective careers in Germany and the United States. Koegler pronounced it, 'a magnificent achievement – four acts of stern, dark and uncompromising modern dance of great originality'.[35] As had been the case with its predecessor *Iphigenie*, *Orpheus* is a completely choreographed dance opera, an approach that characterises a brief stage of Bausch's experimental process. Jan Minarik and Marlis Alt performed in the original production, while the titular roles were danced by Mercy and Airaudo.

Orpheus was reprised by Tanztheater Wuppertal after a lengthy hiatus in 1991 and reconstructed with the assistance of Mercy and Airaudo. In 2005, it was acquired by the Paris Opera Ballet, who elected to retain the German supertitles of the score rather than translating them into French. The ballet follows the narrative of the music score very closely, though, in her version, Bausch elected for the tragic ending of the myth rather than the depiction of love triumphing over death that characterises Gluck's opera. In a more obvious manner than *Sacre*, which was premiered just a few months later, *Orpheus* draws on a range of dance techniques. It evokes Graham's aesthetic as well as the neoclassicism of George Balanchine in its refined yet expressive response to the mythical narrative. In the body of literature on Bausch's *oeuvre*, there is very little detailed analysis of this piece and, within this, only scant discussion of the international reference points contained within its movement vocabulary. This fact is made all the more surprising when we consider that *Orpheus* was created at a crucial turning point in her career. Examining Bausch's early work, it is apparent that a patchwork of creative influences informed her approach to making dance. This is particularly evident in the case of her *Orpheus*, a piece that serves both as a complex homage to her teachers, but also to the transnational and migratory legacy of modern dance in Europe and the United States.

Gluck's opera has been repeatedly revisited throughout the twentieth century. Balanchine choreographed two versions of the myth, the first in 1936 set to the Gluck score, and the second in 1948 as part of his trio of Greek works (the others being *Apollo* [1928] and *Agon* [1957]). Adolphe Appia had designed an experimental stage for Dalcroze in 1912 for a dance work set to the second act of Gluck's opera. However, disagreements over style led to Appia walking away from the school, and he did not return for the performance of the full production the following year.[36] In Germany, Dalcroze's 1913 mounting of *Orpheus* at Hellerau constituted an important milestone in the evolution of avant-garde scenography. Dalcroze's Eurhythmics method serves as an important association between many of the major figures in avant-garde dance history, and in fact several of Bausch's most influential forebears retained connections to Dalcroze's school. In 1912, when Appia was designing his *Orpheus* set, Wigman was still studying at Hellerau under Dalcroze; in 1947, she would stage her own version of Gluck's opera with students at her school in Leipzig. Significantly, in the same year Sergei Diaghilev visited the school along with Vaslav Nijinsky and Nikolai Roerich in preparation for their new production, *Le Sacre du printemps*.[37] They would subsequently engage Marie Rambert, who had been a resident tutor, to teach the Ballets Russes dancers the Eurhythmics method in order for them to better comprehend the challenging rhythms of Stravinsky's score. This connection between *Orpheus* and *Sacre* is curious in light of Bausch's decision to stage her own versions of both pieces within the same year.

Bausch's *Orpheus* is set to an edited score of Gluck's opera and is divided into four sections: *Trauer* (grief), *Gewalt* (violence), *Frieden* (freedom) and *Sterben* (death). The characters of Orpheus, Eurydice and Amore each have a double role, represented by a singer and a dancer. In Bausch's version of the myth, however, each character has been renamed – Orpheus is here marked as *Liebe* (love), Eurydice as *Tod* (death) and Amore as *Jugend* (youth). The musical accompaniment for this work is performed live, with the chorus offstage, while the singers of the three central roles remain onstage with the dancers. This arrangement demonstrates one of the earliest examples of the German playwright Bertolt Brecht's influence on Bausch's stage construction: placing the musicians in sight of the audience, she employs a direct *Verfremdungseffekt* (distancing effect) in an otherwise traditional rendering of the narrative. At points, the singers also appear to be onstage observers of the action rather than fully embodying their roles; Koegler observed that Bausch's split characters allowed them to avoid 'clumsy' miming of the narrative. The splitting of characters is something that recurs in a series of Brecht's works, including *Die sieben Todsünden* (*The Seven Deadly Sins*, 1933), *Puntila* (1948) and *Der gute Mensch von Sezuan* (*The Good Person from Szechuan*, 1943). In Brecht's theatre, this division allows for the exploration of the conflict between reason and instinct, something that would often result in tragic failure. A similar struggle lies at the heart of *Orpheus*' narrative, where the male protagonist must resist the urge to look directly at Eurydice – in doing so, he shatters the spell that would otherwise allow him to lead her out of the underworld.

The European precedents for Bausch's evocation of the Orpheus myth are quite clear and, in Germany specifically, her version is preceded by Dalcroze's early avant-garde staging as well as Wigman's *Ausdruckstanz* imagining. Yet the classical subject matter also serves as a reference point to Graham who, throughout the 1940s, had choreographed a number of signature works based on Greek mythology. By the time Bausch came to study in the United States, Graham was still creating explicitly narrative-driven dance works (a tendency that was rapidly becoming unfashionable with the advent of postmodern dance practice). Equally, Graham's highly dramatic and decorative 'Greek' pieces would have been an established part of her repertoire in the period Bausch was dancing in New York. Indeed, from the very beginning of Bausch's *Orpheus* (Figure 1.1), the dancers' movements are strikingly evocative of

Figure 1.1 *Orpheus und Eurydike*, Stephanie Berger

Graham technique. In the opening *Trauer* section, for example, dancers from the female chorus are sprawled across the stage, and rise up in what appears to be a classic Graham 'pleading' exercise (a movement in which the dancer uses their abdominal muscles to draw the upper body and knees from a prone position to a seated one, using the same core strength and control to return to the floor). The same aesthetic is at play in Alvin Ailey's seminal work, *Revelations* (1960). In the solo section, 'I Wanna be Ready', a male dancer repeatedly rises from the floor in the same pleading-like position. Ailey's aesthetic was heavily informed by his training under Lester Horton, whose technique, in turn, drew on Native American ritual dances as well as more formalist approaches (though Graham also expressed a deep fascination with Native American spirituality, as reflected in works such as *Primitive Mysteries* and *El Penitente* [1940]). That Bausch chose to open her new ballet with a movement that is almost a signature of American modern dance was a bold statement, one that directly referenced her formal training in the United States and the development of her technique that would not otherwise have been possible in Germany at the time.

Even the costumes of Bausch's *Orpheus* bear strong similarities with Graham's early work, with the women clothed in long, simple, monochrome dresses, forming a sculptural impression of a wall of identical bodies. The aesthetic effect is comparable to that of Graham's *Heretic* (1929), or her 1931 three-part ballet, *Primitive Mysteries*, pieces that emerged in what was sometimes referred to as her 'long woollens period'.[38] The character of Orpheus/

Liebe, however, is clad only in flesh-coloured underwear, pre-empting the minimalism that would come with *Sacre*. The works from this early period are characterised by such simplicity in costume and design – where Bausch's company members are now most often costumed in sharp suits and beautiful evening gowns, here the female dancers have their hair slicked back into classical buns. The monumental figure of Eurydice sits on a vertiginously high chair at the back of the stage. Clutching a bouquet of flowers and dressed in a diaphanous wedding gown that reaches the floor, she oversees the mourning rituals of the dancers as they move around her glass coffin. Amore/Jugend enters holding a dead crow, which she then places inside Eurydice's casket. The chorus of dancers draw lengths of white fabric – extensions of the wedding gown – across the stage as their slow, agonised movements reflect Orpheus' suffering. Thus, both setting and movement reveal the narrative strands of Bausch's production. Her partner and set designer Rolf Borzik created an otherworldly yet minimalist environment for this piece, and the visual effect generated by the towering Eurydice is especially arresting in the otherwise bare setting. Though it is rarely identified as such, *Orpheus* is the first work in Bausch's *oeuvre* to include organic elements in its design, with a symbolically laden felled tree located at the back of the stage in its first act.

The movement quality of *Orpheus* is strongly balletic and highly expressive – the dancers continually arch their backs and perform expansive *port de bras* to accentuate the willowy nature of their arms. The use of these repeated movements, accompanied by *ronds de jambe en l'air*, is strikingly similar to the choreography of the first section of *Sacre*, indicating an emerging stylistic tendency that can be seen even in her late works. The undulating use of the upper body is something of a trademark in Bausch's choreography, a tendency that Alessandra Zanobi connects to Isadora Duncan's focus on the solar plexus as the originating location of dance movement.[39] There is also a resemblance with Wigman's 1929 solo *Pastorale*, specifically in the rippling movements of her arms and the flick-like *ronds* of the legs. The first act of Bausch's *Orpheus* is punctuated by moments of absolute stillness evocative of a *tableau vivant*, and is highly reminiscent of both Wigman's early group dances and Laban's *Bewegungschor* exercises. Though she would make a major departure from linear plot and recognisable choreography over the next few years, Bausch was clearly evolving a distinct movement vocabulary in works such as *Orpheus*. Various motifs will also re-emerge in much later works: a short part of this opening section, in which the women travel across the stage in a group forma-tion, seems to foreshadow the red-haired woman's solo in Bausch's celebrated *Café Müller* (1978).

Each section of Bausch's *Orpheus* has its own identifiable aesthetic, reflected in the movement vocabulary as well as the visual language of the stage design. *Gewalt*, the second act, is much more theatrical in tone than the opening, taking place in a nightmarish vision of the underworld. The male dancers assume a more visible role in this section, most of them dressed in dark suits with bare feet. A trio of men are costumed in greasy leather butchers' aprons, their role alluding to Cerberus, the three-headed guard dog of Hades. The movement quality in this act is more urgent as performers hurl themselves across the stage, and there is a percussive quality to the choreography when the dancers audibly slap themselves and strike the stage floor. A woman reaches futilely for an apple suspended from the ceiling, a reference to the myth of Tantalus' eternal punishment. As the action progresses, several individuals tie long threads across the set in a spider web formation, locking themselves within the confines of their own design. Orpheus/Liebe appears panicked, racing between points as if realising that he is trapped. The choreography is extremely athletic in this section and, as male dancers fling themselves perilously high into the air, their movements are reminiscent of Roland Petit's 1946 ballet, *Le Jeune Homme et la Mort* (*The Young Man and Death*). Petit's approach espoused a similar level of drama and narrative storytelling to Bausch's dance operas. In *Jeune Homme*, the titular roles are played by a young man and his conniving lover who manipulates and betrays him – Petit represents the youth's anguish with virtuosic and gravity-defying leaps where the dancer's legs are drawn up behind his body in mid-air, threatening an injurious fall back to earth. In her expressive and balletic movement language for the dancers of *Orpheus*, Bausch draws on several significant reference points in modern dance history, while maintaining an important link to classical formalism.

The oppressive mood of the second act changes abruptly with the shift into *Frieden*, the most aesthetically striking section of the production, which opens to the 'Dance of the Spirits' component of Gluck's opera. The setting has moved to Elysium, where Orpheus has been permitted entry and is reunited with Eurydice. The structure of this section is overtly classical in form, to the extent that it is almost unrecognisable as one of Bausch's choreographies. The lack of pointe work, however, stands as a direct reminder that *Orpheus* was not to be considered classical dance despite heavily referencing elements of neoclassical ballet. In this scene, a chorus of women dance in flowing gauze dresses, with the fabric accentuating their otherworldly nature. There are immediate aesthetic parallels with the Wilis of Adolph Adams' *Giselle* (1841), though Bausch's use of the arms is decidedly modern, with a rippling, almost Oriental quality.

The emphasis on aestheticism in the third act of Bausch's *Orpheus* draws on another crucial reference point, namely George Balanchine's *Serenade* (1934). This landmark work was the choreographer's first ballet created in the United States, and is danced to Tchaikovsky's 'Serenade for Strings'. Balanchine claimed it was simply 'a dance in the moonlight'.[40] Like Bausch's *Orpheus*, his choreography is set to an evocative classical score, and features rows of female dancers clad in long, flowing dresses derived from the Romantic period of classical ballet when tutus were largely discarded in favour of more delicate costume. Balanchine increasingly favoured a stripped-down aesthetic, often clothing his dancers in plain leotards and tights to emphasise movement quality over storytelling and decoration. His neoclassical approach to ballet promoted a new athleticism in dance, similar to that of Petit's choreography, but he also espoused a desire to create non-narrative and progressively more abstract works. Balanchine is a pivotal figure in modernist dance, bridging an international gap between Europe and the United States, and creating a new language and range of possibilities in an otherwise rigidly traditional art form.

The opening sequence of *Serenade* depicts seventeen women in long dresses standing with their feet in parallel, each holding one hand to her temple. In a single synchronised movement, they open their feet to a turned-out first position, which, as Elizabeth Kendall has observed, marks 'the foundation of ballet [technique]'.[41] Shortly thereafter, a woman rushes onto the stage to find her place in the formation, misses, and stumbles to the ground. This image was based on the actual events of a rehearsal, and Balanchine elected to include it in his final choreography. In the same manner, then, that Paul Taylor would later incorporate the image of a woman running for a bus into his 1975 work, *Esplanade*, and dancers such as Yvonne Rainer would construct postmodern dance pieces around the idea of entirely pedestrian movement, Balanchine seamlessly embedded an everyday occurrence into his work. Once she had largely abandoned traditional dance movement, Bausch began to explore the same concept, structuring entire pieces around a complex framework of quotidian movements and cyclical repetitions. *Serenade* was seen as Balanchine's most emblematic work, and is now widely interpreted as a tribute both to his Russian heritage and to his newfound American identity. In a similar sense, Bausch's *Orpheus* represents an homage to her training in the United States and Germany, a reflection of the transnational nature of modernism in dance throughout the twentieth century. In this respect, Bausch can be termed an heir to Balanchine in her internationalist, syncretic outlook.

Orpheus comes to a muted conclusion with its final act, *Sterben*. The chorus of dancers has departed, and the stage opens to a bare set. Only Orpheus/Liebe and Eurydice/Tod remain, the latter now clad in a long, bright red dress, foreshadowing the costume that will identify the sacrificial victim in Bausch's *Sacre*. The two singers are joined once more on stage by their dancing counterparts; they stand back to back, articulating verbally what the dancers express through movement. The final act is perhaps the most spare, minimalist element of the production, but still heavily narrative-led. The movement vocabulary in this act again features swirling, circular movements and expressive use of the arms; it is still balletic, but more theatrical in form than the preceding sections. There is also a stronger connection between music and movement as the two singers move around the stage and the dancers mirror one another's movements. Bausch's dramaturgical eye begins to dominate her choreographic hand in this section, and it is an early indicator of the innovative staging that will characterise her approach as a blurry amalgamation of dance and theatre.

An overriding sense of torment pervades the scene, and Bausch edited Gluck's score to match her narrative accordingly. In Gluck's original opera, Eurydice is brought back to life after Orpheus, in his grief at losing her again, decides to commit suicide in order to join her permanently in the afterlife. The benevolent character of Amore intervenes and resurrects Eurydice. Bausch, however, opted for the tragic ending of the myth – in this version, when the dancers embrace each other and Eurydice/Tod dies for a second time, the singers mimic the action. Orpheus/Liebe lays Eurydice/Tod over her singing counterpart, who has also expired. Stricken, Orpheus staggers from one side of the stage to the other, his back to the audience and doubled over in grief. Thematically, there are strong connections here with *Sacre* in terms of the sacrificial motif, as well as a similarity in movement quality and colouring (neutral colours are employed for the rest of the cast, while Eurydice/Tod, the object of the sacrifice, is clothed in red).

Eventually, it is the singing version of Orpheus/Liebe who embraces the dancer Eurydice/Tod's lifeless body. These shifting character roles underscore a distinctly modernist tendency in an otherwise straightforward narrative, embodying a Brechtian distancing device that is otherwise at odds with ballet formalism. The division of the characters into those who move and those who sing (in place of speech) hints at the expressive shortcomings of both roles. The male dancers in aprons gently push Orpheus between them as the rest of the cast enter the stage in order to perform a slow, flowing sequence mimicking the opening *Trauer* section – as shall become clear when analysing Bausch's later work, she would often reiterate opening motifs as a conclusion to her *Tanztheater* pieces. The men and women fall to the floor, slowly rise, and exit the scene backwards, processing in a formation reminiscent of a medieval Dance of Death. At this point, the music stops completely, and the action continues on a silent stage for around thirty seconds.

Bausch's *Orpheus* is a striking early indicator of the form her *Tanztheater* would ultimately take. It melds multiple languages – a melange of dance techniques is presented in Borzik's innovative staging, and many tendencies that will become points of recurrence are explored here for the first time. At the same time, *Orpheus* acknowledges Bausch's training and the rich choreographic legacy she is heir to. Reviewing a revival of the piece in 2012, it is significant that *The New York Times* critic Alastair Macauley identifies several key modernist reference points in her choreography. He draws parallels with Tudor's landmark *Dark Elegies* (1937), observing that:

Several gestures and motifs recall Graham. It's probable that Bausch, here and elsewhere, intended to restore to dance some of the poetic ambiguity that was so striking and baffling in Graham's choreography in the 1940s. Yet whereas ambiguity in Graham was charged by expressionist urgency, Bausch's language is physically softer, expressively more evasive, structurally devoid of progress. Graham's dance theater, with the body at war with itself, forces you to consider meaning; Bausch's dance theater encourages you to think there must be meanings you can never understand.[42]

Bausch may not have experienced Wigman performing live, but she would have been unable to escape the aesthetic impact of her *Ausdruckstanz* training as a dancer in Germany. The legacy of Wigman and Laban is evident here in the choral arrangements of figures and bas-relief imagery. The influence of Jooss, too, is clear in terms of the merging of theatrical narrative and classical ballet, as well as in the Dance of Death theme. These parallels with her forebears would further crystallise only a few months later with the premiere of Bausch's landmark *Sacre*.

'IT'S NOT A METAPHOR. IT IS WHAT IT IS': *LE SACRE DU PRINTEMPS*[43]

Of all musical scores composed for dance, perhaps the most influential – and certainly one of the most frequently revisited – is Igor Stravinsky's *Le Sacre du printemps* (*The Rite of Spring*). The ritualistic elements of primitivism embedded in Stravinsky's score have a timeless quality and hold an enduring appeal for dance makers seeking to challenge existing boundaries of form and structure. Indeed, since the premiere of Nijinsky's choreography for an unsuspecting Parisian audience in 1913, *Sacre* has been staged by a wide variety of classical and contemporary choreographers across the globe.[44] Modris Eksteins even posits that Nijinsky's *Sacre* represents a starting point for the history of modernism, a direct result of its composition and premiere taking place on the eve of the First World War. It can be inferred that the popularity of Stravinsky's anti-classical, anti-traditional rhythms is indicative of an enduring interest in primitive aesthetics. It is not surprising, therefore, that such influential choreographers as Wigman, Graham, Taylor and Bausch each created their own distinct version of the score. As such, *Sacre* can be framed as a choreographic rite of passage, a modernist shibboleth.

Nijinsky's ballet tells a simple narrative – that of a pagan sacrificial rite in which a virgin is martyred to the fertility-god Yarilo to guarantee a good harvest and ensure a secure future for her tribe. The ballet's plot was devised with Stravinsky at Talashkino, a progressive art and design studio at the estate of Princess Maria Tenisheva.[45] Their artistic collaborator Nikolai Roerich's long-held interest in the rituals of Russian pre-Christian culture underscored his designs for the ballet, and the melodic lines of the score were drawn from rearrangements of traditional Russian folk music. Nijinsky's new vision of ballet choreography inverted the beauty and illusionism of classical dance in favour of turned-in feet, bent legs and caricature-like grotesquery. His movement vocabulary was erratic and sharp, mirroring its musical accompaniment. Nijinsky stripped away the ethereal artifice of ballet and turned the dancers' legs inwards, their stomping feet a notable precursor to Wigman's percussive early solo dances, even anticipating Graham's use of parallel feet and piercing, violent jumps. This outright and aggressive negation of classical ballet heralded the beginning of modernism in European dance.

While Nijinsky's ballet marked the beginning of his career as a choreographer and brought him a new level of fame and notoriety, Wigman's *Sacre* (1957) was to be one of her last large-scale works. This version of the theme bore striking resemblance to the aesthetics of Graham technique. It was an unusually angular piece, with frequent use of flexed hands and feet, and alluded to no particular culture or specific point in time.[46] The choreography revolved around circular patterns of movement, reflecting the oval platform of the raked stage. The constant reiteration of circular, rotating motions resulted in a hypnotic, mesmeric dance which, in turn, reflects the cyclical nature of life and death central to the narrative. Wigman's choreographic spectacle, therefore, became a kind of rhythmic, ritualised performance, with the dancers working themselves into a trance-like state through endlessly repeating circular movements.

Wigman costumed her Chosen One in a red dress, while the rest of the cast were clad in rather sober and minimalist designs; the women in simple, long gowns, and the men in tights with a band of fabric worn across the chest. Following her selection as sacrificial victim, Wigman's Chosen One was crowned by her community's elders. Similarities can be drawn between Wigman's piece and Bausch's version, in which the sacrificial victim is effectively ritualistically bestowed with the red dress after being selected. Considering the widespread awareness and appreciation of Wigman's work in Germany at this point in time, it is conceivable that Bausch's choice of costume was a deliberate reference to her predecessor, with the red dress forming a recognisable trope to be associated with this score.

The work was well received, and both Walter Sorell and Hedwig Müller have referred to Wigman's *Sacre* as the last great success of her career.[47] Gabriele Fritsch-Vivié cites one contemporary reviewer who commented that Wigman had proven *Sacre* was, 'not a ballet, but a cultish dance-act, one that is not about pirouettes and gestures, but line and rhythm'.[48] Wigman's ritual sacrifice is calmer than Nijinsky's: it is less of a violent assault on the victim, and ends on an almost celebratory note – that the female victim was selected by a group of elder priestesses and crowned as part of her sacrifice suggests a rather triumphant depiction of human sacrifice. While the victim was hardly a willing participant in the rite (she was forcibly separated from the male partner she had chosen, before being bound with rope), she went to her death with less evident fear than Nijinsky's knock-kneed, trembling heroine.

The *Sacre* theme has been adopted by a significant number of German choreographers despite performances of the score having been banned under fascism. Manning posits that clusters of revivals have occurred during times of crisis in German theatre, noting a 'seemingly unending succession of *Rites*' since 1970.[49] Bausch's *Sacre* emerged in the midst of one of these periods, as debates raged throughout the 1970s with the emergence of *Tanztheater* as a rejection of both classical and expressive dance. Her *Sacre* was conceived as the third part of a trilogy of dances, an evening headed *Frühlingsopfer* (*The Rite of Spring*) which followed two other works – *Wind von West* (*Wind from the West*) set to Stravinsky's Cantata (1952), and *Der zweite Frühling* (*The Second Spring*), premiered at Wuppertal Opera House on 3 December 1975.[50] Soon after, the final section, *Le Sacre du printemps*, was presented as a separate work.

The piece is instantly recognisable for its dramatic setting, in which the floor is covered with a dense, pungent layer of earth. Borzik's conception transforms the stage space into a haunting vision of a primitive wasteland, the soil soon turned into mud by the perspiration of Bausch's exhausted dancers. By the end of the performance, the performers are caked in filth, and their laboured breathing is audible. Gone is the illusionism traditionally associated with classical dance, and instead the audience is confronted with a cast of highly skilled dancers pushed to the limits of their capabilities – they break another taboo of classical ballet in making their exhaustion overt, rather than concealing the effort behind a balletic mask of artificial serenity. In doing so, Bausch maintains a tradition that had been established with Nijinsky's choreography of the *Danse sacrale*, the final section of Stravinsky's score. In the 1913 version of the ballet, this closing Dance of Death was held to be one of the most physically demanding sections of the ballet repertoire. In the first major revival of Stravinsky's score in 1920, Léonide Massine also adopted this tendency towards excess; after performing in the premiere of his first version of the ballet, principal dancer Lydia Sokolova recalled that she collapsed at the last note of the music behind the stage curtain.[51] Physical exhaustion and endless repetition of specific movements would become a recurring and immediately recognisable motif of Bausch's *oeuvre*, a tendency that is rooted in Nijinsky's dissonant choreographic avant-gardism.

Bausch's *Sacre* opens with a woman lying face down on a red dress, caressing the material in a trance-like state. The red fabric stands in stark aesthetic contrast to the female dancers in their nude shift dresses, who assume the behaviour of a flock of anxious birds. While one dancer holds the dress away from her body, there is a dawning realisation among the wider group that the dress represents a threatening unknown. As the dancer drops it to the floor, the women gather together in tight formation, and the music erupts into a heavy, percussive rhythm while the ensemble move in a repetitive cycle. The dancers throw their heads back, beat their clasped arms against themselves, and sink towards the earthy floor in deep, weighty pliés. This is the first movement sequence to underline the primitive, ritualistic elements of the score in Bausch's choreography and, after a number of repetitions, the dancers' heavy breathing is clearly audible. It is compulsive movement, creating the impression that some external force is driving the group. Like a vision of mass possession, the swirling, cyclical movements are initiated by gradual recognition of the sacrificial nature of the red dress.

The earth-covered stage inhibits the dancers' movements, forcing them to work harder in order to enact the choreography. The resistance of the soil works against the cast, the sweat bestowing animacy to Borzik's stage setting. They evoke more than an impression of exhaustion with their mud and sweat-covered bodies, portraying a visible fatigue, something the audience is able to hear in their increasingly ragged breathing. This is not a performed version of weariness, but real, visceral exhaustion. The dancers work themselves into a hysterical, muddy frenzy, coming to an end only with the collapse of the Chosen One once she has effectively danced herself to death. In a 1994 interview with Ciane Fernandes, dancer Ruth Amarante described the sacrificial solo as follows:

> The whole solo is a progression. In that moment it is more startling – 'what is happening?' – a mortal fear of death. It is as if no more blood were left in your brain . . . Her interpretation is strange. The sacrificed could even feel honored and have some calmness. But in Pina's version, she wanted to show this instinctive fear of death.[52]

Norbert Servos has alluded to the peat-covered stage floor as a 'battlefield', an observation that gains greater significance viewed alongside Eksteins' analysis of Nijinsky's choreography as a portent of global conflict.[53] Adopting a more gendered analysis, Gabrielle Cody comments that, 'by all accounts, *The Rites* became a frightening ritual of male dominance which turned the culminating fertility dance into a predatory and terrifying form of erotic warfare'.[54]

Costume plays a major role in this impression of physical suffering, with the women clad only in thin, flesh-coloured dresses akin to nightgowns (Figure 1.2), and the men bare-chested. Their bodies are clearly on display, though the effect is not necessarily one of sexual titillation; quite the opposite, the spectator's proximity to the dancers' raw flesh heightens the overexposure and exhaustion. As Johannes Birringer has observed, one of Bausch's unique choreographic skills was the simple notion of putting 'everyday rituals' onstage, and

Figure 1.2 *Le Sacre du printemps*, Oliver Look

in doing so, leading the audience to become acutely aware of their shifting role from spectator to voyeur. [55] Here, every twitch of the dancers' lean muscles is visible to the audience – they are completely exposed, and the physical and emotional toll exerted by Bausch's choreography is uncomfortably plain to see.

There is little joy in Bausch's sacrificial ritual. Instead, her tribe evoke a stark, animalistic response to their duty in surrendering a member for the good of the community. However, this ferocious episode of sexual congress is not necessarily the 'mass rape' that Sally Banes has identified in Nijinsky's choreography.[56] Rather, the image of sex Bausch presents is one of orgiastic indifference: ecstatic movements are contradicted by the evident exhaustion in the facial expressions and bodies of the nameless mass of dancers. Schlagenwerth, for example, asks, 'what other piece has this dichotomy of strength, brutality, power and gentleness, calm and devotion, as irrevocably linked as that of Pina Bausch, in this, her thirteenth work for an ensemble?'[57] Like many critics observing Bausch's work, Birringer has read this piece as a play of gender roles, claiming that:

> The ritual dance was constantly repeated – to the point of total exhaustion – as a central metaphor for the well-rehearsed behavior of men following the rules of society and selecting women as sacrificial victims, even as the women themselves envision and anticipate the selection.[58]

Sexuality is clearly present in Bausch's *Sacre*, and its depiction here lays the groundwork for what will become a recursive theme in Bausch's repertoire.

In one section of ensemble dancing that occurs immediately after the selection of the sacrificial victim, the female dancers leap into the arms or onto the shoulders of their male partners (who are seemingly chosen at random). The men grasp the women around their waists, while the female dancers contort themselves in the manner of frantic, ecstatic sexual coupling. It is short, wild and uninhibited, yet simultaneously appears somewhat soulless, cold or even violent with regard to the treatment of the women. This duality of male/female relationships remains one of the most recognisable reference points in Bausch's *oeuvre*. In the case of her *Sacre*, the spectator could well read the entire performance as an exploration of the correlation between sex and death. Here we may identify another underlying aesthetic connection between Bausch and Graham – the twisting, pulsating bodies of Bausch's *Sacre* show similarities with the contraction and release of Graham technique, a visceral device that was used to heighten emotional impact in her work. Meanwhile, in a review of a 1999 revival of *Sacre*, Michaela Schlagenwerth called Bausch's impression of gender roles 'slightly anachronistic', drawing a link between the frenetic impulses of the cast and elements of German *Ausdruckstanz* of the 1920s.[59]

By 1975, Stravinsky's score had been adopted by a variety of choreographers worldwide, with Maurice Béjart's 1959 version being particularly well-known. In Germany, Wigman's elaborate staging had received positive reviews, and a tentative tradition had been established in revising Stravinsky's work. Bausch, however, made her mark not through a traditional rendering of the score. In terms of its depiction of the subject matter, Bausch's choreography shifts from a pre-established narrative, as Manning has pointed out:

> Bausch departed from the elevated tone of Wigman's *Sacre* and rejected her predecessor's interpretation of the final sacrificial dance as an heroic act. Wigman's staging never questioned that Dore Hoyer represented Woman and that Woman represented endurance and self-sacrifice. In contrast, Bausch's *Sacre* questioned why a woman invariably serves as the victim of social violence – 'The original libretto as if viewed from afar' – and when so viewed, the social ritual that frames the woman as victim became shockingly clear.[60]

Where Wigman's ritual was relatively subdued, and ultimately almost celebratory, Bausch's is brutal and relentless, leaving the audience emotionally drained and the dancers physically exhausted. There is an impulse in Bausch's movement that is almost inhuman, animalistic in its unremitting repetitions. In the piece's final moments – the *Danse sacrale* – the soloist swings her arms in a full circle, throwing them overhead before allowing the weight of her upper body to follow the arc of the pendulum downward. With each repetition, the speed of the movement increases. A recorded rehearsal, filmed in 1987, documents Bausch giving precise and detailed instructions for this sequence to Kyomi

Ichida (substituting the role of the Chosen One for a dancer who had unexpectedly taken ill).[61] In forty-five minutes of rehearsal time, Bausch dissects a few sequences from the final solo: Ichida's efforts are viscerally plain to see as Bausch imparts not just the steps, but the motivation that lies behind them. This tantalising glimpse into Bausch's intimate rehearsal process demonstrates the degree to which she expected both meticulousness and, crucially, strong technique from her dancers. Observing a company rehearsal in Wuppertal in September 2011, I noted that, similarly, the utter fatigue of the two dancers alternating the role of the Chosen One was apparent throughout. In a setting devoid of an audience, there was no acting or playing to the camera – instead, the physical strain on these experienced company members was quite evident. Removed from the theatre context and without a full audience, even the dancers' marking movements were drained by the unrelenting changes of direction and speed.[62]

That Bausch's choreography is designed to challenge the limits of a dancer's training align with Kahn's observation of her work in 1972: 'her peculiar vocabulary, dependent on a unique technique created for her own limber and specially trained body, seems hard on other dancers ... I was told several dancers injured themselves attempting to master some of the moves.'[63] Bausch claimed her original intention was to maintain the possibility that any of the dancers could have been selected as victim, but the complexity of the final solo meant that in practice this would have to be predetermined.[64] In her own words, Bausch stated:

> The starting point is the music. There are so many feelings in it; it changes constantly. There is also much fear in it. I thought, how would it be to dance knowing you have to die? How would you feel, how would I feel? The Chosen One is special, but she dances knowing the end is death.[65]

In her *Sacre*, Bausch opted to explore the sacrificial ritual in an empty, almost apocalyptic, landscape. Her dancers emote a sense of terror once the confusion around the mysterious red dress is lifted, huddling together for security before joining together en masse to perform a celebratory, yet joyless, choral dance. As the score progresses and the dancers' thin costumes become ever more soiled, the overall appearance of the massed performers begins to resemble a group of concentration camp inmates. They are a nameless assembly – slender, weary bodies and fearful expressions – clad in identical, stained, ragged clothing. The dancers perform movements as though compelled by some dreadful unseen force, exhibiting palpable relief when a sacrificial victim has been chosen. The bare stage setting contributes to this impression, the blankness of the space beyond the earth-covered floor implying a form of primordial emptiness, or resembling some kind of muddied prison yard. The starkness of the stage, with its lack of decoration beyond the muddy floor, implies a primitive, elemental setting; a 'zero hour' of sorts, where the dancers act out what Rika Schulze-Reuber has called 'a ritual of earth-worship'.[66] It is not surprising that one German critic called this piece a 'death dance'.[67]

Bausch's desire to demonstrate a palpable fear of death is a distinct shift from the almost celebratory ritual of her predecessor Wigman. The two women belonged to separate generations that, in postwar Germany, shared an uneasy relationship. Bausch belonged to the generation of young people seeking answers to difficult questions about the recent past, some of whom went as far as to request that their parents admit responsibility for what had happened under Nazism. Wigman, on the other hand, was a member of this parental generation, accused, whether explicitly or implicitly, of collusion and sympathy with fascism. Thus, where Wigman's *Sacre* formed an attempt at atonement, Bausch's was angrier, more urgent and, in this sense, characteristic of her generation's questioning, resolution-seeking worldview.

The legacy of the Second World War is evident throughout numerous examples of Bausch's early choreography, demonstrated by themes of violence that have come to characterise a significant proportion of her *oeuvre*. More recent critical responses perhaps better comprehend the complexity of Bausch's work, delving beyond the surface shock value of her early reviews. Simon Murray and John Keefe, for instance, observe that, 'for Bausch pain is the corollary of living, loving and desire. It is also an existential condition born out of the monstrosities of fascism and the Holocaust.'[68] For many young Germans of Bausch's age, collective anger was directed at the so-called *Tätergeneration* (generation of perpetrators) and much of the visual and performance art that emerged from this conflict was designed to be a complete break from the pre-war lineage. Moishe Postone has observed that the weight of the Nazi past meant that traditional methods of 'coming to terms' with the past were rendered effectively useless:

> Although the German student movement shared many features with its counterparts in other Western countries, it also, very self-consciously, involved a repudiation of the Nazi past and of the degree to which elements of that past continued to inform the present. The conflict engaged in by the students and other young people was, of course, also generational – but the generation of parents was one that largely had supported the Nazi regime.[69]

The political undertones in Bausch's *Sacre* serve as a connection to another important embodiment of the modernist legacy, namely her mentor Jooss. His anti-war ballet, *The Green Table* was a blend of classical and contemporary dance styles, with the female dancers performing in pointe shoes, but exhibiting decidedly modernist tendencies in the percussive movements and mobile spines of the cast. Jooss was an advocate of ballet training, arguing that ballet and modern dance techniques could complement each other. Premiered at the Théâtre des Champs-Élysées in Paris on 3 July 1932, this landmark work has never been retired from international ballet repertoires, and was adopted by the Joffrey Ballet Company in 1967 (Bausch performed the role of The Old Woman in a 1960s revival). Jooss' partnership with Sigurd Leeder – a young artist and designer who had studied movement with Laban, taken acting classes and was also a mask-maker – was a highly influential factor in the development of *The Green Table*. Indeed, an early mask-design experiment in creating a range of pieces to reflect different emotions laid the groundwork for the development of Jooss' ballet. The masks of the Men in Black in the opening scene of *The Green Table* derived from Leeder's original project. They deliberately exaggerated, to grotesque effect, the features of the brokers and bureaucrats negotiating over the baize-lined table of the ballet's title.

Much discussion of Jooss' piece is, understandably, rooted in political as well as social analysis, as the narrative focuses on the breakdown of diplomatic negotiations, leading to war, violence and death. It is somewhat ironic that, in an interview conducted in 1976 and shown on the American PBS network in 1982, Jooss stated, 'I am firmly convinced that art should never be political, that art should not dream of altering people's convictions . . . I don't think any war will be shorter or avoided by sending audiences into *The Green Table*.'[70] Ultimately, however, his narrative espouses a palpable anti-war sentiment, disconcertingly foreshadowing the violence and trauma that awaited in the years leading up to the Second World War.

Decades after the 1913 premiere of Nijinsky's now infamous *Sacre*, Bausch's choreography proved that there was still the potential to shock audiences with Stravinsky's now canonical score. She created a work that unconsciously connected her *Tanztheater* with a modernist legacy in dance, one that from its inception sought to jolt audiences out of their passive enjoyment of spectacle. Bausch's *Sacre* also connects her to Wigman, her *Ausdruckstanz* predecessor. Where Wigman's imagining of a matriarchal tribe is abstract in its conception, parallels still exist with Bausch's visceral ritual. As German choreographers in the postwar landscape, both women enacted rituals of purgation, of stripping bare and starting anew, albeit in the context of human sacrifice. Bausch's *Sacre* lies in no man's land; an earthy, timeless setting, playing out ritualistic and tribal behaviours in its supposedly unspecified context. Viewed in light of their socio-political setting, it is almost impossible to divorce their ritual sacrifices from their immediate, and shared, historical background.

*

Dance theatre is a malleable, shape-shifting label, a term that does not define an individual movement but refers to a collection of modernist and postmodern dance vocabularies. While their individual approaches to choreography remain distinct, Bausch and her generation of *Tanztheater* practitioners became associated with a sense of postwar angst, their work often drawing upon contemporary socio-political issues. This wave of choreographic experimentation emerged from a backdrop of upheaval and crisis, impacted upon not only by the immediate fallout of the Second World War, but also the international protest culture of the 1960s. German dance in particular reflected a deep underlying anxiety about humanity's cruelty, marking out *Tanztheater* choreographers from their American counterparts.

After Bausch's return to Germany in 1962, she continued to perform as a guest artist in the United States, often to great acclaim – Kahn's 1972 review of the Sansardo Company referred to her as 'the highlight of the concert'. Her training in the United States exerted a powerful impact on the works produced in the formative years of her career at the helm of Tanztheater Wuppertal. Yet the legacy of *Ausdruckstanz* is also evident in Bausch's early interest in more formal dance, imbuing the cool classicism of Balanchine with the swirling patterns of Wigman and the charged emotional content characteristic of Graham and Jooss. In the first years of her directorship in Wuppertal, the pure dance works were heavily informed by aesthetics drawn from both facets of her dance education. Even in predominantly balletic pieces such as *Orpheus*, Bausch makes continual visual references to an intercultural aesthetic dialogue, something that heavily informed the evolution of contemporary dance throughout the twentieth century. Drawing on specific mythological themes, Bausch locates her own work within this vital legacy in modern dance.

The early pure dance works are central to understanding Bausch's progression as a choreographer; viewed in light of her complete *oeuvre*, *Orpheus* and *Sacre* represent a crucial yet transitory moment in her career. In both of these pieces, a straightforward and identifiable narrative is explored through conventional modern dance technique. Despite what appears to be a rather conventional, conformist approach, however, in these key works, Bausch makes a number of significant reference points to major figures in modern dance, including Balanchine, Graham, Jooss, Nijinsky and Wigman. These artists all form important precedents to Bausch's own experimentation with avant-garde performance, and in the early dance works, she explored the limits of her creative potential working within the boundaries of linear narrative. *Sacre* may be read as a particularly notable milestone in this respect, as it belongs to a clear continuum connecting Bausch with Nijinsky, the first dancer to confront audiences with the possibilities of modernism on stage.

By the end of the 1970s, Bausch had largely abandoned choreographing around dance alone and had begun to work in a completely different way, structuring larger scale pieces around a process of posing questions to her dancers, asking them to respond both with language and movement. Thus, the pieces surveyed in this chapter represent a short but significant period in

Bausch's career, and signal the end of her engagement with pure dance. A new phase emerges in the years following *Sacre*, one in which she begins to evolve a style of *Tanztheater* that is uniquely her own, but informed by concepts associated with modernist theatre. Bausch's radical works did not emerge *sui generis*, but were heavily informed by existing precedents in international performance. Accordingly, *Orpheus* and *Sacre* come to represent a kind of artistic homage to her predecessors, reflecting the breadth of her education both at home and abroad.

NOTES

1. Bausch, 'What Moves Me'.
2. Ibid.
3. Manning, *Ecstasy and the Demon*, p. 228. Climenhaga also claims that, while the postwar government made significant hand-outs in funding the arts, favour fell largely with classical or more traditional forms of expression, and that, 'modern dance was often overlooked in favour of ballet'. *Pina Bausch*, p. 8.
4. Bausch, 'What Moves Me'.
5. Manning, 'Pina Bausch', p. 10.
6. Many writers translate *Ausdruckstanz* into English as 'Expressionist dance', which is both linguistically and historically incorrect. 'Expressive dance' is a more accurate translation, as it should be noted that this form of dance was not simply a branch of the German Expressionist movement (though personal and artistic links certainly did exist).
7. Müller, *Mary Wigman*, pp. 22–7.
8. Wigman, 'Aus Hellerau'. Unless otherwise indicated, please note that all translations throughout this volume are my own.
9. Müller, *Mary Wigman*, p. 37. The promotional brochures of Wigman's Dresden school advertised that classes were accompanied with percussion, as well as offering percussion lessons as part of the overall curriculum.
10. Fraleigh and Nakamura, *Hijikata Tatsumi and Ohno Kazuo*, p. 14.
11. Ibid., pp. 9, 14.
12. Baird, *Hijikata Tatsumi and Butoh*, p. 11.
13. For a more detailed analysis of the evolution of dance theatre in Germany and Austria, see Schlicher, *TanzTheater* and Schmidt, *Tanztheater in Deutschland*.
14. Burt, *Alien Bodies*, p. 124.
15. Toepfer, *Empire of Ecstasy*, p. 112.
16. Manning, 'An American Perspective on Tanztheater', p. 58.
17. Hardt, 'Alwin Nikolais – Dancing across Borders', in Gitelman and Martin (eds), *The Returns of Alwin Nikolais*, pp. 64–81.
18. Soares, *Louis Horst*, pp. 74–5.
19. Loney, 'I Pick My Dancers as People', p. 17.
20. While this is a marginalised element of his work, the influence of three key writers – Rupert Doone, T. S. Eliot, and J. B. Priestley – on Tudor's work is examined in Sawyer, 'Antony Tudor and English Theater', pp. 217–36.
21. Homans, *Apollo's Angels*, p. 473.
22. Van Praagh, 'Working with Antony Tudor', p. 57.
23. Meisner, 'Come Dance with Me', in Climenhaga (ed.), *The Pina Bausch Sourcebook*, p. 168.
24. Müller, 'Offenheit aus Überzeugung' in Regitz (ed.), *Tanz in Deutschland*, p. 100.
25. Linke studied at the Mary Wigman School in Berlin before coming to Essen where

she worked under Bausch. She would go on to succeed her mentor as director of the Folkwang Dance Studio from 1975 to 1985, founding her own company a few years later, and directing the Bremer Tanztheater until 2000.

26. Kahn, 'The Paul Sansardo Dance Company' p. 86.
27. Schmidt, quoted in Daly, 'Tanztheater', p. 46.
28. Müller, 'Offenheit aus Überzeugung', in Regitz (ed.), *Tanz in Deutschland*, p. 101.
29. Jennings, 'Obituary'.
30. Koegler, 'Germany [reviews]', p. 52.
31. Mercy, quoted in Meisner, 'Come Dance with Me', in Climenhaga (ed.), *The Pina Bausch Sourcebook*, p. 168.
32. Cattaneo, 'Pina Bausch: You Can Always Look At It the Other Way Around', in Climenhaga (ed.), *The Pina Bausch Sourcebook*, p. 83.
33. Agnes de Mille was an American-born ballet dancer. She moved to London to study with Rambert, and eventually joined Tudor's company, London Ballet. While she choreographed several classical works, most have been lost, and it is largely her contributions to Broadway dance that remain in existing repertoire; *Rodeo* was perhaps her most successful creation.
34. In April 2013, Förster was appointed artistic director of Tanztheater Wuppertal Pina Bausch, succeeding Dominique Mercy and dramaturge Robert Sturm, who had shared the role since Bausch's death in 2009.
35. Koegler, 'Germany: Season's Round Up', p. 35.
36. For more detailed discussion of Appia's work with Dalcroze, see Tallon, 'Appia's Theatre at Hellerau', pp. 495–504.
37. Levitz, 'The Chosen One's Choice', in Dell'Antonio (ed.), *Beyond Structural Listening*, p. 84.
38. Siegel, 'Re-Radicalizing Graham', p. 101.
39. Zanobi, 'From Duncan to Bausch with Iphigenia', in Mackintosh (ed.), *The Ancient Dancer in the Modern World*, p. 252.
40. Kendall, *Balanchine and the Lost Muse*, p. 234.
41. Ibid., p. 234.
42. Macauley, 'Squeezing All the Love Out of a Love Story'.
43. Bausch on *Sacre*, quoted in Bentivoglio, *Pina Bausch oder die Kunst, über Nelken zu tanzen*, p. 38.
44. There are numerous descriptions of the riotous reaction to Nijinsky's premiere, though Eksteins provides a detailed and reasonably measured account in his *Rites of Spring*, pp. 31–40. A detailed list of versions produced throughout the twentieth century is provided in Jordan, *Stravinsky Dances*.
45. Homans, *Apollo's Angels*, p. 309.
46. Wigman's *Sacre* was never recorded on film. However, the piece exists in a series of choreographic notes and photographs documenting the rehearsal process and final production, now held in the Mary Wigman archive at the Akademie der Künste, Berlin.
47. Sorell, *Mary Wigman*, p. 241.
48. Anonymous critic, cited by Fritsch-Vivié, *Mary Wigman*, p. 126.
49. Manning, 'German Rites', p. 130.
50. *Wind von West* was reconstructed in 2013 by former company members Jo Ann Endicott, Mari DiLena and John Giffin for students at the Julliard School as part of the 'New Dances Plus' series.
51. Sokolova, *Dancing for Diaghilev*, p. 164.
52. Amarante, quoted in Fernandes, *Pina Bausch and the Wuppertal Dance Theatre*, p. 117.
53. Servos, *Pina Bausch*, p. 37.

54. Cody, 'Woman, Man, Dog, Tree', p. 120.
55. Birringer, *Theatre, Theory, Postmodernism*, p. 136.
56. Banes, *Dancing Women*, p. 102.
57. Schlagenwerth, 'Nicht eins, nicht zwei sein können'.
58. Birringer, 'Pina Bausch', p. 92.
59. Schlagenwerth, 'Nicht eins, nicht zwei sein können'.
60. Manning, 'German Rites', p. 146.
61. *Sacre: Probe.*
62. In dance terminology, marking choreography refers to the act of rehearsing movement with an emphasis on keeping to appropriate time or spatial limits, without giving a full performance of the movement.
63. Kahn, 'The Paul Sansardo Dance Company', p. 86.
64. As stated by Sturm, 'Illustrated talk on the work of Pina Bausch'.
65. Riding, 'Using Muscles Classical Ballet Has No Need For'.
66. Schulze-Reuber, *Das Tanztheater Pina Bausch*, p. 105.
67. Michaelis, 'Tanzangst. Angsttanz'.
68. Murray and Keefe (eds), *Physical Theatres*, p. 70.
69. Postone, 'After the Holocaust' in Härms et al. (eds), *Coping With the Past*, p. 236.
70. Quoted in Walther, *The Dance of Death*, p. 72.

2

NEW BEGINNINGS: THE ORIGINS OF BAUSCH'S *TANZTHEATER*

Bausch's decision to return to Germany set in motion a chain of events that would lead to her appointment as artistic director of an established ballet company at the relatively young age of thirty-three. With this new role came intense public scrutiny, and Bausch's choreographies elicited mixed responses. While relatively conventional pieces such as *Orpheus* and *Sacre* were successful with local audiences, unorthodox offerings like *Fritz* stoked greater controversy. However, it is the collection of works produced in the late 1970s that represent the first major experimental period in Bausch's *oeuvre*, where, emboldened by the gradual success of the rather more traditional preceding works, she began to test the boundaries of the stage.

The pieces Bausch devised between 1976 and 1978 reveal a fundamental desire to break the conventions of modern dance. Amalgamating theories and techniques encountered through her bilingual dance education in Essen and New York, she created these works in a style that would form the root of her *Tanztheater* method. However, while the early experimental pieces demonstrate radical innovation in terms of Bausch's practice, many elements of their construction and presentation are foregrounded in modernist theatre practice, a process Marvin Carlson terms 'ghosting' in his 2001 study, *The Haunted Stage*. Carlson proposes that a sense of déjà vu stimulates the theatrical memory of the spectator, recalling images of other directors, actors, themes and designs. According to his model (one which is itself a continuation of a theme explored already by writers such as Herbert Blau and Jacques

Derrida), all theatre is haunted by the past, and all theatrical material is, to some extent, recycled. Bausch's *Tanztheater* is similarly haunted by important predecessors. Her working method is highly evocative of Bertolt Brecht and Jerzy Grotowski's anti-naturalistic approach to theatre making, and the resulting works are permeated by the influence of Samuel Beckett in particular. However, her collagist reimaginings of well-known themes never constitute straightforward revivals, as is evident in her unique revisions of Brecht, Beckett and Shakespeare.

EARLY CONTROVERSIES: THE BRECHT/WEILL EVENING

Bausch's first modernist 'adaptation' came in the wake of her mythological trilogy. On 15 June 1976, she presented a new and brutally uncompromising work: *Die sieben Todsünden* (Figure 2.1) was a two-part dance evening, its first act based on Brecht and Kurt Weill's 1933 production of the same name. Bausch's piece forms an allegorical account of the seven cardinal sins as experienced by two sisters – Anna I (the cynical, conniving manager, played by a singer) and Anna II (her naïve but impulsive foil, represented by a dancer) – who travel from their home in Louisiana to various cities across the United States to seek their fortune. Anna II fails to indulge in any of the sins she encounters, and while she succeeds in finding the money to buy a house for their family, she is left envying the people encountered along the way (who, unlike her, are able to indulge in 'sinful' behaviour). The tale is ultimately ironic, as Brecht inverts the concept of vice; sins become virtues in his anti-capitalist model, and Anna I and Anna II form the physical manifestation of the divide between consumers and producers.

Brecht's writings on theatre practice were well known and widely disseminated in Germany by the mid-1970s and, as David Barnett has observed, his work was mounted so often that he had become 'a familiar and blunted classic'.[1] Bausch's piece, however, was not an immediately recognisable restaging of the Brecht/Weill original. Her dance evening was divided into two separate pieces: act one, *Die sieben Todsünden der Kleinbürger* (*The Seven Deadly Sins of the Petit-Bourgeoisie* – the full title of the original work), approximately followed the Brecht/Weill narrative, while the second act, *Fürchtet Euch nicht* (*Don't Be Afraid*), was a revue arranged around a loose plot structure, set to a compilation of songs from earlier Brecht productions. Borzik's stage design came from a cast he had made of a street in Wuppertal which he used to mould the set. There is a curious contrast between the supposed naturalism of the set and the visibility of the spotlights and musicians to the audience – the obvious artificiality of the stage setting reveals a Brechtian rejection of illusionism that would come to characterise the works of Bausch's early experimental period.

However, in contrast to Brecht's overt critique of capitalism, Bausch's version focuses entirely on the objectification of women's bodies, dispensing

Figure 2.1 *Die sieben Todsünden*, Laszlo Szito

with the remaining six sins. It is a very dark Lust she evokes here: while Anna II is kissed, groped, weighed, measured and fondled by the male cast, Anna I continues singing the upbeat numbers of the Brecht/Weill score. Anna I functions as a pimp to the naïve, continually exploited Anna II. The role of 'the family' is played by a cast of men in smart suits who stalk Anna II and eventually become the rapists of the second act. Indeed, *Fürchtet Euch nicht* would achieve notoriety in Bausch's *oeuvre* due to the inclusion of a brutal gang rape scene. Her Brecht/Weill evening forms a sharp critique of show business, emphasising the sleaze and exploitation of the entertainment industry. Yet even within the context of Bausch's often dark subject matter, it was a shocking and unusually direct depiction of gender violence, one that garnered some deeply critical reviews.

In addition to its poor public reception, the making of the Brecht/Weill evening saw conflicts arise between Bausch and her dancers. She later stated that, 'for the first time, I was afraid of my dancers. They hated the piece. They would not understand or accept it.'[2] After the premiere, she experienced a severe crisis of confidence, at first refusing to set foot inside the theatre again. Endicott, who had danced the role of Anna II, claims that a 'bad atmosphere' hung over Bausch and her company during the first few months of 1977.[3] As a result of the negative response, Bausch would dramatically shift her approach to dance-making and begin to evolve a new choreographic format. *Die sieben Todsünden* was the last piece that followed a straightforward, linear narrative. The works produced over the next two years demonstrate the beginning of a radical break that would characterise the rest of her *oeuvre*. She developed a method based on a collagist process of questioning her dancers, integrating movement and spoken word into a new theatrical format.

While Bausch evolved an innovative approach to creating dance works, it is nonetheless clear that her first recognisable *Tanztheater* pieces derive significant influence from modernist performance practice. There is a cinematic aspect to Bausch's motifs of interruption, repetition and revision, an onstage 'cutting' and reordering of the action that emerges for the first time in the period following the Brecht/Weill evening, and parallels the development of the East German playwright Heiner Müller's collagist system. Modernist experimentation is a key player in the evolution of her new technique, yet despite the striking parallels with her work, to date, the twin influences of theatre and dance have not been thoroughly interrogated in current debates around Bausch's *Tanztheater*. Specific case study works can aid in illuminating the ghosts of modernist theatre in Bausch's early experimental work.

WORKING FROM THE INSIDE OUT

Amidst the fallout of the *Todsünden* opening, it was the dancer Jan Minarik who coaxed Bausch back to making dance. Around half the company had left after the unsuccessful premiere but, with a much-reduced cast (initially, only four dancers) and Minarik's encouragement, she tentatively began creating a new piece in his small, private studio. Having made each previous piece through a traditional choreographic approach, Bausch could work in a completely new style once sequestered inside Minarik's space, one that was structured around a collage of fragments that incorporated movement, spoken word and everyday gesture. From this point, each time she initiated the process of making a new piece, Bausch was never certain what the result might be called, how it would be framed or what it would look like. Instead, she went into rehearsals with a conviction that when she saw what she wanted, these unknowns would gradually become clear.[4] Her co-workers remained equally in the dark. Wardrobe manager and former company dancer Marion Cito claims that Bausch rarely spoke with her designers during the making of each new work, and this often resulting in them working well into the night trying to fit the last elements together. Peter Pabst, who took over stage design after Borzik's death, claimed that Bausch only ever asked a single question when he showed her a new model: 'And what else can it do?'[5]

The questioning technique is perhaps what most obviously sets Bausch's work apart from that of her contemporaries in the dance world. The process of making a new work would begin with a list of questions Bausch had compiled in advance, what she called *Stichworte* ('prompts' or 'keywords').[6] These were often quite personal or esoteric enquiries:

> Yesterday I asked if anyone had ever been so frightened they'd messed their pants and when was the first time they'd felt they were a man or a woman. Good questions but they don't lead us anywhere. Sometimes I think I've got really good questions, but they lead nowhere. And then sometimes I ask a similar kind of question in a totally different way, until in the end I've change it completely – and then sometimes I get there in a roundabout way.[7]

However, neither she nor the dancers would propose direct answers to these questions. It is a gradual and collagist process – a full day's rehearsal might only lead to five or ten minutes of the overall work. The result comprises a moving collage, a patchwork of open-ended questions that is ultimately left to the spectator to reassemble and interpret. In this respect, Bausch discards naturalism in favour of a Brechtian eschewing of emotional investment in the action. With no clear plotline or conclusion, Bausch offers her audience the opportunity to construct the narrative and, in doing so, defies the autonomy of the traditional theatrical model.

Neither is this questioning process based on a purely improvisational level: there is still a sense of 'performing' in improvisation, something Bausch wanted to avoid by giving her performers open-ended and sometimes surreal prompts.

Rather than expecting her dancers to improvise movements on a specific topic, Bausch would ask questions to lead the group into a collective understanding of a particular issue. In doing so, the search for an answer would lead the individual to excavate the recesses of their mind, rather than limiting themselves to the idea of generating a specific movement. Thus, an underlying motif exists beneath the various questions and the dancers' responses, and this forms the thematic thread on which each work is built. It is an inherently somatic, embodied practice, one that is not based on improvisation for its own sake, nor does it seek to impose a singular movement style or technique upon the cast of dancers. While pedestrian movement comprises a significant proportion of on-stage action, her *Tanztheater* does not resemble the improvisation-led approach of postmodern choreographers such as Steve Paxton or Yvonne Rainer. A closer parallel might be drawn with Cunningham's creative process, in which movement is consciously isolated from the accompanying soundtrack, and the audience is continually reminded that the choreography is not driven or shaped by its score.[8] Bausch's works evolve according to a similar principle. Despite the significant role the soundtrack plays in creating the overarching atmosphere to her productions, Bausch tended not to use music during the rehearsal period in order to avoid the dancers improvising to specific scores. This presents a degree of risk in composing a new work, as the dancers would usually be introduced to the soundtrack at a late stage in the process, having already worked out the general structure and choreography of movement. Matthias Burkert, Bausch's musical collaborator for three decades, claimed:

> It was important for her that the form of the dance had an independent life, an independent story to tell. It was always the most exciting moment, when we dared to let the dance meet a piece of music or the other way around. It was always a courageous step – there was always the risk of disturbing or even destroying something through a wrong choice.[9]

Technically, this approach does not constitute 'choreography' in any traditional sense, and in fact the emphasis on an internal impulse owes a certain debt to Brecht's conception of *Gestus*. Brecht required his actors to maintain a distance from the character to prevent the spectator from too readily identifying with that figure. He rejected the translation of *Gestus* as 'gesticulation', arguing that, 'it is not a matter of explanatory or emphatic movement of the hands, but of overall attitudes'.[10] Emphasising the showing of a character, emotion or mannerism rather than artificial embodiment, Brecht's technique is visible both in Bausch's creative process and finished works. The collagist image the audience consumes is the result of a sometimes difficult and deeply personal creative process for both choreographer and dancer.

Brechtian motifs appear in many of Bausch's works and are an integral factor in the construction of her early experimental pieces. Throughout her *oeuvre*,

Bausch employs multiple distancing effects, a technique that has its roots in Brecht's vision of epic theatre. What Brecht termed the *Verfremdungseffekt* was a way of jolting the audience from passive, emotional engagement with a play's content and inducing a more active engagement with its politicised themes. Chinese theatre was central to Brecht's evolving ideas around distancing effects and breaking the fourth wall – after seeing Mei Lenfang's company perform in 1935, Brecht observed:

> The Chinese artist never acts as if there were a fourth wall besides the three surrounding him. He expresses his awareness of being watched. This immediately removes one of the European stage's characteristic illusions. The audience can no longer have the illusion of being the unseen spectator at an event which is really taking place. A whole elaborate European stage technique, which helps to conceal the fact that the scenes are so arranged that the audience can view them in the easiest way, is thereby made unnecessary.[11]

This format reacted against naturalism in performance as represented by, for example, Konstantin Stanislavski's method, and plays made within this framework often presented the audience with a moral dilemma. Brecht went so far as to praise 'bad' acting, as this further underlined the artificiality of the stage environment.

Formally, there are obvious similarities between epic theatre and Bausch's *Tanztheater*. Both reject naturalism, illusionism and traditional narrative structure, favouring a non-linear and collagist framework. The action is frequently interrupted by distancing effects. However, in Bausch's *Tanztheater*, while the methods of distancing are structurally similar to Brecht's, their purpose is not explicitly politically motivated. Bausch did not advocate a politicised theatre and, with the exception of the Brecht/Weill evening, she largely shied away from exploring overtly politicised themes. Her *Tanztheater* eschews the specifically Marxist impulse of Brecht's work, instead evolving an approach that serves as a mirror for society without proposing necessary solutions or definitive conclusions. I would contend, however, that this method is not necessarily apolitical: Shomit Mitter suggests, 'the utility of estrangement is not propaganda: it teaches insight'.[12]

Bausch's method in this period also demonstrates similarities with Jerzy Grotowski's system, where, in the early 1970s, he abandoned large-scale theatre to work in small groups or one to one with his actors, making plays for smaller audiences. Grotowski's notion of Poor Theatre emphasised that productions ought to be minimalist in form and that theatre makers should reject the notion of spectacle, permitting the audience to see the actual workings of the theatre space. He rejected naturalism, and, in a similar vein to Brecht's fascination with Chinese theatre, drew upon Eastern traditions alongside exercises from Vsevolod Meyerhold's biomechanics model in his performance training regime.[13] Grotowski stressed that actors should seek to reveal the 'inner truth' of a character rather than simply performing or enacting the role:

> The decisive factor in this process is the actor's technique of psychic penetration. He must learn to use his role as if it were a surgeon's scalpel, to dissect himself. It is not a question of portraying himself under certain given circumstances, or of 'living' a part; nor does it entail the distant sort of acting common to epic theatre and based on cold calculation. The important thing is to use the role as a trampolin [*sic*], an instrument with which to study what is hidden behind our everyday mask – the innermost core of our personality – in order to sacrifice it, expose it.[14]

The primary focus thus lies upon the embodiment rather than the 'inhabiting' of a character role. Thomas Richards identifies a crucial distinction between Stanislavski and Grotowski in their attitudes to character, observing that while for Stanislavski the character is a separate entity, for Grotowski it, 'existed more as a public screen which protected the actor'.[15] Grotowski's character emerges from what Richards terms a 'montage' process, and is subsequently assembled by the audience. This methodology equally applies to Bausch's choreographic technique in which her characters conflate aspects of reality with fiction and fantasy, leaving the end product to be interpreted by the spectator. Both represent inherently hybridic approaches.

The importance of regular work and repetition is also emphasised in Grotowski's method. Despite radical differences in their respective acting systems, Grotowski greatly admired Stanislavski for his insistence upon daily training to refine the actor's craft. An unending working process underlies this approach, training both body and mind. Going a step further than Stanislavski, however, Grotowski's practice does not indicate a single prescribed method, and in fact the system is different for each individual performer. Certain endurance exercises test the stamina of the actor, forcing the individual to repeat actions, movements and sequences for long periods of time while maintaining absolute concentration.[16] As Sabine Sörgel has indicated, there are important similarities between dance and drama training, not least the tendency towards working in small groups, in intimate, non-theatre spaces, with an emphasis on honesty and a move away from showmanship or virtuosity.[17] Examining the mechanics of Grotowski's creative model, it becomes clear that Bausch's radical *Stichworte* technique in fact draws upon an established anti-naturalist tradition in modernist theatre making. She insisted on the importance of daily company class, but also increasingly worked one to one with her dancers during the development period. For the dancers, as for Grotowski's actors, such long hours impacted upon the likelihood of taking on outside work and required dedication to an individual director. Just as Grotowski's students were bound by the demands of his technique, so Bausch's durational and intensive creative period fostered an unusually intimate relationship between choreographer and cast.

Grotowski was deeply critical of his students if he suspected they had lapsed into what he called 'tourist' behaviour, improvisations that leapt from one theme to another without interrogating the structure of the proposed sequence. Superficiality is thus firmly rejected.[18] Grotowski's antipathy towards straightforward improvisation as a compositional tool is reiterated in Bausch's *Stichworte* method. He was quick to identify the clichés of what he termed 'paratheatrics', banal and recurring images that Bausch also dissects in her *Tanztheater*: throwing oneself on the floor screaming to represent suffering would be one such example. In Bausch's model, however, such Grotowskian paratheatrics come in the form of clichéd gestures or behaviours. Both advocated that their performers examine deeper underlying motivations, rather than using movement to illustrate an assigned emotion or soundtrack, and this was achieved in both cases through consistent repetitions of improvised sequences.[19] At the heart of this lies a desire for authenticity and to create a performative event that extends further than spectacle, illusion or entertainment. Grotowski asks:

> Why are we concerned with art? To cross our frontiers, exceed our limitations, fill our emptiness – fulfil ourselves. This is not a condition but a process in which what is dark in us slowly becomes transparent. In this struggle with one's own truth, this effort to peel off the life-mask, the theatre, with its full-fleshed perceptivity, has always seemed to me a place of provocation.[20]

Despite the intense nature of his training and performance regime, Grotowski refused to package his individualised work with actors as a unique 'method'. His approach constantly shifted, and exercises were neither formalised nor consistently applied to all performers. Jennifer Kumiega has observed that:

> There is no one technique or exercise which had an *absolute* value for the laboratory theatre and was a permanent feature of their training. Even the very idea of training itself was abandoned for a certain period when it was found to be losing the quality of challenge for the team.[21]

A similar rejection of standardisation characterises Bausch's method, a term that I use in a loose sense throughout my analysis of her work. Certain tendencies and technical approaches recur throughout her *oeuvre*, but the *Stichworte* approach is different for every performer and in each new work. It is an individual process that cannot be easily condensed into a series of exercises. Bausch was not concerned with creating a specific movement vocabulary, but instead sought to create a dance theatre that could be universally comprehensible, communicating with the audience on a deeper level than the purely physical.

It is not the narrative storytelling inherent in Graham technique, nor is it the improvisational approach of Wigman or Laban. Similarly, Bausch's method of creating *Tanztheater* avoids the strong narrative impulse of Jooss' style. While elements are likely derived from Jooss' theatricality and Paul Taylor's embrace of pedestrian movement, Bausch evolved a style that was specifically her own. In place of a recognisable technique, there are returning themes, images and motifs that we might term 'Bauschian', though, as I suggested in Chapter 1, there is a movement quality that recurs throughout her *oeuvre* that is almost immediately identifiable as a marker of Bausch's work. This is particularly seen in the expressive and flowing use of the arms and upper body, seen both in the choreography for male and female dancers (in her late works, which feature longer sequences of 'pure' dance, the tendency reappears more often). The pieces themselves represent a journey both for the dancers and for the audience, though the precise location is often left ambiguous, as is any concrete notion of time. This somatic method is not something that can be structured and sold as 'Bausch technique', however. Rather, as Robert Sturm explains:

> It's a way of thinking. Pina took all the theory out of theatre, all the barriers, there is no distance between the audience and what's happening on stage. You cannot teach that in school but I think it's possible to pass it on. You absorb it by being in the company.[22]

Bausch's *Stichworte* method comes into its most recognisable fruition with *Kontakthof* (*Meeting Place*, 1978), a work that has been extensively discussed in existing literature on Bausch, and is explored in closer detail in Chapter 3.[23] My analysis here focuses on two case studies which characterise her early, more experimental approach to the questioning method, specifically, *Blaubart: Beim Anhören einer Tonbandaufnahme von Béla Bartóks Oper 'Herzog Blaubarts Burg'* (*Bluebeard: While listening to a tape recording of Béla Bartók's opera 'Duke Bluebeard's Castle'*, 1977), and *Er nimmt sie an der Hand und führt sie in das Schloss, die anderen folgen* (*He takes her by the hand and leads her into the castle, the others follow*, 1978). Created in the twelve months leading to the premiere of *Kontakthof* in December 1978, *Blaubart* and the Macbeth Project (so called as the title is claimed to derive from a stage direction in a German edition of Shakespeare's play) constitute key works that are often overlooked in discussion of her *oeuvre*. These pieces demonstrate Bausch's first exploration of various techniques that would be more confidently employed in subsequent work – my analysis aims to contextualise Bausch's radical break from narrative-led dance.

THE HAUNTED SELF: *BLAUBART*

In late 1976, the senior management of the Wuppertal opera house suggested that Bausch produce a new work based on the Bluebeard myth, outlining an approximate structure. They proposed that she create two pieces, one based on the lighter comic opera by Jacques Offenbach (1866), and the other on Béla Bartók's version (1911, revised 1917). However, Bausch became increasingly consumed by the Bartók recording, and the dance theatre work which she was developing would be choreographed to this score alone.[24] Ensconced in Minarik's studio, Bausch initiated the choreographic process by asking the performers a series of questions which primarily revolved around the subject of male–female relationships and the dancers' own memories of the Bluebeard fairy tale. The resulting piece would embody many of the defining components of Bausch's *Tanztheater*. There is little recognisable, choreographed dance in this work, marking a decisive departure from the Gluck and Stravinsky pieces produced only a few years previously. Similarly, the programme notes did not refer to *Blaubart* as a ballet (as with *Sacre*), or a dance opera (in the case of the Gluck works). Instead, the piece was rather esoterically described as a collection of 'scenes'.

Blaubart was a landmark production in the development of Bausch's new approach and represents the first complete *Tanztheater* work in her *oeuvre*. It is, however, a challenging piece – Schulze-Reuber has called it one of her 'most difficult and introverted' choreographies.[25] At Borzik's suggestion, Bausch elected to use recorded music instead of a live orchestra. Having experienced difficulties collaborating with musicians who criticised her method in *Die sieben Todsünden*, working with the tape recording seemed a safer alternative, and opened new possibilities for the overall structuring of the piece. This first departure from previous form, abandoning live music, was made more unusual by the fact that the tape player itself (already referenced in the work's title) would occupy a central position on the stage, in full view of the audience, and that the performers would interact with it throughout. The action of the performance is frequently interrupted by the recording on the cassette player, and the soundtrack determines the course of the action, rather like an elaborate game of musical chairs. As a result, the piece runs at about double the length of the Bartók score. A motif already explored in both *Orpheus* and *Die sieben Todsünden* is also reprised here, as the central characters' personalities are split, represented by Bluebeard and Judith's singing voices on the tape, and the dancers – who are physically present, but largely silent – on stage.

Bausch's early choreographies often revisit well-known themes and myths, and in doing so, she could rely upon the audience's tacit understanding of the content. The earliest known version of the Bluebeard theme can be found in Charles Perrault's 1697 collection of fairy tales, *Histoires ou contes du temps passé*, under the title *La Barbe Bleue*. In Perrault's account, a naïve young woman becomes the latest wife of Duke Bluebeard (so called because of his blue-black facial hair), who presents her with a set of seven keys. He tells her she may explore the castle at will, but that she must not open the seventh door.

When her husband is away, Judith enters the forbidden room, where she finds the bodies of his previous wives. Upon his return, Bluebeard discovers that she has disobeyed him, as the key remains stained with the victims' blood, despite Judith's attempts to wash it clean. Flying into a rage, he threatens to kill her, but she is saved by the arrival of her two brothers, who kill the duke. The young woman inherits his fortune and, of course, lives happily ever after.

Bartók's opera was based upon German versions of the Bluebeard theme, which marks an important thematic departure from Perrault's text. Completed in 1911, Karen Mozingo called it, 'the first European Bluebeard text to fully resist a subversive ending'.[26] Despite the tale's French origins, in her study of multiple versions of the theme, Mererid Puw Davies observes that German authors have tended to alter the ending of the story in favour of a darker narrative. Where the original French version celebrates the wife's curiosity, which is ultimately her saviour, German versions have tended towards a critique of female inquisitiveness and nosiness, punishing the wife for her disobedience. Davies points out that, between 1905 and 1911, a series of particularly violent versions of the tale were published by German writers.[27] This violence is always enacted against the women in the story, becoming more bloody and extreme with the shift into the twentieth century.

Bausch's postwar evocation of the tale would revive this brutal Germanic legacy. First performed at the Wuppertal Opera House on 7 January 1977, her *Blaubart* is a haunting piece that juxtaposes absurdity with the threat of violence. Bausch alters various key details of the myth – the fairy tale castle is transformed into a derelict nineteenth-century home, with autumnal leaves scattered across the floor of the large open lounge that forms Borzik's set. The windows lining the sides of the stage are firmly closed, connoting a sense that the performers are trapped inside, and the only props consist of a tape recorder on a small trolley and a single chair. Cracks visible on the walls reinforce the abandoned house aesthetic but, on closer inspection, it becomes clear that these are gaps in the set, perhaps a deliberate Brechtian motif to remind the audience of the constructed nature of the stage design. The influence of Brecht is palpable throughout. Patterns of interruption and repetition are reminiscent of his epic theatre, as is the notion of editing material live on stage. Brecht is also evoked in the use of distancing devices, most obviously realised in the use of the tape recorder – though as shall become clear, this piece of technology also serves as an important link to Beckett's work.

Bausch's Bluebeard is an unremarkable, clean-shaven Everyman. He is dressed in a heavy dark overcoat, but wears no shoes, a costume reminiscent of both Brechtian minimalism and Beckett's itinerant anti-heroes. The piece opens with Bluebeard sitting in front of the tape recorder, while a woman lies on the floor with her arms bent at the elbows. He throws himself on top of her and shuffles across the floor; she remains impassive, with the only sound coming from the rustling of dead leaves. He stops, stands up and turns the tape on, before continuing to drag her across the floor. Again, he stops abruptly, resets the music and resumes the action. This motif repeats several times, with Bluebeard growing more agitated on each occasion he changes the music. The woman's face is expressionless, though, after several repetitions, it does appear that she is trying to push him away.

Where, in previous works, Bausch had begun to draw on the battle between the sexes as a recurring theme, in *Blaubart* it becomes the central focus of the entire piece. From the opening, the violent nature of Bluebeard's relationship with his wife is made clear and, despite the inclusion of other cast members, it is the couple that occupies centre stage here, with Bluebeard's wife adopting a particularly key role. Where the woman remained unnamed in the Perrault fairy tale, Béla Balázs, Bartók's librettist, bestowed on her an identity, calling her Judith. This particular choice of name is significant: Judith derives from the Hebrew *Yehudit*, meaning 'praised' or 'woman of Judea'. In the Apocrypha, Judith is the redeemer of the Israelites who beheads Holofernes and triumphantly drives the Assyrians from her country. According to Carl Leafstedt, in the early decades of the twentieth century the name 'Judith' was associated with the archetype of the femme fatale, in a manner comparable to popular depictions of Salome.[28] It is in keeping with this theme that in Bartók's staging, as Meg Mumford points out, the role of Judith was first sung by the 'powerfully built Olga Haselbeck', against a much slighter Oszkar Kalmann as Bluebeard.[29] In Bausch's version, however, the trend is reversed: Bluebeard is a towering figure, but Judith is danced by a slender woman clothed in dense, heavy material that threatens to drown her. She constantly reaches out to Bluebeard, who violently rejects her and manipulates her fragile body as if she were an unloved toy. Judith's passivity is underscored in the opening sequence – in this *Tanztheater* reimagining of the myth, she is certainly not the warrior queen of her Biblical namesake.

In Bausch's version of the tale, Judith functions as a mirror for Bluebeard's cruelty, forcing him to look upon his crimes; in one sequence, she drags individual women from a line-up and forces them to look at him, placing his previous victims in the spotlight. Bausch thus alters the storyline, implying that Judith is already conscious of her husband's violent past. This reordering of narrative is a collagist feature of the *Stichworte* method, allowing the audience to form alternative readings of the plot. The relationship between the protagonists is neither loving nor affectionate, and repeated actions of caressing and reconciliation are met with violence and rejection. Each time Judith attempts to take his hand, Bluebeard roughly snatches it away. This hostility becomes infectious – when Bluebeard turns the tape recording back on, couples begin to slow dance, though the women lead aggressively by dragging the men across the stage like puppets. Later, the women grope at the men, who back away sharply. Bluebeard repeatedly carries a limp Judith across the stage and abandons her in a corner, but she chases after him each time. Cycles of abuse are played out much more explicitly than in previous works and, in *Blaubart*, Bausch depicts an almost relentless display of suffering and rejection.

Superficially, *Blaubart* seems to imply that men are the aggressors and perpetrators of violence and women the passive targets of their abuse. Indeed, this reading characterised many of the reviews that the work garnered after its premiere in New York. Nonetheless, Bausch's non-linear narratives are never simplistic, and it seems a somewhat short-sighted interpretation that would limit *Blaubart* to a study of violence against women. Her characters are rarely one-dimensional figures, and the protagonists of *Blaubart* cannot simply be categorised as antagonist and victim. Bluebeard is a hulking yet ultimately pathetic figure who hauls women around the stage like insignificant objects. At the same time however, his appearance is worn and tormented, and as he sits slumped over the table with his head in his hands, he looks utterly defeated by his situation. Later, surrounded by the chorus of women, cooing and stroking him, he appears almost helpless, as if smothered by their unwanted affection. Trapped in this room with the spectres of his violent history, Bausch's Bluebeard inhabits a kind of living hell.

A palpable sense of haunting runs throughout this piece. With Bluebeard tormented by his crimes and his wife by the knowledge of his brutality and misogyny, both protagonists are haunted by events of the recent past. At the same time, Bluebeard is persecuted by Bartók's accompanying score which voices his inner thoughts and murderous desires. He attempts to shut out the singers as if to conceal or deny the evidence but, despite his best efforts, he cannot edit the past or escape the spectral figures of the women he has abused. Yet, in analysing Bausch's *Blaubart*, it becomes apparent that another figure ghosts its construction, namely Beckett's Krapp, the titular character of his 1958 play, *Krapp's Last Tape*. Beckett's work was well known in Germany by the time Bausch began the process of creating *Blaubart*. Beckett himself had directed the extremely successful German revival at Berlin's Schillertheater in 1969 (the play had already been staged at the same theatre a decade previously by Walter Henn), and mounted another performance in the city in 1977 with Rick Cluchey as the protagonist. Several writers on Bausch's work have drawn a connection between *Blaubart* and Beckett's play, largely due to the central presence of the tape recorder. Parallels between the two pieces run deeper than the use of this device, however, and form a significant indicator of Bausch's relationship with modernist theatre.

Just as *Blaubart* runs without an interval, *Krapp's Last Tape* is a one-act, minimalist play. The opening sequences of both performances are fitful and uncertain: Krapp shuffles back and forward across the bare stage setting, eating a banana, retrieving spools of tape and muttering to himself, while Bluebeard continually starts and stops the Bartók recording, rewinding to the same point with each repetition. The starkness of the stage design in each production evokes a misanthropic asceticism, and even the protagonists' clothing is similar – in the second half of Bausch's piece, Bluebeard exchanges his overcoat for a striped bathrobe, which is strikingly reminiscent of Krapp's costume design in the 1977 Berlin revival.[30] Both performances centre on a male anti-hero, and the respective narratives revolve around their personal histories. *Krapp's Last Tape* is structured on a framework of failed love stories. The protagonist sits alone in his room surrounded by recordings he has made each year. On his sixty-ninth birthday, he elects to listen to the tape that he made thirty years before. Despite its litany of failed intimacies, the play ends with Krapp's rather hollow proclamation that he is happy with his solitary existence.

It seems inconceivable that Bausch would have created *Blaubart* with no knowledge of Beckett's play. The tape player is a centrally positioned distancing device that frames the narrative of both pieces. *Krapp's Last Tape* is technically a monologue, but the protagonist is represented in two forms, his voice on tape at the age of thirty-nine and the sixty-nine-year-old self on stage. In a similar manner, Bluebeard is performed by the dancer and voiced by Bartók's score, which speaks the inner workings of his mind and his interactions with Judith. In Beckett's play, just as Krapp interrupts the tape recording, his recorded voice also interrupts his live monologue. The same principle of parallel interruption is at work in Bausch's *Bluebeard*, where the dancer attempts to edit and control the content of the tape, but is ultimately trapped by the recording. Miki Iwata repositions Beckett's play as a dialogue between sole performer and the recorder, and this same model might be applied to *Blaubart*.[31] In Bausch's piece, the recorder functions as a mouthpiece for the protagonist's dark thoughts and actions. Her vision of the myth radically alters the purpose of the musical accompaniment, turning Bartók's opera into a schizophrenic set of voices that foreshadow the violence, articulating Bluebeard's tortured thought processes. Just as Krapp loses himself in his own personal narrative (constantly repeating the word 'spool', the semordnilap of 'loops'), Bluebeard is trapped in this timeless, shuttered space, endlessly repeating patterns of abuse that are punctuated by the singer proclaiming his inner thoughts.

The presence of a recording device also draws cinematic connotations, something that is reinforced by the continual editing and cutting that takes place onstage. In Beckett's play, Krapp is a kind of ouroboros, caught in a self-perpetuating narrative arc – the actor listens to a recording of himself, a younger version who has in turn just listened to another earlier tape. Precipitating this action is the fact that the onstage Krapp is preparing to record yet another monologue. Though Beckett's play is peopled by spectres of the protagonist's past, and ghosted throughout by the younger version of the man himself, the representation of the 'other' Krapp is inherently inhuman. Michiko Tsushima identifies a binary contrast in the frailty of the onstage Krapp with the hardness of the machine and the past version of himself it contains; she posits that the tape recording in fact 'neutralizes' his previous emotions.[32] Thus, there is a sense of containment created by the presence of the tape player. Krapp is surrounded by inorganic records of his past and he lives in a vacuum, bounded by edited versions of his personal history. There is a recycling of old emotions that is directly tied to technology, but is also limited by it. Bausch revises many of these tropes in *Blaubart*, centring her narrative on a man who is haunted by his past and forced to confront it repeatedly. He attempts to control the tape, but fails to silence its voices completely. By fragmenting the operatic score, Bausch signals another shift from her early practice – the recording is no longer a musical accompaniment, and instead the voices of Bluebeard and Judith are isolated and reframed as a dialogue. Indeed, Schmidt went as far as to claim that 'Bausch dismembered the music'.[33] Meanwhile, cycles of repeated movement give the impression that the physical action onstage rewinds just as Bluebeard does with the tape. That the recording device occupies centre stage in Bausch's piece (and even features in its title) seems a direct reference to Brecht – in the same way that he advocated placing musicians within the spectator's viewpoint, his writings show that he also favoured the use of a record player on stage where it could be clearly seen by the audience.[34] The collagist nature of the creative process is laid bare in *Blaubart*, as is Bausch's continual desire to expose the artificiality of the stage setting (David Price comments that, at one point, she even turns on the houselights during the performance).[35]

Several key concepts of Bausch's *Tanztheater* are put together in this work for the first time. As in *Orpheus*, Bausch imbues the piece with her own distinct impression of the narrative, emphasising its undercurrents of violence, sexuality and the cruelties of human relationships. Her *Blaubart* is a bold production that provokes and unsettles the audience through its patterns of compulsive behaviour and multiple breaks from theatrical convention. She rejects recognisable narrative structure, creating the impression that the action takes place in an alternative realm where time can be stopped, started, replayed or looped. Similarly, the movement quality is based on repeating patterns of compulsive behaviour, and the movement vocabulary of *Blaubart* is as disordered as the onstage editing of Bartók's score. The dancers twitch and nod violently throughout, they scream at random intervals, one man shouts, 'ich liebe dich' repeatedly. At one point the men enter the stage dressed in what look like white lab coats, something that, viewed alongside the frantic, neurotic movements of the dancers, gives the impression that Bluebeard's castle has been transformed into a psychiatric ward. The exhaustion motif first explored in *Sacre* is reiterated here and stripped of its choreographic quality; the dancers run into the walls over and over again until they are completely drained and lie slumped on the floor. Thus, images of self-harm emerge in tandem with the dancers' exhaustion, a crucial theme that comes into many of her darker works from the early 1980s. There is no interval, and this was the first piece Bausch presented as a kind of endurance test for her audience. The running time is just under two hours, and the relentless repetitions, violent interactions between the dancers, and incessant clicking of the tape recording become increasingly jarring on the nerves.

In one scene, the male dancers stand in a line, touching their noses and hair, while slowly advancing towards the audience. They move to the back of the stage again where they take off their jackets and shirts, and repeat the original sequence. With the third repetition, they take off their trousers – men's bodies are placed on display here, perhaps in response to the focus on female sexuality in the Brecht/Weill evening. Eventually, the dancers split into couples and begin to slow-dance, though one man strides to the front of the stage where he affects rather comic body-builder poses. Here, Bausch underlines the ludicrous nature of gender stereotyping, and her dancers demonstrate the performativity and inherent artificiality of archetypal gender roles to the audience. Shortly there-after, a woman enters carrying a battered, broken doll. Even though it is quite grubby and broken, missing several limbs, she cradles it like a cherished toy. Her tender caresses soon turn to violence as she yanks its hair and tugs its nose, eventually abandoning it at the front of the stage. Her behaviour invokes an immediately recognisable feature of childhood behaviour in the manhandling of precious toys. Performed by an adult woman, this childish cruelty takes on odd significance, and repositions the violence enacted throughout *Blaubart* as inherently childish in its spiteful and petty nature. After she exits the stage, Bluebeard notices the doll, and begins to perform the same muscle-flexing regime, as if trying to catch the attention of a mate. In the context of a piece that is punctuated by images of violence against women, this portrayal of gen-dered anxiety hints at an undercurrent of bruised masculinity. If the Bluebeard myth is employed here to represent humanity's cruelty more generally, this sequence suggests an indication of Bausch's explanation for violence – that feelings of emasculation or inferiority often lie at the heart of misogynistic behaviour. Bausch's *Blaubart* forms a subversive and difficult exploration of gender violence, one that counters the often-heard criticism of Bausch's images of pathetic women. After all, the performativity of gender is not limited to the men in this piece. When a woman begins to smother her mouth in lipstick, the gender focus switches once more – now *she* is performing for the broken doll, which has inexplicably become a central totem for the inmates of Bluebeard's castle.

The conclusion confirms our initial impression of Bluebeard's dominance. Realising the inevitability of her fate, Judith goes calmly to her death, as Bluebeard piles multiple heavy dresses on top of her as if clothing a doll. He drags her body across the stage while the lighting dims to semi-darkness. Meanwhile, the chorus of dancers stand in a formation at the other side of the stage; as Bluebeard claps his hands, they freeze, moving once again when he claps once more. This game of musical statues continues as the stage lights dim further, until the audience can barely perceive any movement on the stage, though the sound of clapping and shuffling is still audible. Bausch invokes the motif of a children's game to remind us of Bluebeard's power, and his position of dominance within the group. In this respect, her *Blaubart* is not simply a study of male violence, but an abstracted exploration of power structures and social hierarchy, at the top of which remains the murderous yet tortured protagonist. Childhood games and relationships become a metaphor for society's cruelties in Bausch's grotesque, adult fairy tale.

By the nineteenth century, the Bluebeard theme had been subsumed into German *Märchen* literature, its French origins largely obscured by generations of writers imbuing the tale with ever darker, bloodier overtones. As had been the case with the Brecht/Weill evening, Bausch drew on subject matter that was culturally close at hand, establishing a familiar reference point for performers and audiences alike. Mozingo, for example, makes the point that Bausch made her early work for an audience that largely reflected her own working-class origins.[36] This sense of familiarity is characteristic of the experimental period of her *Tanztheater*, as is the overarching theme of memory, and the cycles of repetition she uses to depict it onstage. In *Blaubart*, Bausch explores the disjuncture between inner thought and outer action as her protagonist violently interacts both with his wife and the spectres of his past. He is continually confronted with images of violence, something he is apparently doomed to repeat. Forced to look upon his own actions, Bluebeard is in torment, and the ending is inconclusive in failing to atone for his cruelty. Bausch offers the audience a mirror in the form of her dancers' frantic, compulsive behaviour, suggesting that the shocking images of violence against women that run throughout the piece form a metaphor for violence against mankind more broadly.

Bausch's *Stichworte* method did not evolve in isolation, but developed through a dialogue with various incarnations of modernist theatre and dance, the sources of which are located in her bilingual education. *Blaubart* forms a radical break from Bausch's previous work but, at the same time, a great deal of its avant-gardism is foregrounded in the writings of Beckett and Brecht. A crucial divergence lies in the fact that Bausch replaces Brecht's Marxism with a more generalised critique of human cruelty. Brecht's model is a social intervention, a Marxist challenge to power structures, whereas Bausch's evocation of epic theatre is less overtly politicised, seeking instead to create a more open space for enquiry, engagement and reflection. Her version of *Die sieben Todsünden* is one of her few overtly political works, targeting the commodification of women's bodies but, as her work evolved, the element of social critique becomes increasingly subtle. In *Blaubart*, she utilises a series of distancing effects to induce the viewer to reflect on the nature of violence, all the while reminding them of the artificiality of the theatre environment. Like the Brecht/Weill evening that preceded it, *Blaubart* constitutes a reference to the theatrical past, as well as looking forward to modern dance's future.

A THEATRE OF FRAGMENTS: THE MACBETH PROJECT

Despite its innovations in structure and design, *Blaubart* ultimately remained wedded to the accompanying score, and consequently followed an established and recognisable narrative. While Bausch may have fragmented Bartók's opera, she relied upon it to drive the action of the performance, and this dependence on an external framework reflects the fact that her questioning method was still in its infancy. In the twelve-month period that followed, her confidence in the new *Stichworte* approach grew stronger, and the pace at which she worked garnered speed. Over the course of the next two years, Bausch would abandon the last vestiges of linear plot. *Komm tanz mit mir* (*Come Dance with Me*) and *Renate wandert aus* (*Renate Emigrates*) were fragmented and surreal productions, devised in the same year as *Blaubart*. In these works, the structure is episodic and looping, abandoning any semblance of a straightforward narrative.

Komm tanz mit mir is perhaps the first piece to be based on a framework of the dancers' contributions instead of being structured by the accompanying score. In another nod to the Brechtian *Verfremdungseffekt*, the opening is fitful and uncertain – the fire curtain remains in place, with a gap hinting at a white space behind. Distancing effects are established before the piece even begins; one of the dancers is stationed in the theatre foyer, dragging a rather incongruous fishing rod as he wanders aimlessly amongst the viewers. For the first time in her work, the fourth wall is dispensed with in dramatic form as Bausch locates the performers in the supposedly safe space of the foyer. Inside the theatre, the audience patiently awaits the beginning of the performance and, when the fire curtain is finally raised, the floor of the bare setting is revealed to be covered in brittle tree branches, a self-referential indicator of her *Orpheus*. The title becomes a constant refrain throughout the piece, which takes as its primary themes the struggle between the sexes and an unfulfilled search for intimacy.

1977 was a year of intense creativity for Bausch, one in which she would present three distinct *Tanztheater* works. Described as an 'operetta' in its programme notes, *Renate wandert aus* is staged on a vision of an ice rink, with the performers clad in formal party wear. The title is something of a mystery, as the 'Renate' character never actually materialises. Again, Bausch focuses on romantic relationships, touching on some of the themes of commodification that had been so brutally presented in the Brecht/Weill evening. *Renate* draws on motifs of clichéd nostalgia, gently mocking social stereotypes with its sentimental soundtrack (a compilation drawn from film scores, German pop songs and Henry Mancini records). The music is continually fragmented and, as there is no indication of a linear plot, the content is similarly collagist. As in *Komm tanz mit mir*, the dancers move out of the stage space in order to interact with the audience, but this time in an even more direct fashion, addressing individuals personally to offer them sweets or ask their opinion on items of clothing. Bausch's works become increasingly surreal, direct and fragmented in this period, a style that reaches its zenith with the Macbeth Project.

Although rarely identified as such, *Er nimmt sie an der Hand und führt sie in das Schloss, die anderen folgen* was in fact Bausch's first co-production, created in residence at the Schauspielhaus Bochum at the invitation of its director, Peter Zadek. The premiere was held on 22 April 1978 and was badly received, perhaps even more so than the Brecht/Weill evening. Bausch's biographer Marion Meyer suggests that the audience had anticipated a relatively conventional adaptation of the Macbeth theme, not realising Bausch's piece constituted a deliberate misreading of Shakespeare's text.[37] The performance was interrupted by shouts and heckling, and the first act was almost stopped altogether due to audience interjections. Endicott claimed she nearly fled the stage in fear of the furious response from spectators, while Schmidt has pointed out that some of the loudest dissenting voices in the crowd came from the German Shakespeare Society, enraged at what was supposed to represent 'the crowning event of their anniversary'.[38] At one point, Endicott confronted the audience directly, telling them, 'If you don't want to watch, go home and let us work.'[39]

In much of the literature on Bausch's career, the Macbeth Project receives scant attention, though it is often pinpointed as an important work in the development of her process. Its title has received similarly fleeting levels of analysis, yet Bausch's selection of this specific line merits further discussion. 'He takes her by the hand and leads her into the castle, the others follow' carries several important associations. The title is unusually lengthy, but it is also a fragment, one that makes little sense removed from its context, and only tangentially corresponds to the action on stage. In her selection of a stage direction that no audience member would automatically associate with this canonical play, Bausch makes the very title of her piece a distancing effect. The unveiling of stage directions is an important feature of Brecht's epic theatre, as it aids in reinforcing the audience's awareness of the play's artificiality. In this case, Bausch also mitigates the authority of Shakespeare's text, diminishing its historical significance by removing the primary identifying markers from its framing. Yet examination of available German editions of the play has not revealed Bausch's original source – the stage direction in question seems only to read 'exeunt'. The direction, which we may assume is written by Bausch rather than the original author, refers to Duncan taking Lady Macbeth's hand and entering the castle where he will meet his grim fate; this is the same hand that Lady Macbeth will obsessively attempt to scrub clean of the phantom traces of the king's blood following the murder she has orchestrated.[40] This fragmentary line thus represents the step that precipitates the focus of the play's narrative, demonstrating a developing subversive tendency in Bausch's approach that shifts the focus from physical action to the dynamic drive that underlies it. It also highlights that, in the canonical play that is *Macbeth*, the key point of narrative shift occurs not in a speech or soliloquy, and is not made explicit to the audience, but rather is concealed in the (potentially reimagined) stage directions. Bausch elucidates these points for her audience with the framing of her Macbeth Project.

From the opening, there are lengthy stretches of inaction, and there is almost no recognisable dance choreography throughout (Figure 2.2). Mulrooney claims that this work is where Bausch's approach 'approximates or comes close to Stanislavski's "method of physical actions"', demonstrating the relationship between cognitive and physical functions.[41] The stage opens in semi-darkness, with a jukebox in the background casting a red light across the performers laid out on the floor. Seemingly asleep, they begin to stir slightly, but the movements become more erratic, as some are clearly suffering nightmares.

Figure 2.2 *Er nimmt sie an der Hand und führt sie in das Schloss, die anderen folgen,* Gert Weigelt

The set design is chaotic and colourful, giving the impression of a playroom, though one inhabited here by slightly deranged adults. A thick carpet lines the floor, and the stage is full of toys and furniture that have seen better days. The haphazard arrangement of items does not reflect a specific period, and instead the kitschy items of furniture come from different eras, cast in vibrant, clashing colours – a green shower cabinet, for example, sits rather incongruously in the middle of this disordered space. The inertia of the opening sequence suggests that the audience have intruded on the personal, intimate space of the performers. Slumped in their worn armchairs, the cast look directly into the theatre, and there is a sense that the spectator is under similar observation in this curious environment.

The Macbeth Project was created on an even smaller cast than previous works, featuring just ten performers in total. Having first introduced non-dancers into the company for the Brecht/Weill evening (the actress Mechthild Großmann had been given a central role in *Fürchtet Euch nicht*, singing four songs in the revue), this piece broke further with convention by casting a range of dancers, singers and actors who did not make use of their specific talent or mode of training. Bausch herself observed that the Macbeth Project marked a radical departure from existing form:

> The very big change in my work was with *He takes her by the hand and leads her into the castle, the others follow*: a production with not too many people, but I had singers who didn't sing, dancers who didn't dance, actors who didn't act – each one did different work. It had as starting point a scene from *Macbeth*, but the piece is not Shakespeare's *Macbeth*.[42]

In place of dance steps, everyday behaviours form the Macbeth Project's choreographic makeup; the performers adjust themselves, sniff under their arms, and bite their nails. Devised through a collaborative, cross-disciplinary process, the final piece inverts audience expectation by removing the possibility of recognisable dance from the stage altogether. At the same time, Bausch refuses the spectator an orthodox retelling of one of Shakespeare's most famous plays – in dismantling the original text, she bestows responsibility for its reassembling onto the viewer. The Macbeth Project accordingly forms a redefinition of *Tanztheater* in Bausch's vocabulary, dispensing with the narrative structural elements that remained in place in *Blaubart*. Its systematic fragmentation of text, plot and gesture locates the piece at a crucial juncture in the evolution of Bausch's method, aligning her *Tanztheater* more closely with Hans-Thies Lehmann's conception of postdramatic theatre. Lehmann distinguishes this kind of practice from what he terms 'dramatic' or 'mimetic' theatre through its revaluation of the importance of text. Where dramatic theatre is based upon principles of illusion and the willing suspension of disbelief, postdramatic theatre requires that the spectator adopt a more active role in the production, to become, as Karen Jürs-Munby puts it, 'active co-writers of the (performance) text'.[43] Bausch's sharp revision and restructuring of this canonical text mirrors Lehmann's proposal that 'the new theatre confirms the not so new insight that there is never a harmonious relationship but rather a perpetual conflict between text and scene'.[44]

In the Macbeth Project, virtuosity and technique are removed altogether, and there are extended periods of little to no activity onstage, as if to test the patience of the audience. Theatrical conventions are inverted throughout: stage commands are made part of the dialogue and, at one point, the dancers line up rows of chairs to sit facing the audience. The roles of spectator and performer therefore become interchangeable as the fourth wall is broken down. Bausch's cast return the audience's gaze, never allowing the audience to settle into a passive consumption of the performance. In these moments, Bausch challenges the viewer to take an active role in the piece by turning the spectatorial gaze back on itself. She undermines the supposed authenticity of her characters, allowing the audience repeated glimpses of the instruments of the theatre – one performer tells another, 'Jo, it's your cue, smile!', for instance.

Displacement is a key theme. In the Macbeth Project, there are no defined character roles, and dance is represented only in short bursts. This piece sees Bausch take her experimental approach a step further, with most of the content comprised of pedestrian movement. There is no consistency in the overarching framework of the performance, which lurches from comedy to tragedy and back again. Nor is there a uniform narrative that acts as a central thread, what forms the 'through line' of Stanislavski's theatre, for instance. Instead, Shakespeare's plot is lost to petty squabbles. Schmidt has described the piece as, '[a collection of] fairytale parables compressed together into a convoluted cabaret style with no thought for chronological development'.[45] Lying limply across the overstuffed chairs that fill the chaotic set, the strange assortment of characters sing children's songs or fight with one another over toys. The immaturity of the performers is mirrored in their evident self-consciousness. They constantly adjust their clothing and check themselves, as if embarrassed to be been onstage. In one section, to the soundtrack of a peculiarly jazzed-up version of Grieg's Piano Concerto in A minor, the cast march at speed diagonally across the stage, repeating a frantic sequence of self-adjustments, touching their hair, checking their faces, forcing uncomfortable smiles and shyly avoiding eye contact with the audience. Their uncomfortable catwalk implies a sense of failure, like amateur actors overcome by stage fright resorting to a hurried exit from the stage. Bausch's stage direction here forms yet another distancing device – implying that her cast is comprised of non-professionals rather than accomplished performers, she reveals the artificiality of the staging through their supposed failure.

The Shakespearean content is similarly reduced to fragments, creating a very loose framework for Bausch's exploration of themes that are only tangentially connected to the *Macbeth* narrative. Sleepwalking emerges as a recurring image, for instance, drawing the audience back to the content of the original play in Lady Macbeth's nocturnal wanderings. As with *Blaubart*, refrains are established in the Macbeth Project that foreshadow developments in Bausch's own choreographic style; the image of the sleepwalkers here would be made a central focus of her seminal *Café Müller*, premiered one year later. The somnambulist theme is also reflected by the unusual title in its suggestion that the unnamed crowd of followers go passively into the castle, something Mulrooney has compared to the 'herd mentality' of fascism.[46] The tale of Macbeth is told through disjointed snatches of Shakespeare's dialogue, but the order is disturbed. The narrator sits cross-legged on a chair, facing the audience – again, any semblance of a fourth wall is dispensed with, and the performer engages directly with her viewer. Her character is part-child, part-vamp, as she applies garish lipstick and poses like a body-builder, her eyes bulging while she describes the disconnected happenings of the play. This repeated comic action serves as an immediate reminder of *Blaubart* and the surreal posing sequence enacted in front of the broken doll, but also of Brecht's use of comedy as a distancing device. It is a further play on Bausch's elucidation of the theatre's artificiality, allowing the actress/narrator to openly acknowledge that she is being looked at, and that she is in turn looking back at the spectator.

In this disjointed, chaotic spectacle, the sole constant motif in Bausch's adaptation is the presence of water. At the front of Borzik's kitsch set, a garden hose is left running throughout the performance, filling up an incline built into the front of the stage. Water forms an important part of Bausch's aesthetic throughout her career. Images of bathing appear in a significant number of her works, including some of her final choreographies. Water is a deeply symbolic element in Bausch's *oeuvre*, taking on alternately ritualistic, comic and reflective properties. In the Macbeth Project, the running hose is a disconcerting addition to the stage, and increasingly becomes a distraction for the audience as it slowly fills up the incline and begins to soak through the carpet. The constant steady flow of liquid is something Servos has read as 'a symbol of time wasted', running as it does like sand through an hourglass.[47] Crucially, the presence of water also functions as an important and, in the context of this fragmented narrative, unusually direct link to the underlying Shakespearean theme. Returning to the text of the play, the running hose reminds us of Lady Macbeth's conviction that, 'a little water clears us of this deed'. The need to atone for terrible acts is a theme that is reflected in the performers' neurotic rituals of ablution that occur throughout this piece: they wash their hands almost compulsively and, following the murder of the reimagined Banquo character, shower in the green cabinet while still clad in their eveningwear. When the incline at the front of the stage has filled up with water, a man repeatedly hurls himself into it, despite its shallowness. His failed attempt at diving is uncomfortable to watch, and reminiscent of the obsessive rituals of *Blaubart*'s dancers as they throw themselves against the stage walls. The theme of washing also illustrates Bausch's reframing of Shakespeare's narrative, drawing the Macbeth story out of the realm of drama (and, accordingly, high art), and reimagining it through the customs of everyday activity. Just as the performers are limited to pedestrian movement, the melodrama of the original play is reduced to fragments of routine behaviour. In this way, Bausch continues the exploration of cruelty first outlined in *Blaubart*, using Shakespeare's play as a frame for a more generalised exploration of the capacity for childishness and spite in modern society.

The actions of her performers take place in a surreal, fragmented environment that forms an assault on the viewer's senses. Each time a particular piano score starts up, the cast members interrupt their own activities to jump on the furniture in a hysterical game of musical chairs. Interruption is a habitual theme of Bausch's early work, and another key element drawn from Brecht's epic theatre. Here, however, she adopts a style that is increasingly fragmented and collagist to the point that there is no material narrative to follow. Past and present are evoked through the childish emblems of the set, though any sense of time or location is absent. In the Macbeth Project, repeating patterns emerge, but overall it is an inconsistent, shifting piece in which the performers swap characters and any notion of plot is practically non-existent. The central positioning of a stage direction, direct addresses to the audience and inconsistency of character roles have their roots in Brechtian theatre, and the significance of Brecht in Bausch's experimental period is clear. Within the Macbeth Project, however, she also demonstrates an increasing interest in collage that had first emerged in the onstage editing of *Blaubart*. Birringer proposes that montage in Bausch's work is 'inherited' from Brecht's theatre.[48] Yet its roots also derive from a cinematic context, including the highly influential theories of Sergei Eisenstein. Schmidt has drawn similar comparisons with Bausch's collagist process:

> The German dance theater found a new form. It wasn't really new in the arts, because it was in painting and film. It was the form of collage and montage. The works of Pina Bausch are much closer to an Eisenstein movie than to classical or narrative ballet. The Bausch pieces are narrative. They tell things, but they don't tell stories. They tell: then it was this, then that, and that. There are always things going on, and you have to put it together in your head. She knows very well what she is doing and all the things she does are very, very formed.[49]

In Bausch's theatrical montage, narrative is upended and thrown into flux. Her pieces are often disjointed and structured by repeating patterns, phrases or themes rather than a standard or linear plot. While the origins of this disruption can be found in Brechtian theory, the realisation of experimental productions such as the Macbeth Project is situated in postdramatic territory (echoing Lehmann's own definition of postdramatic theatre as 'post-Brechtian'[50]). Significantly, one of the closest points of comparison for this stage of Bausch's new vision of *Tanztheater* lies in Heiner Müller's work, a playwright that Lehmann has identified as exemplary of the postdramatic turn in theatre practice. Müller's increasingly fragmented, collagist dramaturgy came to prominence contemporaneously with the evolution of Bausch's new approach. Perhaps predictably, Brecht also forms a major influence on Müller's aesthetic. His notion of *Kopien* (copies) aligns with Brecht's Marxist approach to creative 'property', arguing that existing texts were not the private preserve of the writer, but incentives for recycling themes and creating new work. A similar principle is at the heart of Bausch's *Tanztheater* montage, and particularly in the productions of her early experimental period that revisit and revise existing themes. Müller's work is also based on a myriad of different sources, but as Jonathan Kalb observes, there is no reverence in Müller's treatment of the material.[51] This is epitomised in Müller's handling of stylised theatrical language in his controversial reworkings of Shakespeare.

Müller's *Macbeth*, written in 1971 and premiered the following year, was resoundingly condemned by East German censors and critics for its pessimistic tone and violent imagery.[52] Like Bausch's piece, Müller's play is not a straightforward revival of Shakespeare's text, but a far bloodier imagining that featured twenty-three rather than five acts (including an extra nine scenes) and dialogue written in coarse, blunt language. It is an unusually violent production, and there is no Manichean division of heroes and victims in Müller's world; even Duncan is depicted sitting on a throne atop a pile of bloodied corpses. Each character is equally murderous and brutal, and the piece ends as the witches welcome Malcolm with the same words they used to greet Macbeth, which, Kalb posits, demonstrates that the 'cycle of killing' will begin anew.[53] In its 1982 staging, Macbeth was split across three different roles, and Lady Macduff and Duncan were played by the same actress. This division of characters can be seen in Beckett's theatre, but also in Bausch's contemporary productions including *Blaubart* and the Macbeth Project. In doing so, Bausch and Müller revisit another of Brecht's epic devices, breaking the elision of a single character with one performer as in the Stanislavski method. In the postwar German context, this splitting of identity can also be read as reflecting contemporary socio-political turmoil, namely the physical division of the postwar state into East and West (Müller would return to this conflation of contemporary politics and Shakespearean text in 1977 with his more widely discussed work, *Hamletmaschine*).

Müller's 1982 staging of Macbeth also echoes certain themes already seen in Bausch's piece, including the sensory overload of Borzik's vibrant set: there is a stronger emphasis on imagery in this work than seen in Müller's wider *oeuvre*. While the stage design reflected the interior of an artist's flat in the Prenzlauerberg district of Berlin, his actors wore thick, grotesque makeup or masks and outlandish costumes, none of which corresponded to a fixed period. The stage was set with unusual props, including a device that seemed to be a cross between a telephone box and an elevator. In both versions, the cast indulge in childlike behaviour – Müller's unusual characterisation of Lady Macbeth was performed by a young actress who played children's games throughout, undermining the traditional portrayal of the scheming temptress.[54] Meanwhile, the role of Lady Macduff's child was represented by a doll.[55] In both Bausch and Müller's postdramatic adaptations, literary characters are fragmented and reduced to signifiers, becoming ciphers of the narrative. Lehmann's description of character roles in Robert Wilson's theatre might easily be applied here: 'they exist as mere images, familiar also to those without an "education". As unconsciously operating figures of cultural discourse everyone "knows" (knowingly or unknowingly).'[56] Bausch does not directly link her performers to identifiable characters – this ambiguity is already at play in *Blaubart*, and develops in tandem with Müller's own radical revision of the theatrical framework.

The parallel evolution of Müller's theatre with Bausch's *Tanztheater* is underscored by their collective, Brechtian rejection of naturalism and the auteur-like nature of their composition, namely their shared function as both writer and director. The postdramatic tendencies at play in their respective *oeuvres* do not represent an anti-Brechtian turn; indeed, Brecht's epic theatre constitutes an important experimental baseline from which their respective works emerge. Reflecting on his decision to recreate the Macbeth theme, Müller observed that he wanted to engage in a 'line by line' discussion with Shakespeare by dismantling and reconstructing his narrative.[57] This statement is reminiscent of Bausch's approach to linear plot, but also reflects the parallel dialogues at play in *Krapp's Last Tape* and *Blaubart*. In this post-Brechtian, modernist-inflected theatre, Müller and Bausch engage in a collagist process that interrogates and dismantles seminal texts and narratives. Revising existing text was a staple element of Müller's theatre, something he had adapted from Brecht's writings and, in the early experimental period, a strikingly similar concept is at play in Bausch's *Tanztheater*. In these avant-garde, German versions of the Macbeth theme, narrative and plot are completely reinvented to create a new and surreal theatre based upon Shakespeare's text. While Müller's play followed a more conventional plotline than Bausch's completely fragmented piece, neither version of Macbeth has a fixed beginning or end – Müller's is a merciless cycle of violence, and Bausch fails to provide a definitive conclusion for the audience. In each, Shakespeare's text is radically altered and the narrative reshaped to fit their specific aim: in Bausch's case, she sought to relocate the Macbeth tale in a more general reflection of social norms and cruelties, whereas for Müller, the dark storyline was reshaped as a stinging critique of power structures and class struggle, and his treatment of language formed a mockery of the East German state.[58] Though Bausch and Müller may diverge in terms of motivation, in their Shakespearean works they express a shared desire to create work that is consciously difficult, inducing the viewer to take an active and questioning role in reassembling the fragmented narrative.

Bausch's rendering of the Macbeth tale ends with the narrator sitting motionless in a chair as tears stream down her face. She remains immobile for almost twenty minutes, the chaos of the preceding acts having lapsed into silence. This reiterates the ending of *Blaubart*, where the protagonist's clapping continues well beyond the apparent conclusion of the action, and the audience is left uncertain as to whether the performance is over. In Bausch's *Tanztheater*, such closing elements are often so ambiguous that her performers will announce the beginning of the interval. Similarly, her pieces rarely end with a clear conclusion or summation of the approximate narrative – usually, the end is signalled by repetition of an opening sequence. Her inconsistent approach to the fourth wall does not allow the spectator to settle for a passive engagement of the spectacle. In *Blaubart* and the Macbeth Project, any realistic sense of time is missing as well as an overarching narrative, and it is for the first time in this latter work that we see Bausch's tendency to create pieces based on patterns of waves or cycles. In place of linear plot, the tempo rises and falls, sequences loop round each other, patterns repeat, and then it simply ends. She permits the audience no conclusion, and, arguably, no sense of catharsis. Instead, Brecht's ghost serves as a continual reminder of the artificiality of the stage setting, and the *Tanztheater* work becomes a mirror for contemplative reflection on themes of cruelty, loneliness and the search for intimacy.

*

It is ironic that, having evolved her method through asking questions, Bausch herself tended to avoid answering them. She generally shied away from interviews, and would rarely answer direct questions about her work or herself as an individual. Rita Felciano reiterates this commonly held conception of the artist:

> Bausch doesn't like to talk about herself. She hates interviews and refuses to give them. When one becomes unavoidable, her resistance is palpable. In a 1993 documentary about her company, for instance, she never

once looked at the camera. A few informal encounters earlier this year revealed her to be an intensely private person: quiet, soft-spoken, but perfectly polite, with the same enigmatic smile often seen on her dancers' faces, but giving the impression that she would really much rather be doing something else. Lutz Forster, professor of dance at Folkwang Dance Studio, and an on-again, off-again member of Bausch's company since 1975, offers another reason for her reticence: 'Pine [*sic*] is very clear about what she does, but she doesn't want to talk about it because she is suspicious of words. They can so easily be misunderstood.'[59]

From an early age, Bausch found solace in movement rather than in words. It is no surprise, therefore, that in later life she remained unwilling to analyse her work for critics or audiences. In the pieces made through the *Stichworte* method, Bausch broke down conventional narrative, creating a space for the spectator to reassemble the content and determine its ultimate purpose. However, this can be a frustrating endeavour, as the constant reiteration of Brechtian distancing devices prevents the viewer from identifying with individual characters. Yet Bausch often asserted that she did not intend to provoke her audiences, despite the critical reactions such pieces garnered.

Banishment becomes an underlying theme in the works of Bausch's early period, a recurring motif initiated by the Gluck dance operas, the ritualistic setting of *Sacre*, Bluebeard's entrapment in his own nightmares and the obsessive repetitions of the Macbeth Project. In some respects, this reflects Bausch's personal experience, finding herself in a kind of artistic exile after the Brecht/Weill premiere. In much of the existing scholarship on *Tanztheater*, the period immediately following *Die sieben Todsünden* is referred to as a time of 'crisis', and Bausch herself admitted she was wounded by the criticism of her dancers and collaborators.[60] Yet without this period of creative crisis, it is difficult to imagine how she might otherwise have evolved the *Stichworte* method. The challenges of creating and the negative reception towards the Brecht/Weill evening collectively provided Bausch the space to enter a phase of experimentation. Indeed, the notion of crisis forms a central theme of the works produced in this period; as Bausch went on to produce several new pieces that moved increasingly further from recognisable dance and straightforward narrative, she would delve deeper into dark and challenging themes. While the seeds for a Brechtian model were sown as early as *Fritz*, and even in otherwise straightforward choreographies as the splitting of characters in *Orpheus*, a decisive methodological shift occurs in the experimental period. Bausch began to reject the limitations and autonomy of theatre production and, as would become increasingly central to her work, notions of theatrical illusionism.

Over the course of the period between 1976 and 1978, Bausch established several of the key motifs that run throughout her *oeuvre*, including fragility and violence, the fragmentation of narrative, cycles of repetition, and an ongoing exploration of male–female relationships. Many of her critics have focused on the depiction of women in her work, an issue that certainly merits further and more nuanced analysis. However, in relying too heavily on a gendered reading of her work, critics are liable to obscure a great deal of the underlying, multi-layered meaning inherent in Bausch's *Tanztheater*. The violence enacted between men and women in works such as *Die sieben Todsünden* and *Blaubart* should not be read simply as a reflection of gender politics; rather, Bausch seems instead to comment on the fragility and potential for cruelty inherent in the human condition. There is a darkness that overshadows the early work extending well into the mid-1980s – as I explore in greater detail in Chapter 4, Germany's recent history and tumultuous political situation seem obvious reference points. Yet, the line between humour and tragedy or violence is often dangerously thin in Bausch's early work, and the dancers transgress the audience's expectations not only of appropriate comic or dramatic performance, but also the boundaries of the stage itself.

Notes

1. Barnett, '"I've been told that the play is far too German"', in Braun and Marven (eds), *Cultural Impact in the German Context*, p. 160.
2. Bausch, quoted in Finkel, 'Gunsmoke', in Climenhaga (ed.), *The Pina Bausch Sourcebook*, p. 155.
3. Endicott, *Ich bin ein anständige Frau!*, p. 89.
4. As stated by Sturm, 'Illustrated talk on the work of Pina Bausch'.
5. Wiegand, 'Let's Tanz'.
6. For an extensive list of these *Stichworte* examples, see Mulrooney, *Orientalism, Orientation, and the Nomadic Work of Pina Bausch*, pp. 152–9. The *Stichworte* texts from the making of *Palermo Palermo* (1989) are given in Bentivoglio, *Pina Bausch oder die Kunst, über Nelken zu tanzen*, p. 151. Bausch's method is also explored in detail, alongside a transcribed interview, in Climenhaga, *Pina Bausch*, pp. 39–68.
7. Bausch, quoted in Servos and Müller, *Pina Bausch – Wuppertal Dance Theater*, p. 235.
8. Copeland, *Merce Cunningham*, pp. 149–50.
9. Burkert, quoted in Wiegand, 'The Sound of Pina Bausch'.
10. Brecht, 'On Gestic Music', *Brecht on Theatre*, p. 167.
11. Brecht, 'Alienation Effects in Chinese Acting', *Brecht on Theatre*, pp. 151–2.
12. Mitter, *Systems of Rehearsal*, p. 44.
13. Kumiega, *The Theatre of Grotowski*, p. 40.
14. Grotowski, *Towards a Poor Theatre*, p. 37.
15. Richards, *At Work with Grotowski on Physical Actions*, p. 98.
16. Ibid., pp. 55–7.
17. Sörgel, *Dance and the Body in Western Theatre*, p. 58.
18. Richards, *At Work with Grotowski on Physical Actions*, p. 40.
19. Ibid., pp. 11–13.
20. Grotowski, *Towards a Poor Theatre*, p. 21.

21. Kumiega, *The Theatre of Grotowski*, p. 112.
22. Sturm, quoted in Cappelle, 'Pina's Ghost'.
23. Climenhaga's chapter on *Kontakthof* details the process of creation and rehearsal through this questioning method (*Pina Bausch*, pp. 69–94).
24. Schmidt, *Tanztheater in Deutschland*, pp. 50–1.
25. Schulze-Reuber, *Das Tanztheater Pina Bausch*, p. 108.
26. Mozingo, 'The Haunting of Bluebeard', p. 97.
27. Davies, *The Tale of Bluebeard in German Literature*, p. 126.
28. Leafstedt, *Inside Bluebeard's Castle*, p. 185.
29. Mumford, 'Pina Bausch Choreographs *Blaubart*', p. 51.
30. As described in Haerdter's account, reprinted in McMillan and Fehsenfeld, *Beckett in the Theatre*, p. 303.
31. Iwata, 'Records and Recollections in "Krapp's Last Tape"', pp. 34–43.
32. Tsushima, '"Memory is the Belly of the Mind"', p. 126.
33. Schmidt, 'Ballet after the fall from Grace', p. 25.
34. Brecht, 'Notes on *Pointed Heads and Round Heads*', *Brecht on Theatre*, p. 165.
35. Price, 'The Politics of the Body', p. 326.
36. Mozingo, 'The Haunting of Bluebeard', p. 98.
37. Meyer, *Pina Bausch*, p. 51.
38. Schmidt, 'Return to Wuppertal, Eleven Years Later', p. 44.
39. Meyer, *Pina Bausch*, p. 51.
40. Brunel, 'Pina Bausch chez Shakespeare', p. 12.
41. Mulrooney, *Orientalism, Orientation, and the Nomadic Work of Pina Bausch*, p. 119.
42. Climenhaga, *Pina Bausch*, p. 172.
43. Jürs-Munby, 'Introduction', in Lehmann, *Postdramatic Theatre*, p. 6.
44. Lehmann, *Postdramatic Theatre*, p. 145
45. Schmidt, 'Return to Wuppertal, Eleven Years Later', p. 44.
46. Mulrooney, *Orientalism, Orientation, and the Nomadic Work of Pina Bausch*, pp. 117–18.
47. Servos and Müller, *Pina Bausch – Wuppertal Dance Theater*, p. 94.
48. Birringer, 'Pina Bausch', p. 90.
49. Schmidt, quoted in Daly, 'Tanztheater', p. 51.
50. Lehmann, *Postdramatic Theatre*, p. 33.
51. Kalb, *The Theater of Heiner Müller*, pp. 89–90.
52. Harich, 'Der entlaufene Dingo, das vergessene Floß', pp. 189–218.
53. Kalb, *The Theater of Heiner Müller*, p. 89.
54. Fiebach, 'Resisting Simulation', pp. 82–3.
55. Barnett, '"I have to change myself instead of interpreting myself"', p. 10.
56. Lehmann, *Postdramatic Theatre*, p. 80.
57. Müller, quoted in Henrichs, 'Die zum Lächeln nicht Zwingbaren'.
58. Kalb, *The Theater of Heiner Müller*, pp. 87–103.
59. Felciano, 'Pina Bausch', p. 68.
60. Bausch, quoted in Servos, *Pina Bausch*, p. 234.

3

UNMASKED, UNFINISHED, UNRESOLVED: A DANCE THEATRE OF THE ABSURD

Bausch's *Tanztheater* defies straightforward categorisation. It exists in the margins of ostensibly distinct artistic modes, and there is no single aesthetic, style or method that characterises her *oeuvre*. Rather, her work can be divided into particular phases that punctuate the evolution of her creative process. In the years that followed her experimental phase, Bausch produced a series of works that demonstrate a growing confidence in her hybridised creative approach. They characterise what some critics have termed her 'golden' or 'vintage' period, which might alternatively be framed as the mature phase of her *Tanztheater*.[1] These pieces take place in liminal settings, environments which become increasingly intangible as her *Stichworte* questioning technique evolves. In this era, Bausch's dancers continually enact a quest for intimacy played out within indeterminate spaces.

The productions devised in this phase do not evoke a sense of realism, nor are they structured around a linear plot, features that are still evident even in radical works such as *Blaubart* and the Macbeth Project. Instead, Bausch's mature *Tanztheater* abandons familiar storytelling and structural form, repositioning aspects of everyday life within irrational or incongruous circumstances. Specific recurring themes characterise the work of this period: indeed, recursion forms the primary structure of these non-narrative performances. Choreography is often comprised of everyday actions, and identifiable narrative is rejected in favour of specific images, the most significant being the search for intimate contact. Social interactions form another common refrain, where breakdowns of communication are almost inevitable.

Throughout Bausch's mature phase, a desire to unveil the mechanics of the theatre becomes a central concern. References to Brecht recur throughout this model in the focus on *Gestus*, the separation of mime and gesture (especially in her emphasis on the artificiality of the stage), and continual breaking of the fourth wall. However, as Price has indicated, while a 'Brechtian vocabulary' is often used by critics analysing Bausch's work, this is a limiting tendency that does not consider the marked shift her work undergoes.[2] Analysis of her mature *oeuvre* demonstrates a structural change of direction from epic theatre convention into an increasingly abstract, almost surrealist format. These pieces seek to undermine the sanctity of the theatre space through the development of an unmasking process: in doing so, her mature works evoke characteristics of absurdist theatre, furthering the Beckettian parallels already present in *Blaubart*. Illogicality, non-linearity and a lack of resolution become common motifs, and the viewer is continually met with ambiguity and multiplicity of meaning. The overarching sense of futility that permeates these pieces recalls Martin Esslin's explanation that absurdist theatre represents the 'sense of metaphysical anguish at the absurdity of the human condition'.[3]

Lehmann rejects the idea that the Theatre of the Absurd embodies proto-postdramatic tendencies, arguing that it remains too thoroughly wedded to text and dramatic form.[4] While language occupies a central role in absurdist drama, I would counter that, in this kind of theatre, gesture and movement begin to take precedence over verbal communication and contribute to its sense of futility and fragmentation. Indeed, Esslin tell us that absurd theatre:

> tends toward a radical devaluation of language toward a poetry that is to emerge from the concrete and objectified images of the stage itself. The element of language still plays an important, yet subordinate, part in this conception, but what *happens* on the stage transcends, and often contradicts, the *words* spoken by the characters.[5]

This contradictory relationship between text and action thus marks an important precedent for many aspects of Lehmann's conception of the post-dramatic, especially in the revolt of language and slide into illogicality. In the mature period of Bausch's repertoire, we see numerous parallels with Beckett who, despite Lehmann acknowledging as a precursor to the postdramatic, is inextricably linked with Esslin's choice of signature text in defining absurdist theatre: *Waiting for Godot* (1953). Beckett forms my primary point of comparison in the analysis that follows, centring on the unmasking and resulting deconstruction of theatrical frameworks and theoretical principles. In this respect, Bausch's mature *Tanztheater* constitutes a kind of choreographic metatheatre.

'AN ARCHAEOLOGY OF THE EVERYDAY'

The antagonism that met controversial works such as *Die sieben Todsünden* and the Macbeth Project ran deeper than a few negative press reviews. Bausch was publicly criticised by the head of the department of culture, faced walk-outs of her shows and protests outside the Wuppertal opera house and, for more than a year, received anonymous threats from an aggrieved member of the public.[6] Yet despite the weight of negative criticism and the personal and professional crises that followed the Brecht/Weill evening, Bausch continued to create new productions through her *Stichworte* method. This also precipitated significant changes in the makeup of the Wuppertal dance company. After the Bochum premiere, Bausch invited Großmann to join the company on a formal basis, despite her not being a professional dancer. This presented the actress with a difficult decision: not only did friends warn her that Bausch was 'artistically dead' in Wuppertal following the terrible reaction to the Brecht/Weill piece, but working with Bausch also meant that she would be unable to take on external roles due to the company's complex development and rehearsal process.[7] Nonetheless, Großmann accepted her offer and, as a result, the Tanztheater Wuppertal became an amalgamated dance/theatre troupe.

These changes signify an important factor in the new creative approach Bausch began with *Blaubart* – specifically, the evolution of her method through the diversification of the company. Bausch's creative process centres on a search for authenticity, excavating human gesture and motivation through the probing and time-consuming *Stichworte* process (the dancers would often work with Bausch for up to eight hours a day). As her confidence in the technique grew, Bausch increasingly removed herself from the work, creating pieces based on a script designed in collaboration with the dancers. Accordingly, it is perhaps more appropriate to frame Bausch not as the author, but as the architect of these works.

Bausch's most quoted summation of her practice – that she was 'not interested in how people move, but what moves them' – refers to a desire for her dancers to embody a genuine inner impulse rather than resorting to improvisation.[8] There is a deliberate attempt to do away with virtuosity for its own sake. As Bausch stated:

> The steps always come from somewhere else – never from the legs. The movements are always worked out in between times. And gradually we built up short dance sequences which we memorise. I used to get scared and panic and so I would start off with a movement and avoid the questions. Nowadays I start off with the questions.[9]

Bausch's *Stichworte* method espouses a transparency suggestive of Brecht's epic theatre in its desire to reveal the mechanics of the stage. Central to Brecht's approach is the notion of 'demonstration' in place of 'acting' – a clear distance is established between the performer and their role, the audience is prevented from emotional identification with a fictional character, and the artificiality of the theatre is made apparent. Bausch's own distancing effects often refer to the illusory nature of performance. Her dancers usually perform under and address one another by their own names on stage and, rather than immersing themselves in identifiable characters, consistently blur the boundary between themselves and their stage personae. They frequently allude to the rehearsal process and occasionally make explicit references to Bausch herself, acknowledging the hand of the creative director that, in a traditional theatrical set-up, would remain deliberately veiled. That the dancers speak on stage is a common feature of her works from the late 1970s onwards, but also marks a significant departure from standard dance vocabulary. There are, of course, much earlier exceptions to this tenet in modern dance, including several of Bausch's predecessors – Wigman's *Totenmal* (*Call of the Dead*, 1930) and Graham's *Deaths and Entrances* (1943) include lengthy spoken word sequences, for example – and it would become a common tendency in postmodern dance as seen in the performances of the Judson Dance Theatre. Yet Bausch's use of the device transcends more common applications of voice in dance. Her cast go a step further when they directly address the audience, often leaving the environs of the stage to enter the realm of the spectator.

The works produced during the experimental phase of the late 1970s essentially reject dance as a medium, eschewing recognisable choreographic convention in favour of a collagist approach. Yet amid this period of radical experimentation, Bausch's *Café Müller* (1978; Figure 3.1) marks a brief reversion to more familiar territory. Her last piece in which the dancers do not speak at all, *Café Müller* evokes themes that run throughout Bausch's entire *oeuvre*, namely memory, nostalgia and the search for intimacy. It bridges the choreographed, dancerly aesthetic of her early work and the fragmentation of narrative, form and characterisation that accompanies pieces made through the *Stichworte* method. Lasting forty-five minutes in total, and featuring only six dancers, this Bauschian chamber piece is considerably reduced from the scale of preceding works like *Komm tanz mit mir* or *Renate*: indeed, the simplicity of its arrangement bears more commonality with the Macbeth Project. In *Café Müller*, the patrons of the eponymous café desperately try to make contact with one another but are lost in echoing cycles of rejection and isolation. The cast is comprised of unconscious sleepwalkers and anxious wakeful figures that seem unsure of how to interact with or aid their dreaming counterparts. There are brief moments of tenderness amidst movement passages that border on hysteria, but no plot is proposed, nor is there any sense of resolution as the dancers gradually exit the darkening set.

Significantly, *Café Müller* demonstrates evident structural and thematic

Figure 3.1 *Café Müller*, Laszlo Szito

similarities with Eugène Ionesco's 1952 play, *Les Chaises* (*The Chairs*), a work Esslin considers characteristic of the Theatre of the Absurd. Servos hints at this connection in his description of Bausch's work, but few critics have pursued these parallels further.[10] Ionesco's work is similarly dark and recursive. It takes place inside a tower located on an unnamed island, in which an elderly couple are preparing for the arrival of a group of esteemed guests. They are convening a meeting in order to publicly proclaim the old man's message, an unrevealed missive that, Ionesco seems to suggest, might explain the meaning of life. Invisible guests arrive, and the couple frantically pack the set with chairs, but throughout they struggle to communicate with one another. Their exchanges revolve around alternate attempts to relive and forget the past, and they appear to be caught in a constantly repeating loop. When the Orator arrives (the audience is likely surprised by the fact the role is played by a real actor, following the stream of non-existent guests), the old man announces that he and his wife can die happily knowing his message will be communicated at last. The couple commit suicide by throwing themselves out of the window. However, when the Orator begins to speak, he makes only unintelligible sounds, and thus the old man's message is ultimately lost.

Visually and, indeed, structurally, the similarities between these two productions are evident. Nameless characters populate both works, who frantically arrange and rearrange the furniture in these otherwise minimalist, bare sets:

Bausch and Ionesco's pieces occur in liminal zones cluttered with empty chairs, and the symbolism of absence weighs heavily over both stages. Their inhabitants are lost in worlds of their own creation, and it is unclear how they relate to one other. *The Chairs*, which seems to take place in a post-apocalyptic world, essentially plays out the breakdown of a relationship. The sleepwalkers and their conscious counterparts of *Café Müller* suggest the same theme – they reach for one another, but are unable to make lasting connections. Character roles are not clearly defined in either production: Ionesco's protagonists are nameless, absurdist archetypes, and their assembled guests do not physically exist (suggesting that the actions of the play could be an unconscious fantasy, or simply that the elderly couple have no living friends left). Equally, Bausch's performers do not adopt clearly delineated identities. Instead, characters morph and shapeshift through the course of a work, with the dancers often taking on multiple personae simultaneously. Certain archetypes continually recur, however. These figures emerge in Bausch's work in her experimental period: we first meet them in the Macbeth Project, and they continue to metamorphose throughout her *oeuvre*. In *Café Müller*, they are divided into two groups, the wakeful and the sleepwalkers, but there is no further character development beyond this demarcation.

In their respective fragmented languages, *The Chairs* and *Café Müller* depict the unravelling of communication: in each piece, the characters' attempts to connect with one another – whether represented in word or gesture – repeatedly fail. The audience cannot escape from the sense of loss connoted by the empty chairs, a pointed symbol of anticipated but absent guests. Albert Bermel suggests that, in Ionesco's work, such symbolism evokes discomfort on the part of the viewer, as 'there is an implied continuity between the semicircular cyclorama onstage and the auditorium; between the stage chairs and the theater seats . . . The latter has been co-opted into the play.'[11] Bausch's audience could be forgiven for expressing a similar sense of unease in response to the self-destructive actions of *Café Müller*'s sleepwalkers. Both works end without providing a clear resolution – the old man's message is lost, and Bausch's dancers simply exit the set – leaving the audience with a profound sense of futility. Narrative is upended, just as linear time is abandoned. Behavioural patterns are endlessly reiterated, and such repetition only serves to undermine the inherent pointlessness of the characters' actions. An analogous tendency emerges in Lehmann's theorisation of postdramatic theatre, which he claims is characterised by an '*aesthetic of repetition*'.[12]

Movements and sequences are continually repeated to emphasise the missing connections between Bausch's characters, a theme to which she habitually returns. Indeed, repetition is one of the most recognisable characteristics of her work, and analysis of its significance has come to dominate much of the literature on her *Tanztheater*.[13] Discussion of repetition in Bausch's work tends to centre on specific reference points. One of the most commonly invoked is the 'dropping' scene of *Café Müller*: a woman is repeatedly placed in a sleepwalking man's arms, though he gradually releases his support and allows her to drop to the floor. The sequence is repeated multiple times, increasing in speed and violence. Moments such as this suggest the impossibility of resolution and imply a cycle of suffering inherent in the ongoing search for comfort and intimacy. In Bausch's dance theatre, the search for intimacy inevitably ends in failure or violence but, regardless, her dancers continue ceaselessly playing out these patterns: Adrian Heathfield, in this respect, has called her work 'an embodied language of desire'.[14]

For Bausch's audiences, the repetition device also forms an aide-memoire of the creative process behind the making of the work. The intertwining of repetition and rehearsal is perhaps not surprising: the director Peter Brook drew attention to this parallel in his 1968 text, *The Empty Space*, observing that the French term for 'rehearsal' is *répétition*.[15] Equally, a rehearsal director in classical ballet is generally referred to as a *repetiteur*. Repetition is an integral facet of creating a new work but, crucially, this part of the process is usually concealed from the intended audience. In Bausch's *Tanztheater*, this becomes a further development of her distancing effect, reminding the viewer of theatrical artifice while simultaneously shifting everyday activities into the realm of the nonsensical. Rituals of routine behaviour are similarly fragmented throughout her *oeuvre* when repetitions centre on quotidian behaviours, motifs or events. Broken down to their most basic gestures, ordinary motions become increasingly ludicrous. This excavation of commonplace behaviour is what Servos frames, in his analysis of Bausch's *1980* (1980), as 'an archaeology of the everyday', a description that can equally apply to her wider corpus of work.[16] Pedestrian movement and everyday tasks are obsessively, almost pathologically reiterated.

Although repetition serves multiple functions in Bausch's *Tanztheater*, each incarnation inevitably results in a distancing effect. The continued repetition of an action undermines its authenticity, estranging the viewer from the events on stage and reinforcing the artificiality of the action and surrounding set. Equally, it defies audience expectation, providing the viewer with recurring images of ordinary activities and quotidian behaviours in place of a narrative arc: Fernandes proposes that: 'Bausch's pieces do not intend to break the barriers between performance and life. She incorporates live elements and daily movements precisely to demonstrate that they are as artificial and representational as are stage performances.'[17] There is no clear sense of a beginning or end in Bausch's model; exposition and resolution are conspicuously absent. Her works pose ambiguous questions but suggest no answers. In this respect, interpreting their content can pose a significant challenge. Yet it is precisely this litany of uncertainties that aligns Bausch's mature *Tanztheater* with absurdist theatre practice. Linear plot and a coherent, conventional framework is frequently lacking. Absurdist plays characteristically omit defined openings or conclusions, and mundane, everyday behaviours and interactions replace traditional dramatic progression: Billie Whitelaw, one of Beckett's closest collaborators, described his play *Happy Days* (1961) as an account of 'the universal human task of *getting through the day*', despite the fact that her character spends its duration inexplicably buried in sand.[18] In such works, dialogue between characters can be ludicrous, utterly mundane or comic, thus highlighting the ineffectiveness of language. The absurdist play's underlying meaning is not immediately apparent, or even non-existent, as summarised by Vivian Mercier's now famous review of *Waiting for Godot* as a play in which 'nothing happens, twice'.[19] There is no evident internal motivation in this form of theatre, with events seeming to occur chaotically without clear reason or purpose. Esslin terms such events 'reflections of dreams and nightmares'.[20]

This critical phase in which Bausch rejects choreography in favour of an absurdist outlook begins with *Blaubart*. These tendencies become more visible in the works produced after *Café Müller* that abandon dance and theatrical tradition. It is a process of de-familiarisation. Bausch takes elements of dance practice, daily activity, pedestrian movement and the mechanics of the theatre, and situates them in unfamiliar territory. She devises productions lacking narrative that occur in liminal spaces and run according to their own internal logic. In this phase, a series of significant parallels arise connecting Bausch's theatre with Beckett's. They demonstrate a shared interest in absurdity and liminality, providing few recognisable reference points for audiences of traditional theatre. Bausch's works are structured in a strikingly similar way, though she transcends his absurdist approach by using Beckettian techniques to unmask the theatre itself. It is a process of unveiling that begins in the experimental period and arguably reaches its zenith in *Walzer*, an unsettling production that seeks to undermine the sanctity of the theatre space and reveal the workings of the company, but ultimately leaves the audience uncertain of its authenticity. In the end, the pieces made in this period function as, what I term, glimpses behind the *mise en scène*.

RETURNING THE GAZE: *KONTAKTHOF*

The fourth wall, an imagined barrier that separates audience from performer, is a fundamental component of conventional theatrical practice. In realist or naturalistic theatre, this invisible distinction tends to remain unbroken, aiding in the viewer's willing suspension of disbelief. The spectator remains a passive observer in this ultimately conformist theatrical model. When direct address is used in dramatic theatre (it is a common trope of Shakespeare, for instance), it is usually to serve a specific function, explaining a difficult plot point or emphasising a moral or ethical message such as Puck's salutation to the audience in the final scene of *A Midsummer Night's Dream* (1595). With the turn towards naturalist theatre in the late nineteenth century, the fourth wall became more firmly established, and by the early twentieth century this complete separation of dramatic action from the realm of the audience had become a dominant conception. Accordingly, it is primarily with developments in modernist dramatic practice that theatre-makers began to question the purpose and efficacy of the fourth wall as an established device.

Interrupting the fourth wall is anticipated in Stanisław Witkiewicz's Theatre of Pure Form, a tendency that, Daniel Gerould proposes, emerges in works such as *W małym dworku* (*Country House*, 1921).[21] Its disruption lies at the root of Brecht's highly influential conception of the *Verfremdungseffekt*: he states that one of the primary conditions of the distancing effect is the necessity to 'drop the assumption that there is a fourth wall cutting the audience off from the stage and the consequent illusion that the stage action is taking place in reality and without an audience'.[22] Brecht's theatre features multiple distancing actions that are designed to prevent the viewer from sliding into passivity or easy identification with the characters onstage, such as announcements projected onto a screen to indicate time and scene changes.[23] He sought to dismantle the suspension of disbelief, preventing the audience from engaging with the content on an emotional level and denying them the possibility of catharsis. Instead, Brecht's audience is encouraged to engage in objective rather than subjective analysis of the content. The emphasis in this model lies on greater criticality. Mitter's comment on distancing in Brecht's theatre serves analogously for Bausch's use of the device in her mature period:

> The actor's 'truth' in this situation stems from their acknowledgment that the dramatic text stands in relation to life outside the theatre as metatext does to text. Theatre's 'reality' is now the reality of comment upon life; it is not the thing itself.[24]

As I discuss in greater detail in Chapter 4, Antonin Artaud's conception of the Theatre of Cruelty espouses a similar attitude to the fourth wall, advocating for its disruption in an effort to jolt the spectator from passive voyeurism, and to merge the spaces of audience and performer. Grotowski also aimed at creating a unified space between performers and spectators, enabling the viewer to become a 'participant' in the action: this is evidenced in works such as *Dziady* (*Forefathers' Eve*, 1961), and *Kordian* (1962), in which the performance space reflects the layout of an asylum and, by extension, the viewers come to represent patients.[25] From the 1960s onwards, generations of dramatists have seized upon the radical potential of fourth wall disruption – Lehmann states:

> The aesthetic distance of the spectator is a phenomenon of dramatic theatre; in the new forms of theatre that are closer to performance this

distance is structurally shaken in a more or less noticeable and pro-vocative way. Wherever this unsettling blurring of boundaries happens in postdramatic theatre, it is invaded by the qualities of a *situation* (in the emphatic sense of the term), even in cases where all in all it seems to belong to the genre of classical theatre with its strict division of stage and theatron (auditorium).[26]

Peter Handke's 1966 work, *Publikumsbeschimpfung* (*Offending the Audience*), is a notable example of completely plotless theatre in which the performers address the audience directly throughout. The viewer is continually reminded that what they are watching does not even constitute a play and, accordingly, that none of their theatrical expectations will be satisfied. The Living Theatre, a collective established by Julian Beck and Judith Malina in 1947, has also used direct address and audience participation for similarly confrontational ends, not least in the case of their 1968 play, *Paradise Now!*, in which the performers extended an invitation to spectators to join their near-nude onstage melange (ending in a memorable group chant of the slogan, 'fuck means peace'). Indeed, confronting the audience arguably now forms a standard element of performance vocabulary in much contemporary theatre practice (Erika Fischer-Lichte discusses the marked shift in relationship between audi-ence and performer throughout her analysis of the postmodern 'performative turn'[27]).

Yet Bausch's treatment of the fourth wall, which might be better termed a manipulation of the device, departs from these prevailing trends of the 1960s. In the works of her mature period, she adopts a peripatetic attitude to its visibility and purpose that is more akin to the Theatre of the Absurd. Her per-formers regularly transgress the boundary between the stage and the audience with sudden or unexpected gestures – a particularly common example is her tendency to turn the lights on the audience, a device she used for the first time in *Blaubart*. This portal is rarely open for long, however, as Bausch continu-ally reinstates the fourth wall, and the process of removal and reinsertion is repeated throughout these durational works. Her approach is unusual for its inconsistency. She transgresses the concept of audience immersion, blurring the boundaries of narrative theatre and personal interaction between performer and spectator. In works such as *Kontakthof* (1978), the changing nature of the fourth wall presents a challenge to the parameters of theatrical space. Here, Bausch extends the fourth wall break beyond the limitations of the Brechtian device. My analysis explores the extent to which Bausch's spectator is made an active participant in the spectacle through the shifting of boundaries between fiction and verisimilitude.

Kontakthof is one of Bausch's most well-known productions, having toured regularly since its premiere and, more recently, undergone two restagings with non-professional casts. Devised at a crucial stage in the development of her new choreographic technique, *Kontakthof* also represents the gateway to Bausch's mature era, emerging in the same year as the Macbeth Project and *Café Müller*: Servos indicates that, 'the reality of the production of theatre activity is explored more starkly here; it becomes the defining theme of the piece'.[28] The breaking of the fourth wall is used as a tool to emphasise self-consciousness and self-awareness. *Kontakthof* thus represents a critical juncture in the evolution of an unmasking process that began in *Blaubart*.

The stage design of *Kontakthof* is reminiscent of an old-fashioned dance hall, and a sense of faded grandeur permeates the piece. The cast is clad in similarly outdated eveningwear, though this choice of apparel is not unusual for Bausch. Her dancers are often costumed as if attending a formal event, reflecting her proclamation that, 'I never create pieces for leotards.'[29] This tendency is reminiscent of her mentor Jooss' attitude to design. His dancers were often clothed in everyday wear, extending the use of pedestrian elements in his choreography to costume as well as movement. Under the proscenium arch, Bausch's dancers evoke rituals of human behaviour that are reflected in their dress, like guests at a formal gathering or dance party.

Kontakthof is the last of Bausch's works to take place in a seemingly identifiable temporal–spatial location. Much of the soundtrack is composed of popular German songs of the 1930s and 40s, and the costume and set design similarly evoke the European dance hall tradition. While there is no clear narrative proposed, there does seem to be an overarching theme of the battle of the sexes. Men and women divide into distinct groups and their interactions with one another form the 'script' of this piece in place of dialogue. They perform 'at' rather than with one another, with the women playing coy or fleeing their counterparts and the men often grabbing or lunging at them (Figure 3.2). One sequence sees the female dancers line up against the wall, squirming as if frantically trying to escape while the men (all seated on chairs) desperately reach for them, shuffling gradually closer across the stage. These interactions grow more confrontational as the piece progresses, as when they stand opposite one another in groups, screaming the words for individual body parts at one another. Fragmentation of the body through language (that is, screaming or drawing the audience's attention to specific parts) is a theme that evolves and expands through Bausch's mature period.

A melancholic air hangs over the proceedings of *Kontakthof*, with the cast endlessly playing out cycles of childish games and spitefulness. The title, which can be translated as 'meeting place', is also suggestive of the negotiation 'salon' of a brothel. Climenhaga has argued that the theme of prostitution implied by the title is a metaphor for the treatment of young performers within the world of professional dance, observing that this designation was only chosen halfway through the choreographic development of the work.[30] Throughout,

Figure 3.2 *Kontakthof*, Oliver Look

the dancers enact a public and, at times, uncomfortable quest for intimate contact, and a warped sense of intimacy is reflected in the performers' flirtatious interactions with one another. From the very beginning, the fourth wall is broken down as the dancers display themselves one body part at a time to the audience. They stride to the front of the stage and present themselves as if standing before an audition panel. At first individually, then in small groups, they scrape their hair back from their faces, stand in profile and suck in their stomachs to correct slouches, and confront the audience with teeth bared in an emotionless grimace. Bausch allegedly devised this sequence by asking her dancers to present the parts of their bodies they most disliked. In this respect, self-consciousness is immediately evoked, as is a sense of negativity and shame. Beginning with a reference to the audition process also marks an early instance of Bausch's theatrical unmasking, referring to the time and space before the finished piece exists. Accordingly, *Kontakthof* situates the spectator in the role of casting director from its very opening. The viewer cannot easily revert to a passive, detached role, but unwittingly (and, perhaps, unwillingly) becomes a kind of participant in the action. Recalling his first experience seeing this production, Climenhaga claimed that the eye contact between dancer and spectator was extremely unsettling, stating, 'that direct gaze was exposing, and exposure always feels self-consciously personal'.[31] However, the direct relationship between audience and performer is not consistently maintained.

Instead, Bausch's dancers alternate between interacting with their audience and retreating into their self-contained world on stage.

Drawing attention to theatrical artifice similarly forms an integral facet of Beckett's *oeuvre*. While direct address does occur in his work, this aspect of his own tendency towards unmasking has not received a significant degree of critical attention. Nathaniel Davis proposes that one reason for the relative lack of discussion around the fourth wall in Beckett's work is due to its shifting nature, that in Beckett's theatre, the barrier is never 'static'.[32] In this respect, another key commonality with Bausch's methodology emerges. Both utilise patterns of repetition around mundane activity as a kind of distancing effect. In the case of Beckett's *Endgame* (1957), the play even opens with a repeated sequence: Clov's pronouncement, 'Finished, it's finished, nearly finished, it must be nearly finished', undermines the spectator's conception of recognisable time and space, suggesting the play has ended before it has even begun.[33] Themes of encasement and the abandonment of linearity are regularly evidenced in Beckett and Bausch's theatres through patterns of repetition. However, the stage directions accompanying Clov's opening line – *He goes to door, halts, turns towards auditorium* – implies the presence, and puncturing, of the fourth wall from the play's outset. Further on, Clov's use of a telescope when gazing out into the audience, 'I see . . . a multitude . . . in transports . . . of joy',[34] is curious not only in suggesting the permeability of the fourth wall, but also the implied distance between performer and spectator.

The boundaries between the performance space and the audience remain similarly fluid throughout Bausch's *Kontakthof*. At one point, a woman speaks directly to the audience, requesting change to animate the coin-operated rocking horse onstage. In this respect, Cody states that:

> Bausch openly confronts the complicated motivations of our desire as spectators and explores the genesis of performative acts by examining the power relations underlying representation . . . This brief negotiation and her subsequent performance of sexualized passivity in which she blankly gazes at the audience as she rocks to the horse's artificial cadence expose the tacit rules of a representational economy which regards femininity as a compulsory public service.[35]

However, when the action shifts into short sequences of cruelty and spitefulness, the audience is once more relegated to passive observer. One sequence features two dancers prancing gaily in the background while a man attempts to conceal his partner's limp, seemingly lifeless body. Nonetheless, he, along with the grinning women behind him, play to the crowd with exaggerated comic gestures. The spectator becomes an accomplice to the action as the performers directly address the audience, often making and maintaining eye contact with individual viewers. The physical structure of *Kontakthof* is built upon small gestures of self-consciousness, which escalate into more aggressive movements, as awkward shuffling and tweaking give way to pinching and slapping. The dancers critique one another, playing out impressions of a rehearsal through-out the performance itself, distorting the boundaries between what could be considered 'real' (the rehearsal process) versus 'unreal' (the choreographed performance event). The male/female courtship ritual is played out painfully: a woman bites her partner's ear; a man grabs a woman's hand and roughly yanks her fingers backwards; another pulls the hair from his partner's head as their fellow performers limply applaud. While a couple appear locked in a seemingly loving embrace, a glance at their feet reveals that the woman is actually grinding the high heel of her shoe into her partner's foot. Such childish cruelty is what Norbert Servos chiasticly calls 'affectionate violence and violent affection'.[36]

This sense of complicity, as well as the increasingly aggressive search for intimacy (the *Kontakt* of the title), reaches its conclusion with the controversial closing sequence. A woman stands centre stage, surrounded by male dancers who tenderly stroke her. What begin as gestures of consolation become increasingly heavy-handed, until gentleness gives way to outright physical abuse. Meryl Tankard, a former company member who regularly performed this role, admitted that she often spontaneously wept during this part of the piece, claiming that, 'it felt like being raped'.[37] Throughout this sequence, the woman gazes out at the audience, once again breaking the fourth wall to unset-tling effect, as the passive spectators become complicit in the action. Through their inactivity, they tacitly allow the men's abuse to continue for a duration of more than seven minutes, after which the performers exit, leaving the stage in darkness. The audience is left in a tenebrous state to reflect on their collective permissiveness, as an accusatory air hangs over the now empty stage.

Fischer-Lichte suggests moments of unsettlement in performance have the capacity to jolt the viewer into becoming a participant in the action or, at least, can leave us asking what we are supposed to do next: she makes clear that 'contradictory emotions' are at play in such circumstances.[38] Similarly, Lehmann proposes that, in such moments in postdramatic theatre practice:

> We witness a displacement that all questions of morality and behavioural norms undergo through theatre aesthetics, in which there is a deliberate suspension of the clear line between reality (where, for instance, the observation of violence leads to feelings of responsibility and the need to intervene) and 'spectatorial event'.[39]

Ramsey Burt puts forward a dual reading of this specific scene. He argues that the men are at once committing an act of violence, but also clinging to the woman in search of some kind of tenderness themselves.[40] Their gestures begin as gentle reassurances, and eventually became more violent and forceful. It is this interplay of violence and longing that characterises a considerable quotient of Bausch's *oeuvre*. Indeed, loneliness and longing feature heavily in the many direct audience addresses throughout *Kontakthof*. These often take the form of open pleas seeking to transcend the barriers put in place by the fourth wall: consider the moment when one dancer announces,

> I stand on the edge of the piano and threaten to fall, but before I do it, I scream, so that no-one can miss it, then I crawl under the piano and peek out, and do it as if I want to be alone, but actually I want someone to come to me.

Bausch's reiterations of cruelty, enacted by a cast seemingly trapped within their surroundings, demonstrate evident parallels with Beckett's framing of *Endgame*. Obsessive iterations of meaningless behaviour estrange the spectator from the action onstage and impede any significant identification with the characters (such as they are). In *Endgame*, the blind, crippled Hamm repeatedly insists Clov, his tormented servant, return him precisely to the centre of the stage. His fixation is undermined by the broader context of the play: these characters are each trapped, unable to escape either their dingy surroundings or their attachment to one another. As this is made increasingly clear, Hamm's constant demands become all the more absurd. Beckett's characters are trapped within repeating patterns of behaviour, with no real hope of escape or any kind of resolution. As Katherine Weiss asserts, 'quite literarily, Beckett imprisons his storytellers perhaps to show how the past – their histories – imprison them'.[41] Hamm's parents, Nag and Nell, are confined to their dustbins for the duration of the play, even following their respective deaths. Clov and Hamm spar with one another throughout and the threat of abandonment pervades the proceedings, but ultimately rings hollow. They are locked in a grotesque, almost sado-masochistic relationship, but it becomes clear that these characters are unable to leave, regardless of the cruelties they visit upon one another. Bausch's performers depict a similar sense of unhealthy dependency, returning to an unhappy stasis after each childish rejection or spiteful interaction. The grimly humorous inevitability of this fact is reflected in Nell's observation that, 'Nothing is funnier than unhappiness.'[42]

Estrangement is the recursive tendency that underpins *Endgame*. Even confined within the same setting, genuine intimacy or contact remains impossible. Nag and Nell attempt to kiss, but cannot reach one another. Endeavouring to extract themselves from each other, Hamm and Clov reach a similarly futile conclusion:

> HAMM: I can't leave you.
> CLOV: I know. And you can't follow me.
> (*Pause*)

HAMM: If you leave me how shall I know?

CLOV (*briskly*): Well you simply whistle me and if I don't come running
    it means I've left you.

(*Pause*)

HAMM: You won't come and kiss me goodbye?

CLOV: Oh I shouldn't think so.

(*Pause*)

HAMM: But you might be merely dead in your kitchen.

CLOV: The result would be the same.[43]

Some time later, Clov and Hamm have a terse exchange over the windows in their cell. Hamm demands to be brought under the window so that he can hear the sound of the sea, but he hears nothing and feels no effect from the light. Their discussion casts doubt on the veracity of the windows themselves, as if the characters onstage are equally conscious of the artificial set design as the audience. The windows in Beckett's play provide no real sense of perspective, nor do they afford the possibility of escape. They are merely dressing, a decorative aspect of set design. This is a concept both Beckett and Bausch's characters seem to obliquely acknowledge. Naoya Mori proposes that:

> The window, in general, has a dual function; it makes a threshold of inside and outside. It constitutes a wall against the outer world, but through its transparency the exterior merges into the interior, and vice versa. The duality of Beckett's window, however, parts company with this traditional notion. Not only are Beckett's windows more complex . . . they do not actually let in the outer world at all.[44]

Windows in Bausch's *Tanztheater* similarly hint at an outside world, a possible escape route, that does not even exist within the piece's internal logic. The revolving doors of *Café Müller* similarly lead nowhere, but hint at a void, an expanse of nothingness beyond the limits of the stage. The unstable role of the fourth wall is, it seems, the only real window in these works, opening a temporary portal into another dimension (namely, the realm of the audience). In Beckett and Bausch's theatres, windows thus serve as an unusual reminder of artifice. When the action taking place onstage is nonsensical and ultimately meaningless, such ciphers of quotidian reality are also thrown into doubt. Each time the performers acknowledge the presence of the audience, they starkly remind their spectators that they are watching a play. Their onstage world, with its windows opening out onto an impossible landscape, becomes all the more ludicrous.

Bausch's dreamlike choreographies seek to further blur the boundaries between performer and spectator than is realised in Beckett's dramaturgy. In her dance theatre, while dancers may speak, either to one another or directly to the audience, their voices do not drive the narrative of the performance. Indeed, there is often a tendency to confuse the spectator further through their dialogues, whether they are nonsensical diatribes, requests for help, or amusing or painful anecdotes. Short vignettes, often nonsensical or bizarre, move out of the stage environment, where they are safely 'contained', and into the audience. The role of the spectator is made active, and the understanding of reality as opposed to theatrical fiction is thrown into a degree of flux.

With this, she increasingly abandons the vestiges of Stanislavskian technique and the notion of immersion is shifted. The audience is constantly reminded that what they are watching is not reality. In doing so, Bausch employs elements of everyday life to break down any remaining idea of spectacle that the viewer might have in mind. Audience expectation is continually confounded: in *Kontakthof*, Bausch includes several sequences of broken-down, awkward dancing performed by the whole ensemble. Their deliberately clumsy, even ugly, movements form the only recognisable dance choreography in the piece. Bodies in Bausch's work, as in Beckett's, are frequently depicted as distorted, fragmented or malfunctioning. Disembodiment is a common feature of the evolution of their respective methods. As Beckett's *oeuvre* progresses, his performers become increasingly incapacitated and immobilised: all the characters of *Endgame* suffer from specific disabilities that keep them trapped within the stage set; Winnie, the protagonist of *Happy Days*, is progressively buried in sand; *Play* (1963) features three performers encased within urns; and *Not I* (1972) centres on a disembodied mouth illuminated by a single shaft of light. Bausch initiates a similar process of bodily estrangement in her mature work that emerges as a direct result of the *Stichworte* technique. Her fragmentary queries and prompts often centre on individual body parts or movements, reducing choreography to repeating patterns and everyday gestures. In *Kontakthof*'s shuffling dance routine, the graceful bodies of Bausch's classically trained dancers jar with the uncoordinated and jerky dance moves. It is this rejection or denial of embodiment that simultaneously unravels the viewer's expectations around dance (and the anticipated 'quality' of the performance) and furthers the unmasking process of Bausch's mature *Tanztheater*.

The pinnacle of theatrical unveiling in *Kontakthof* is realised when a screen is lowered onto the back wall of the stage and the cast assemble their chairs, turning their backs to the audience, to watch a short documentary film on the mating rituals of moorhens. The theatregoer is now placed in the unusual position of seeing the objects of their gaze adopt the role of spectator themselves. That is, the audience watches the performers become an audience. Bausch opens the piece by shifting the role of the viewer to that of a voyeur. Thus, from the outset, roles are unfixed and unreliable. Yet this inconsistency also indicates that Bausch, the creator of the work, has already conceived of you, the audience member, watching the performance. In turning the gaze back on the viewer, she evokes a sense of deliberate discomfort. The audience member has entered into a willing contract by purchasing a ticket and taking their place in the theatre. Having paid the price of admission in order to be entertained, however, the viewer of Bausch's work has, to a degree, been duped: in productions such as *Kontakthof*, the spectator must temporarily adopt new identities, as if they have been drawn into playing a part that they have not rehearsed or had time to prepare.

Bausch's inconsistency in maintaining the fourth wall is problematic. Without a clear boundary, the audience is left unsure of its role. Performers regularly address the spectator, yet in the uncomfortable and lengthy final scene, there is no clear direction for the audience member – whether to stand up and intervene, or to accept that the fourth wall has been put back in place. It is this vacillating attitude towards the boundaries between spectator and performer that exemplifies Bausch's technique. In her *Tanztheater*, not even the seasoned theatregoer can be completely confident in the validity of their passive enjoyment of the spectacle. It is an attempt to show us the vulnerabilities of theatre. At the same time, *Kontakthof* can be also read as an allegory of the failure of communication. Pleasantries and tender gestures steadily give way to acts of cruelty. The performers address their audience directly, drawing them in to the enclosed world on stage, then ignoring them, returning to their own domain with its rules and nonsensical functions. When they turn their backs on the audience to watch a film, the viewer is even further estranged from the action. As everyday activity is played out onstage, it becomes increasingly de-familiarised. The audience member is tacitly asked to detect where the quotidian meets the artificial, to demarcate between reality and fiction. *Kontakthof* is, in this sense, a theatrical hall of mirrors.

Mirroring also forms a framing device in Bausch's *Tanztheater*. Her reiterations of particular sequences, lines or jokes are often used to structure productions in place of a linear narrative. Her pieces are usually cyclical, in a similar manner to absurdist theatre, and repetition is substituted for resolution. Indeed, Rosette Lamont's analysis of Beckett and Ionesco's theatre could easily be applied to Bausch's work: 'Their literature is in no way didactic: they neither preach nor teach. They direct a gaze as impersonal, as lucid and transparent as a spotlight, upon the creature they place upon the stage.'[45] Mirroring the opening and closing scenes of a performance marks another important parallel with absurd theatre, where repetition, just as in Bausch's *Tanztheater*, often relates to the notion of failure. Humanity's capacity for foolishness is emphasised in these works, and the futility of everyday routine is magnified by the bare, liminal space in which these actions are played out. As the fourth wall is alternately removed and reinstated, the spectator is asked to question their own role in proceedings as well as working out the underlying meaning of the performance. As a result, audience expectations of theatrical convention are unmet and, ultimately, unsatisfied.

Kontakthof represents a cornerstone of Bausch's mature *Tanztheater*. It is a synthesis of elements, drawing upon personal experience, rehearsal material, and toying with audience expectation and the boundaries of theatrical form. It stands at the forefront of a new phase of her work that is in many respects more radical than the experimental pieces. Here, she uncovers a more clearly defined dramaturgical language. A crucial aspect of this is the fact that the mature works demonstrate a shift further away from the tendencies of Brecht's epic theatre towards a more absurdist model, one that has important parallels with Beckett's theatre, not least in its shared inconsistent approach to the fourth wall.

'AND THEN, PINA SAID . . .': *WALZER*

A key recurring image in Bausch's *oeuvre* is the theatre itself. Her interest in making visible the constructed nature of performance is first tentatively explored in the experimental period, and initially appears to derive from the influence of Brecht's epic theatre. In her mature phase, however, the Brechtian *Verfremdungseffekt* transitions into a Bauschian estrangement, one that is particularly focused on the artificiality of theatre, performance and dance training. In a period when she grows increasingly confident in her new creative method, Bausch further strips away the illusionism associated with classical dance.

Walzer (*Waltzes*, 1982) represents the apotheosis of the unmasking process that characterises Bausch's mature period. It is a thoroughly intertextual and self-reflexive production, revealing the workings both of the theatre space and of Bausch's own creative practice. Its narrative is non-existent, and instead comprises a seemingly random assortment of ludicrous stories and bizarre vignettes. The action is partly directed by a figure who conducts surreal games. These interactions often descend into farce, as when a woman chases a male dancer while both bark like dogs. In these absurdist scenes, Bausch illustrates the thin veneer that separates polite society from chaos. She abandons the framing of a straightforward narrative and rejects any recognisable location for the action, something that is still perceptible in *Kontakthof*. This gradual rejection of linearity begins with *Blaubart*: where in that piece time (represented by the tape recording) stops and restarts, there is still an approximation of a plot that follows a relatively conventional model. More significantly, *Blaubart* centres on a single score which, though fragmented, provides an identifiable narrative line to follow. In the mature era of her *Tanztheater*, Bausch's works change shape. They become cyclical, not linear, and fragmented rather than narrative-driven.

Artifice is unravelled at almost every stage in *Walzer*. The dancers address the audience directly, telling jokes and nonsensical stories, though language often descends into nonsensical or inane repetition. The stage is stripped back to the extent that the viewer is able to see the lighting galleys. This deliberate visibility of the stage mechanics evokes the Brechtian *Verfremdungseffekt*, but here Bausch continues her own process of theatrical estrangement introduced in *Kontakthof*. The fourth wall remains an unstable constant, again undermining the authenticity of the action onstage and the environment in which it occurs. The key themes of *Walzer* centre around memory and identity. The piece also builds upon the durational aspect of preceding works and, in its original form, lasted almost four hours in total. It is an unmasked spectacle, run through with a sense of angst and longing that ultimately remains unresolved. The length and lack of narrative structure presents a challenge to the audience, breaking the convention of allowing the viewer a return to the real world.

Despite the titular suggestion that *Walzer* might draw upon musical themes, its central interest lies in language, perhaps to a greater degree than other productions of Bausch's mature period. Her emphasis on non-literal and nonsensical word play suggests dissatisfaction with the capacity of language to appropriately express relevant emotions. Impossibility thus represents a commonality between absurdist theatre and Bausch's mature dance theatre, in which the loss of communication or its gradual breakdown forms the loosest sense of a plot. Where in previous works, including the experimental *Blaubart*, movement and narrative were connected to the central score, in *Walzer*, the music is largely disconnected from the events onstage. Waltzes by Schubert and Schumann feature at intervals throughout the piece alongside Latin dance music and various national anthems. This estrangement between soundtrack and action bears some relation to epic theatre: one of Brecht's preferred distancing effects was the use of songs, which he saw as 'highly gestic'.[46] At the same time, it reflects a tendency in postdramatic theatre more broadly, where musical form is known to shift and warp.[47]

Waltzes physically materialise in the repeating motif of the dance lesson, a recurring sequence in which cast members draw an outline of the appropriate dance steps in chalk on the stage floor. They are repeatedly taught the steps and, as the piece builds towards its conclusion, the whole ensemble is able to execute the waltz to the vocal applause of the audience. The manifestation of the steps as physical marks on the stage represents a further unmasking of per-formative artifice as choreography is reduced to its most basic form. Audience expectation is confounded once more as Bausch presents a cast of highly trained dancers seemingly struggling to learn a basic social dance step. This is a continuation of the breakdown of dance technique initiated in *Kontakthof*, though in *Walzer* the awkward, jerky routine is replaced with a dispassionate, almost lacklustre process of 'going through the moves'.

By the early 1980s, Bausch had hired dancers from a broad global spectrum, and themes of travel and border-crossing prefigure the transient approach that the company would imminently adopt. *Walzer* is the first piece in Bausch's *oeuvre* to explicitly play upon the international makeup of her company. The piece opens with the dancers moving around a semi-lit stage while a recording of the public-address system in Hamburg's harbour plays announcements that greet and bid farewell to travellers. One welcomes us aboard *The Prince Hamlet*, a reference that recalls Bausch's avant-garde Shakespearean adaptation. A series of national anthems are played at deafening volume – Germany's Deutschlandlied is followed by The Star-Spangled Banner. Anthems form a major recurring theme of the first act and blare out at regular intervals, interspersing the musette waltzes of the title. Thus, the main themes established early in this piece relate to travel and national identity, reflecting the diverse constitution of Tanztheater Wuppertal.

As is typical of Bausch's *Tanztheater*, no specific location is evoked in this piece, nor has any attempt been made to connote a realistic impression of a port in terms of set design (the presumed site for the actions of *Walzer*). Instead, a group of eccentric characters appear to have encountered each other either whilst waiting to travel or while in the process of travelling. The lighting is stark and the stage sparsely furnished: Ulrich Bergfelder's setting is significantly more minimalist than in previous works such as *Kontakthof* or the flooded stage of *Arien*.[48] Huge pots of flowers lining the set constitute the most notable feature of *Walzer*'s design. Some chairs, a table and a piano comprise the remainder of the props. These elements consistently recur in Bausch's mature work, quotidian symbols of the rehearsal studio that find their way into her otherwise abstracted settings. Nonetheless, the dancers' movements lead the audience to surmise that the action seems to be taking place on or around a ship. Multiple references are made to the motif of swimming, establishing a connection to other 'water' pieces such as the Macbeth Project and *Arien*, though in the case of *Walzer* this elemental factor is implied rather than made explicit through stage design.

The ambiguity of *Walzer*, and its use of visual and thematic signifiers, serves as a link to Brechtian semiotics. Consider, for example, his *Leben des Galilei* (*Life of Galileo*, 1943) in which a doorway is used to illustrate the prince's palace. The rest of the stage is otherwise empty, starkly contrasting with the single signifier. A similar device is used in *Walzer* where, rather than constructing a recognisable harbour, ship or sea environment on stage, the set is comprised of minimalist signifiers of the setting. When the stage goes dark, the dancers lie down in formations that reflect the underlying nautical theme, imitating the form of ships. This recurring motif is usually accompanied by the 'welcome to Hamburg' announcement over the public-address system. As the lights come up again, the dancers move across the stage carrying small paper boats, and at points mime the motions of swimming. The Brechtian connection is taken even further in the cast's use of the chairs which line the walls of the set.

When they are not directly involved in the action, Bausch's performers sit and observe the scenes played out on stage. Indeed, they appear to be watching the show along with the audience in the auditorium. The voyeurism of this motif is reminiscent of Brecht's enduring fascination with Chinese theatre: he was especially interested in the notion that the actor is conscious of being watched as he performs. At the same time, the stripped-back setting of *Walzer* is evocative of the rehearsal space, an environment in which this casual, observational relationship between dancers is quite common. This set-up immediately recalls the fourth wall breakages of *Kontakthof*. The chairs, constantly in use, serve as a reminder to the audience that they are watching a work of fiction, while the largely empty set implies that the production might even be a work in progress.

The theme of work left unfinished runs throughout *Walzer*. In addition to the bare stage and the dissonant accompanying score, the dancers make multiple references to the *Stichworte* questions Bausch proposed in the process of the piece's creation. This further unmasking of theatrical artifice permits the audience a new level of engagement with the process that lies behind the construction of *Tanztheater* pieces. It is also in this reduction of stage design that further parallels with Beckett's absurdist theatre are evidenced. Thus, *Walzer* questions the boundaries of theatrical space in a manner that begins to transcend Brechtian principles. Visual signifiers may point us in the direction of a nautical theme, but the location of the work remains undefined and its internal goings-on become increasingly absurdist. Even the distancing device evoked by the dancers watching one another seems to literalise Brecht's desire in a more direct manner than evidenced in his own work. The starkly lit, largely empty stage focuses audience attention on the actions of the dancers, but no moral message is proposed, nor is the spectator left with a clear sense of purpose behind the piece's content. Indeed, Mercier's oft-cited summary of Beckett's *Godot* might equally apply in the case of Bausch's *Walzer* – in the end, nothing happens here.

Both productions take place on stages where set design is completely minimised, with *Godot* featuring only a rather bare tree and a small mound. Beckett's instructions delineate the play takes place on 'a country road', though no indication of a specific location is provided – Anna McMullan observes that when Beckett staged *Godot* in 1975 at the Berlin Schillertheater, he collaborated with designer Matias Henrioud to 'maintain as unspecific a location as possible'.[49] As a result of his increasingly reduced sets, bodies are continually foregrounded in Beckett's theatre. By clearing his stages and minimising potentially distracting elements of set design, plays such as *Endgame* and *Godot* focus the audience's attention almost entirely on the physicality of the performers and the action being played out. The lack of a clear narrative arc further emphasises the attention on the performers themselves. In *Godot*, for example, the plot merely extends to the action indicated by the title – the characters achieve little beyond waiting for the eponymous character, who never appears. Davis suggests that this unadulterated minimalism impacts on the integrity of Beckett's fourth wall:

> With Godot, we are presented with a stage, a plot, and characters that are all so extremely reduced as to barely register as theatrical, let alone real or natural. With Godot, we are neither here nor there, and thus the fourth wall separating the audience from the stage takes on a strongly ambiguous character.[50]

Revealing theatrical artifice thus destabilises the imagined barrier between audience and performer; the viewer is denied the possibility of a willing suspension of disbelief when confronted with a largely empty stage and the presence of obviously artificial scenery. Beckett further estranges his audience from passive engagement with the narrative through several jarring instances of fourth wall rupture. On these occasions when his characters refer to the theatre space itself, the unnerving nature of direct address is emphasised by the austere setting. In the first act, for instance, Estragon observes his surroundings and wryly acknowledges the presence of the audience:

> ESTRAGON: Charming spot. (*He turns, advances to front, halts facing auditorium.*) Inspiring prospects.[51]

At the mid-point of the same act, he seems to break from the internal pseudo-narrative (waiting for the mysterious Godot) when directing Vladimir through the physical space of the backstage area:

> VLADIMIR: I'll be back.
> (*He hastens towards the wings*)
> ESTRAGON: End of the corridor, on the left.
> VLADIMIR: Keep my seat.[52]

In the second act, this recognition of the reality of the theatre environment focuses upon its limitations, reiterating the notion that, despite the insecurity of Beckett's fourth wall, his characters remain trapped within the boundaries of the stage. The back wall represents a real, physical barrier for the pair, but the realm of the audience becomes an empty, potentially threatening expanse:

> VLADIMIR: We're surrounded! (*Estragon makes a rush towards back*) Imbecile! There's no way out there. (*He takes Estragon by the arm and drags him towards front. Gesture towards front*) There! Not a soul in sight! Off you go! Quick! (*He pushes Estragon towards auditorium. Estragon recoils in horror*) You won't? (*He contemplates auditorium*) Well I can understand that. Wait till I see. (*He reflects*) Your only hope left is to disappear.[53]

In both Beckett and Bausch's theatres, the fourth wall represents a temporary portal to a world outside the narrow confines of the stage, but the performers are never permitted a proper escape route as a result of its inconsistent form.

Onstage, the absence of logical plot development prevents any kind of resolution. The title of Beckett's work reflects the hopelessness of its non-narrative – Godot never appears, and the waiting thus never ends. There is a curious link here with Bausch's earlier work, *Renate wandert aus*. As in Godot, the titular character does not materialise, and as such the nature of her 'emigration' is not clarified. Beginning with the Macbeth Project, however, Bausch initiates a process of estrangement in the titling of her productions that moves beyond Beckett's suggestion of impossibility. *Godot* remains a descriptive title, illustrating the onstage action. Bausch on the other hand moves from the literal (*Orpheus*, *Sacre* and *Blaubart*) to increasingly abstracted designations that often bear little relation to the content. As in absurdist theatre, language in Bausch's work is often estranged from the action taking place on stage, and new meanings are ascribed to specific words and phrases. In *Arien*, for example, when a woman covering herself in makeup is asked, 'What do you think of arias?' she replies, 'I associate them with blood-red nails and torture.' This unanticipated response is jarring for the audience member who might automatically associate operatic arias with art, theatre and beauty. Yet it is precisely this sense of disjuncture that mirrors the progressive breakdown of semantics recurring throughout Beckett's *oeuvre*. An overarching sense of self-awareness characterises Bausch's mature work and serves a similar function to that of Beckett's slyly cognizant characters.

It is also in this period that absurdist humour emerges as a central theme in Bausch's *Tanztheater*. In *Walzer*, Großmann performs an amusing turn in the guise of a drunken woman, by turns charming and then abusive. She lies at the edge of the stage with her legs up the wall, refusing to go home until she's had 'noch ein Weinchen, noch ein Zigarettchen – aber noch nicht nach Hause' ('just a little wine, just a little cigarette, but let's not go home yet'), interspersing her pleas with an alternative history of God's creation of the earth. Großmann's constant reiteration of the same lines is played for comic effect in this sequence, with each (increasingly inevitable) refrain eliciting laughter from the audience. Throughout Bausch's mature period, jokes and anecdotes are often repeated multiple times over the course of a single production, but, as Fernandes has discussed, repetition of humour or fits of laughter serves primarily to undermine authenticity.[54] After the same joke has been told several times, the audience is aware of the punchline in advance, and the performers' resulting laughter is read as increasingly artificial with each reiteration.

Großmann claimed that this specific scene was derived from the rehearsal process for the Macbeth Project. The cast would work together for lengthy periods of time, but afterwards when Großmann insisted she was going home,

Bausch would attempt to delay her with this very line.[55] By working her catch-phrase into the script of this new piece, Bausch references her own role in the artistic process (and in her performers' lives). In this regard, *Walzer* is a deeply self-referential production. Shortly after the opening sequence, a man strides up to a microphone which is located centre stage and announces, 'and then, Pina said . . .' The repeated use of this aposiopestic line becomes a structuring device for *Walzer*, and continually reminds the audience of Bausch's ghostly authority. Though she is not physically present on stage, the dancers will not let one another (or the audience) forget her role in the creation of this piece. We can read this fragmentary refrain as the ultimate removal of the fourth wall. Each time the dancers reveal another of Bausch's *Stichworte* prompts they unambiguously acknowledge the mechanics not just of the theatrical space, but of the specific rehearsal process Bausch evolved. It foregrounds an unusually explicit aspect of the workings of the company, a process of theatrical dissection first suggested in the Macbeth Project: where in the earlier piece Bausch uses a supposed stage direction for the title, in *Walzer* stage directions and rehearsal questions are presented for analysis.

Later, Bausch is referenced again when a dancer reads to the audience from a piece of paper. He recalls a conversation with her that leads the viewer to question the veracity of his tale:

> And then Pina wanted to hear some good news.
> So I said to her 'the president's died, there'll be an amnesty soon. And this year we'll have a summer again.'
> Then I put a green branch in my mouth.[56]

The ambiguity of this absurdist anecdote throws further into question the supposed location of this production. The reference to the president's death as a glad tiding and the prospect of an imminent amnesty suggests *Walzer* takes place in wartime. In turn, this framing indicates the nomadic cast might in fact be refugees fleeing some unspecified conflict. This indeterminate temporal–spatial setting is similarly evoked in Beckett's theatre: Vladimir and Estragon await the arrival of the titular Godot to provide them with a sense of purpose. They do not seem to know where they are or what will happen next, only that they must wait for Godot. Both Beckett and Bausch locate (and arguably trap) their performers in liminal, otherworldly spaces, but neglect to give them further direction beyond obsessive reiterations of the same lines, actions and behaviours.

The last sentence of the dancer's account reflects the surrealism inherent in Bausch's increasingly absurdist dance theatre. Questions addressed to the audience are often non-sequiturs and usually remain unanswered. In one scene, a woman holding the microphone leads a row of men across the stage. The woman giggles to herself as she asks a series of questions, including, 'Where do you live?' and 'Are you hungry?' She continues laughing as she announces, 'I'm so stupid. I gave it my all.' The men follow meekly behind her, hands joined like a row of small children in formalwear, with mournful looks on their faces. The woman then exchanges them for a row of female dancers. The same pattern repeats, but this time as her questions cease the group take their shoes off, tuck their dresses up and perform a snaking dance step across the stage to the soundtrack of another waltz. Unreciprocated address and incomplete actions continually recur in *Walzer*, leaving the audience to question whether any element of this production will be finished.

In this durational piece, Bausch does not permit her viewer much respite. Light-hearted and comic sequences are countered by moments of darkness and the threat of violence: a man throws a stone into the air, only narrowly missing being hit as he moves out of its way; a woman is dropped from a man's shoulders to be caught by the rest of the dancers; a dancer lights a fuse that is connected to a piano, but each time he ducks for cover underneath, the spark goes out. Random acts of violence are similarly evoked throughout *Godot*, not least in Pozzo's brutal treatment of his slave, Lucky, and Estragon's offstage beating during the night. Bausch's cruelties are rather subtler, however, and often merely implied, as when a woman discusses methods of killing insects, then nails another dancer's dress and tapes her hair to the wall. The image of the pinned woman comprises another reference to the opening nautical theme, as her splayed hair and dress resemble the paper ships the dancers hold aloft in the opening sequence.

Similarly, direct audience address shifts between comedy and confrontation. In a well-known scene, a woman enters the stage clad in an unflattering blue swimming costume and an incongruous pair of black stilettoes (this role was originally performed by Endicott, with whom it is now synonymous). She stalks across the stage glaring at the audience, sits down and begins to draw a chalk outline around her splayed legs on the stage floor. While doing so, she bites into an apple, spitting the chunks across the set. The scene progresses uncomfortably slowly, though the audience erupts into laughter as she barks a monologue about the difference between holding oneself 'properly' and allowing the body to relax – for instance, sitting with one's knees together is preferable to allowing the legs to splay and look 'fat and revolting'. She then proceeds to perform a series of ballet warm-up exercises (balances, tendus and grand battements), holding onto the chairs that litter the set. This time, dance training is unmasked and revealed to be an uncomfortable burden on the performer: as she points her impressively arched dancer's feet, she groans, suggesting that the basic steps cause both physical pain and intense frustration. Where classical dance seeks to conceal the effort that goes into its production, Bausch presents ballet as a miserable exercise in obligation. At the same time, the viewer cannot help but laugh at the scene and the dancer's unrelenting fury.

She resembles an enraged beauty pageant contestant, throwing the gaze back at the audience while furiously screaming at her peers onstage (Mercy comes in for particular criticism here). The self-deprecation initiated in *Kontakthof* is revisited in this dancer's treatment of her own body and her balletic demonstration to the audience. The scene also forms another distancing effect in its revelation of the mechanics of dance training. The artificiality of the stage is made clear in the uncomfortable exposure of this dancer, who plays out her physical insecurities for the audience.

Walzer might be read as an analogy for the construction of selfhood. In its early scenes, this motif is invoked through frequent reiteration of travel imagery and the blaring national anthems played over the theatre's sound system. As the action progresses, however, the focus appears to shift from collective (national) to individual identity. The dancers each display an item given to them by a relative. Later, as they introduce themselves to the audience, they recall a piece of advice they have previously been given. Throughout, objects are handled and described to the audience which further emphasise the notion of legacy. There are numerous references to genealogy in the dancers' interactions with one another and in their addresses to the audience. For around fifteen minutes, the stage is cast into near darkness as a screen descends from the back of the stage on which a film of a birth is projected. The men spread their legs wide while the women nestle in their laps, a gendered reversal of the events taking place on screen. Notably, in its first stagings, the cast of *Walzer* included a heavily pregnant dancer. While watching the birth film, she slowly draws an image of a baby upon her swollen belly. This moment requires special consideration, as multiple layers of unmasking occur simultaneously. Firstly, the inclusion of film as a medium in the works of this period is significant. It functions as a technologically updated version of the absurdist play-within-a-play, a nested story. Here, the recursive dimension of the audience watching the performers watching a production is markedly de-familiarising, just as in the film sequence of *Kontakthof*. In doing so, Bausch destabilises the perception of reality to the extent that we cannot but help wonder who might be watching us. The image of the birth reflected in the actions of the pregnant dancer is another example of the recursion that characterises Bausch's *Tanztheater*. The swollen belly of the dancer is an immediate reminder that the image captured on film will soon become a reality for this individual. As she draws a baby over the skin covering her own foetus, she becomes a physical manifestation of a *mise en abyme*. At the same time, this infinite reproduction of the act of childbirth evokes Baudrillard's schism between simulation and simulacra.

That birth should feature so explicitly in this piece might well relate to the birth of Bausch's own son, Salomon, born a year before *Walzer* was first mounted. Several of her peers have anecdotally noted a change in the choreographer following her transition into motherhood; Bausch herself frames the experience in her typically understated manner, observing that:

> I don't want to sound banal but really [childbirth] is a miracle. At the moment, I'm discovering things practically every day which seem almost inexplicable, quite incredible things. I suddenly see how things connect within my own body. You run around with a pair of breasts all your life and of course you know what they're for, but all of a sudden you feel their function. These are very simple things, I know. But it is a tremendous experience.[57]

Birth also forms a useful metaphor for analysing this difficult piece, as, in *Walzer*, Bausch reveals the difficult process of creating her *Tanztheater* works. This represents a shift from a Brechtian model of estrangement to a more immersive format in which Bausch grants the audience intimate access into her actual creative processes. In the productions of the late 1970s and early 1980s, Bausch is most willing to allow the spectator a glimpse behind the curtain and into the rehearsal studio, rather like a magician revealing how the trick is done. In *Walzer*, this extends further, with Bausch permitting us a brief insight into her home life and her experience of motherhood. It is one of the very few occasions in her *Tanztheater* that the 'human' Bausch is made visible, rather than her directorial persona.

Death, however, must inevitably make its appearance. In Servos' review of a performance of *Walzer* at the Holland Festival in 1982, he points out that the dancers refer to former cast members throughout.[58] This list includes dancers who moved on to other companies as well as those who have died. Bausch thus rather baldly emphasises the notion of lineage through the visceral depiction of birth and direct reference to her own deceased former colleagues. This also forms a link to the repeated theme of incompletion, as the dancers repeatedly refer to performances or events interrupted by illness on the part of the performer. The circle of life is not presented here as a natural progression of events, but rather death occurs *in media res*, interrupting the order of events. It is a reiteration of the aposiopesis initiated by the 'and then, Pina said' refrain. The bare stage design, repeated jokes and actions, and recursive references to interruption suggest *Walzer* might best be understood as a work exploring different forms of failure. Bausch refuses her audience an easy sense of catharsis through a clear narrative structure. Instead, her works remain unresolved, moving further away from resolution as the technique evolves.

Walzer ends on this motif of work left unfinished. The cast sit on the chairs lining the stage listening to a recording of the pianist Wilhelm Backhaus' last concert. Once again, the spectator observes the performers becoming an audience themselves. However, this live copy features an abrupt break in which Backhaus interrupts his own playing to announce a last-minute alteration to the programme, shifting to Schubert's Impromptu No. 4 in A-flat major. In a piece that is characterised by the motif of incompletion, we see the evolution of Bausch's 'unfinishing' process. Her work does not adhere to a single interpretation or propose answers to the difficult questions that arise. There is no single way of interpreting her dance theatre, no correct response from the audience, and no resolution promised. Rather, like Beckett's plays, everything and nothing happens. In *Walzer*, she does not present a polished, finely honed production, but a work in which deliberate gaps are left to allow the spectator into the inner workings of her *Tanztheater*.

*

Emerging from one of Bausch's *Tanztheater* performances, it is often difficult to describe the event that has just taken place. There is no narrative to retell, only memories of the cast enacting recurring patterns of everyday activity in their continual pursuit of intimacy. Their exchanges rarely suggest the possibility of a happy ending. Rather, affection often gives way to abuse, and an air of resigned loneliness hangs over pieces such as *Café Müller*, *Kontakthof* and *Walzer*. Tenderness remains tantalisingly out of reach, though, throughout Bausch's *oeuvre*, her dancers demonstrate an impressive degree of indefatigability, persistently reaching out to one another regardless of the painful results. In these lengthy, oneiric productions, the fourth wall is a malleable barrier between performer and spectator. It is frequently ruptured, allowing Bausch's dancers to acknowledge, address and interact with their audience. Yet these cracks in the wall are only with us temporarily and do not permit the inhabitants of the stage reprieve from the ongoing cycles of mundane activity and quotidian cruelties.

The works of Bausch's mature period are surrealist spectacles that synthesise fact and fiction, memory and the imaginary. For the time that we share the theatre space with Bausch's work, we cannot help but see ourselves reflected in the continual repetitions of everyday life on stage. The imaginary boundary of the fourth wall becomes more porous, allowing us to recognise the shared connections between performer and perceiver. The relentless recursion of individual sequences is often difficult to watch, especially on occasions where physical contact becomes increasingly heavy-handed. Just as her dancers are trapped within the confines of the stage, the viewer who chooses to stay in their seat becomes a tacit part of the production. Birringer has cited Bausch's explanation of these challenging repetitions: '"We must look again and again," Bausch once said in defence of her excessive repetitions, "and maybe the saddest thing about our obsessions is that they often look so cheerful."'[59] Bausch's *Tanztheater* fragments ordinary social behaviours through these cyclical and uncomfortable patterns of repetition. In this respect, her dancers hold a mirror to the audience in place of a definitive fourth wall: Bausch dismantles a fundamental theatrical mask by destabilising the barrier between performer and spectator. The power structures of the theatre space are thrown into question, and preconceived notions of boundaries, appropriate behaviour and expectation are left open-ended.

This unmasking process raises certain questions regarding the authenticity of Bausch's supposed 'archaeology of the everyday'. Heidi Gilpin proposes that, 'Pina Bausch constructs performances in which the audience is presented with material that *appears* to be "events as they really occur."'[60] She presents an impression of everyday activity which, in reality, is carefully constructed and calculated. It is this fragile distinction between the manifestation of daily experience on Bausch's stage and the underlying truth of its fictionalisation that runs as a constant thread through her mature work. Such an attitude reflects Brecht's consideration of the relationship between reality and fiction:

> For choreography, too, is again given tasks of a realistic kind. It is a mistaken belief of recent times that it has nothing to do with the illustration of 'people as they really are.' If art reflects life it does so with special mirrors.[61]

As Bausch's *Tanztheater* evolves from the experimental productions of the late 1970s into a more fully developed method, the gap between performer and spectator increasingly narrows. Her dancers regularly engage with the audience, occasionally encroaching upon the supposedly safe environment of the auditorium to address individuals directly. These works rather provocatively call into question the limits of the theatre space, and the audience is continually challenged, even in seemingly innocuous or humorous interactions. The spectator of Bausch's mature work, having been tacitly drawn in to proceedings, must grapple with difficult questions regarding the nature of the production and its underlying meaning. If it becomes too challenging, however, we can take our lead from Endicott's proclamation to the disgruntled patrons of the Macbeth premiere and 'go home'.[62] This intimate relationship between viewer and performer is reminiscent of Grotowski's definition of theatre – 'what takes place between spectator and actor' – in which he declares that 'all other things are supplementary – perhaps necessary, but nevertheless supplementary'.[63]

In opening up her stage, revealing the physical structure of the set and even allowing the audience an insight into her unique working method, Bausch invites this deeper level of engagement from her audience. The mature dance theatre works consciously strip away the layers of artifice that occlude theatrical processes and dance training. This revelation of the inner workings of the theatre constitutes an important parallel with Beckett's writing, in which questions are continually posed, but resolution is never provided. In both Beckett and Bausch's work, patterns repeat, non-sequiturs prevail and narrative is altogether absent. Where in classical Greek theatre the viewer experiences the heightened comedy (Thalia) and tragic nadir (Melpomene) of a narrative arc, in these cyclical and non-linear productions, the audience observes a process in which the performers are entombed in cyclical recursions. Thus, the Beckettian/Bauschian spectator is never granted the resolution of narrative that is arguably required to provide a sense of catharsis. It is in this respect that we can discern the emergence of a dance theatre of the absurd in the evolution of Bausch's *oeuvre*.

NOTES

1. As stated by, for example, Elswit, 'Ten Evenings with Pina', p. 217.
2. Price, 'The Politics of the Body', p. 322.
3. Esslin, *The Theatre of the Absurd*, pp. 23–4.
4. Lehmann, *Postdramatic Theatre*, p. 53.
5. Esslin, *The Theatre of the Absurd*, p. 26.
6. Hoghe, *Pina Bausch*, p. 20.
7. Großmann, quoted in Linsel, 'Pina Bauschs Wildgruber'.
8. Bausch, quoted in Servos and Müller, *Pina Bausch – Wuppertal Dance Theater*, p. 227.
9. Ibid., p. 235.
10. Servos, *Pina Bausch*, p. 64.
11. Bermel, 'Ionesco', p. 415.
12. Lehmann, *Postdramatic Theatre*, p. 156.
13. Repetition forms the thematic basis of Fernandes' volume on Bausch, where she explores Bausch's process in-depth through the lens of Lacanian theory and Laban Movement Analysis.
14. Heathfield, 'Dance-Theatre and Dance-Performance', in Kelleher and Ridout (eds), *Contemporary Theatres in Europe*, p. 188.
15. Brook, *The Empty Space*, p. 138.
16. Servos, *Pina Bausch*, p. 82.
17. Fernandes, *Pina Bausch and the Wuppertal Dance Theatre*, p. 6.
18. Whitelaw, *Billie Whitelaw*, p. 148.
19. Mercier, 'The Uneventful Event', p. 6.
20. Esslin, *The Theatre of the Absurd*, p. 22.
21. Gerould, 'Introduction', in Witkiewicz, *Country House*, p. xviii.
22. Brecht, 'Short Description of a New Technique of Acting Which Produces an Alienation Effect', *Brecht on Theatre*, p. 184.
23. Kiebuzinska, *Revolutionaries in the Theater*, p. 33.
24. Mitter, *Systems of Rehearsal*, p. 49.
25. Kumiega, *The Theatre of Grotowski*, pp. 36–7.
26. Lehmann, *Postdramatic Theatre*, p. 104.
27. Fischer-Lichte, *The Transformative Power of Performance*.
28. Servos and Müller, *Pina Bausch – Wuppertal Dance Theater*, p. 69.
29. Bausch, quoted in Servos, *Pina Bausch*, p. 238.
30. Climenhaga, *Pina Bausch*, p. 66.
31. Ibid., p. 69
32. See Davis, '"Not a soul in sight!"', pp. 86–102.
33. Beckett, *Endgame*, p. 12.
34. Ibid., p. 25.
35. Cody, 'Woman, Man, Dog, Tree', p. 122.
36. Servos, *Pina Bausch*, p. 69.

37. Jennings, 'Obituary'.
38. Fischer-Lichte, *The Transformative Power of Performance*, p. 15.
39. Lehmann, *Postdramatic Theatre*, p. 103.
40. Burt, *The Male Dancer*, p. 190.
41. Weiss, 'Beckett's "Happy Days"', p. 40.
42. Beckett, *Endgame*, p. 20.
43. Ibid., p. 33.
44. Mori, 'Beckett's Windows and the Windowless Self', p. 358.
45. Lamont, 'The Metaphysical Farce', p. 319.
46. Kiebuzinska, *Revolutionaries in the Theater*, p. 83.
47. Lehmann, *Postdramatic Theatre*, pp. 91–2.
48. Rolf Borzik, Bausch's partner and artistic designer, died in 1980 at the age of thirty-five. He was instrumental in the design of almost every piece Bausch made for the company from the beginning of her directorship. The last piece on which Bausch and Borzik collaborated was *Keuschheitslegende* (*Legend of Chastity*, 1979), named after the 1919 novella of the same name by Rudolf Georg Binding. Her enduring collaboration with designer Peter Pabst would begin with *Nelken* in 1982.
49. McMullan, *Performing Embodiment in Samuel Beckett's Drama*, p. 32.
50. Davis, '"Not a soul in sight!"', p. 97.
51. Beckett, *Waiting for Godot*, p. 6.
52. Ibid., p. 28.
53. Ibid., p. 66
54. Fernandes, *Pina Bausch and the Wuppertal Dance Theatre*, p. 36.
55. Großmann, quoted in Schwarzer, 'Ein Stück für Pina Bausch'.
56. Minarik, quoted in *Walzer*, p. 72.
57. Bausch, quoted in Servos and Müller, *Pina Bausch – Wuppertal Dance Theater*, p. 235.
58. Servos, 'Und dann hat Pina gesagt . . .', p. 19.
59. Birringer, 'Pina Bausch', p. 91
60. Gilpin, 'Amputation, Dismembered Identities, and the Rhythms of Elimination', in Jankowsky and Love (eds), *Other Germanies*, p. 175.
61. Brecht, 'Short Organon for the Theatre', in *Brecht on Theatre*, p. 254.
62. Meyer, *Pina Bausch*, p. 51.
63. Grotowski, *Towards a Poor Theatre*, pp. 32–3.

4

VIOLENT ACTS: TRAVERSING THE POSTWAR LANDSCAPE

In the first decade of her directorship, Bausch proved to be a highly prolific choreographer, producing several new full-scale productions each year. By the mid-1980s, however, the speed at which she premiered new pieces began to decelerate, and the work made in this period demonstrates a sharp change in tone, reflecting the darker elements of some of her earliest choreographies. These complex pieces are emblematic of a difficult period in Bausch's career, a phase in which her dance theatre often garnered poor reviews for its despairing content.

Violence is a recurring concern in this controversial phase of Bausch's *Tanztheater*. Her needy, interdependent characters continually lapse into patterns of maltreatment, and attempts to form intimate attachment often degenerate into spitefulness or brutality. Repressed unconscious desire and taboo behaviours become central features of this period. These tendencies, first explored in experimental works such as *Blaubart* and the Macbeth Project, recur with increasing frequency in her mature *oeuvre*. In this phase, microcosmic instances of violence serve as analogues for macro manifestations of cruelty. In the complex, multi-layered works produced during this period, Bausch creates environments where her audience might negotiate the recent past and interrogate our intrinsic potential for destructive behaviour. Yet, in doing so, Bausch's *Tanztheater* does not adopt an explicitly politicised message: as indicated in Chapter 2's analysis of her experimental period, there is a clear distinction between her use of distancing devices and the motivations

of Brecht's socially conscious epic theatre. Similarly, her dramaturgical collaborator Sturm has claimed that, while Bausch was personally interested in
politics, it did not form the driving force behind her *Tanztheater*.[1]

In examining the works of her 'dark' period, it is clear that Bausch does
not explicitly refer to current affairs in her work. Rather, a central concern
of her dance theatre lies in interpersonal relationships, something she often
explores through ubiquitous images of rejection, loneliness and pain. The
work produced throughout the mid-1980s is unusual for its candid depiction
of cruelty and suffering. In these diverse, multisensory pieces, the gap between
audience and performer becomes increasingly narrow, with audience address
verging into hostility or confrontation. The apocalyptic images she creates in
this period constitute simultaneous, implicit allusions to recent history and
humanity's innate capacity for violence. Evocations of authoritarianism and
brutality are abundant in this period, though the resulting works require that
the audience make a metaphorical leap from the examples of specific onstage
cruelties to wider issues of violence. Mapping the development of this process,
parallels begin to emerge between Bausch's dark *Tanztheater* and Antonin
Artaud's Theatre of Cruelty. Both rely upon spectacle, shock and the invert-
ing of traditional theatrical frameworks. Significantly, Bausch and Artaud's
respective approaches also emerge from the aftermath of global conflict and
destruction. In these cruel theatres, where language is reduced to absurdism
and actions drive the narrative of the performance, we might be reminded of
Walter Benjamin's observation: 'Was it not noticeable at the end of [the First
World War] that men returned from the battlefield grown silent – not richer but
poorer in communicable experience?'[2] In the dark phase of her *Tanztheater*,
Bausch's method provides a movement vocabulary for that which cannot be
easily communicated: like Artaud's prioritising of gesture and stylised movement over the written word, Bausch's darker pieces privilege visual spectacle
over text. This chapter centres on what might be termed Bausch's Theatre of
Cruelty by examining three manifestations of violence in her work, ranging
from the macro (the art form as tyrannical), to the meso (cultural heritage and
the difficult past), to the micro (interpersonal intimacy).

Performing Authoritarianism: *Nelken*

The process of unmasking that emerges in Bausch's mature *oeuvre* system-
atically fragments the theatrical event, beginning with the performance space
itself, and progressing through the supporting text or soundtrack to the
underlying narrative. In works such as *Walzer*, the mechanics of theatrical
production are unveiled and the audience is provided with a voyeuristic
glimpse of the creative process. However, a recurring facet of this unmasking
lies in the metaphorical representation of the body. In *Kontakthof*, this theme
of fragmentation forms the opening sequence of the piece, as a series of dancers

present their body parts for inspection by the audience. Destabilising the fourth wall and facing the audience directly, her performers continually confront the spectator and undermine their expectations of the theatrical experience. Such unsettling and unexpected interactions shatter illusions of the dancer's body as a perfect, artificial whole.

Throughout this period, Bausch's dancers appear increasingly estranged from their own bodies, treating them as objects of amusement, inconvenience or abuse. In a similar manner to Beckett's characters, they are trapped within their circumstances and dislocated from their (often malfunctioning) physiques. In the mature work, Bausch evokes a sense of bodily crisis that is underscored by overarching threats of authoritarianism or violence. Her dancers push themselves to the limit of physical exhaustion, berate one another, spurn acts of tenderness or cower in fear of unknown forces. While the pieces produced in the 1980s are markedly distinct in appearance and structure, recurring themes of discomfort and unease form a point of connection for these productions. This is not to frame Bausch's mature work as unremittingly dark: indeed, humour is a crucial component of her work, and most *Tanztheater* pieces produced in this era alternate between gloominess and genuine comedy. Satire is regularly employed to bridge the gap between light and dark, often in relation to failed amorous advances or displays of exaggerated self-consciousness. Similarly, the formalities of classical dance training are repeatedly mocked in this period. The ballet class is regularly dismantled and exposed for its unreasonable demands on the dancer's body. However, ballet is also invoked as a metaphor for totalitarian control and, accordingly, becomes a potent symbol of cruelty.

My categorisation of Bausch's mature work encompasses the range of productions that span the period from 1978 to the early 1990s. It is a broad grouping, and one that would benefit from further subdivision. Accordingly, those pieces which continually refer to the artifice of the theatrical setting and upend conventional audience expectation can be classed as part of the unmasking or estrangement phase. Related to this, but distinctive for its unsettling content, are the works devised between 1981 (beginning with *Bandoneon*) and 1989 (where the co-production model becomes a dominant new framework). It is within this period that Bausch's *Tanztheater* approaches a contemporary revision of Artaud's Theatre of Cruelty, eschewing traditional dance and theatrical convention in favour of creating collagist, dreamlike productions on an epic scale. In doing so, she increasingly confronts the audience with difficult imagery that, viewed in light of global events of recent history, takes on a new level of significance. In the aftermath of loss in both world wars, the Holocaust and the division of the country, a resulting distrust of authoritarianism takes on a unique significance in the German context.

Artaud's conception of the Theatre of Cruelty rejects traditional theatrical frameworks in favour of a confrontational aesthetic, provoking the audience in order to bring to light the inner workings of the unconscious. The roots of Artaud's theories can, of course, be drawn back to Surrealism and its dissolution of logic.[3] However, his writings on cruelty explicitly derive from a belief that theatre, and by extension, the world generally, is in need of radical change. Artaud does not speak of rebirth as a positive act, rather he proposes that it reflects the extreme violence and apocalyptic devastation characteristic of recent history. The essays that comprise his most celebrated text, *The Theatre and its Double* (1938), were begun in the interwar period, an environment profoundly impacted by the destruction of the First World War. Thus, the notion of crisis is central to his manifestos on cruel theatre, with Artaud referring to 'the anguished, catastrophic times we live in'.[4] His theorisation of this new theatre is visceral and highly embodied: as Adrian Morfee states, 'when Artaud does move away from his theorizing and polemics to describe his experience of thought, it is striking how thoroughly the two realms of mental and bodily fuse'.[5] Artaud's conception of cruelty is often misinterpreted given its frequent application to works that utilise genuine sadism or literal manifestations of violence. Here, my use of the term aligns more with Artaud's figurative conception of cruelty – Bausch's performers may be pushed to physical extremes, of course, but violence is never actually enacted. It is specifically the framing of her theatre, and the choice of thematic subject matter, in this period that can be defined as Artaudian. Her use of violent imagery to jar spectators into a more active engagement with the spectacle not only forms a useful counterpoint to the Brechtian tendencies that emerged strongly in her earlier experimental work, but also demonstrates a further evolution of her technique.

Artaud's highly ritualistic conception of performance seeks to elicit an emotional response from the spectator. In Bausch's *Tanztheater*, theatrical conventions are similarly manipulated in order to confront the audience more directly. As in Artaud's model, she intensifies the routine components of existence, heightening emotion, confronting the audience's senses with innovative stage design, and relocating elements of the everyday to surreal new settings. We thus see a further shift from the Brechtian model: his epic theatre also uses shock as a device for awaking the audience, but ultimately aims for some form of resolution. In Artaud's conception (and, as we shall see, in Bausch's work also), this is not the case. In works that take place on the cusp between dreams and reality, ultimately the question of responsibility is left almost completely open-ended – there is no resolution, only room for reflection on how we might respond to and interpret the content.

One of Bausch's first productions to synthesise patterns of estrangement with aspects of Artaud's cruel theatre is *Nelken* (*Carnations*, 1982). It is a visually arresting piece: the stage is entirely covered in pink and white carnations, and dancers wear brightly coloured dresses or smart suits, though

Figure 4.1 *Nelken*, Oliver Look

several of the male dancers later reappear in silk dresses. A smiling woman, clad only in high-waisted white briefs, crosses the stage carrying an accordion. Contradicting audience expectation, she never once plays the instrument in her various appearances on stage. The surreal visual impact of a stage bedecked in flowers and the playfulness of the performers contributes to a dreamlike impression of innocence (Figure 4.1). However, this is immediately tempered by the presence of police dogs and their minders standing guard at the corners of the stage. Meanwhile, a sinister master of ceremonies periodically interrupts the dancers to check their passports and papers (a similar figure also features in *Kontakthof*, regularly interrupting the action to note the physical dimensions of the dancers). Devised in the midst of the Cold War, *Nelken*'s master of ceremonies alludes to the surveillance states of both the Third Reich and German Democratic Republic. It is in this alternately ethereal and nightmarish vision of a Garden of Eden that Bausch most directly addresses the paranoia of the police state.

The eponymous carnations, reminiscent of celebratory as well as funerary flower arrangements, invite a dichotomous response from the audience. Elements of nature and the world outside the theatre are blended into the stage space and become part of the surreal environment of Bausch's *Tanztheater*. Yet in this case, the unmasking process that begins with *Kontakthof* continues, manifested in the artificiality of the flowers. This design decision confounds audience expectation in the wake of works which have used genuine organic matter on a large scale – *Sacre, 1980* and *Arien*, for example. In doing so, Bausch toys with the more knowledgeable dance theatre spectator, the viewer who, by this stage, is able to read her work intertextually.

The increasingly elaborate stage design of her mature period reflects an Artaudian conception of *mise en scène*: Artaud argues that theatre ought to transcend its traditional form to reflect the inner workings of the subconscious. Accordingly, the script does not form the centre of the production, rather spectacle takes precedence. A new language of the stage is proposed in this model, replacing traditional dialogue and the narrative arc associated with it. Dream imagery and the unconscious provide a vital conduit for Artaud's irrational theatre which, at its core, is designed to confront and unsettle its audience. Artaud is unambiguous on this point, stating, 'I propose a theatre where violent physical images pulverise, mesmerise the audience's sensibilities, caught in the drama as if in a vortex of higher forces.'[6] The cognitive dissonance inherent in works such as *Nelken* is, it seems, indicative of Artaud's proposal.

Throughout its two-hour duration, *Nelken* oscillates between humour and menace, depicting the search for love in an often hostile and divided world. Lighter moments are juxtaposed with the menacing presence of guard dogs and the Gestapo or Stasi-like master of ceremonies. The actions of the dancers heighten this underlying sense of unease. Throughout, they break the sanctity of the fourth wall to address, confront or plead with the audience. In the midst of the performance, several members of the cast leave the stage and wander into the auditorium, asking individual spectators for a moment of their time. The relative privacy afforded by the fourth wall is transgressed when the performers enter the personal space of the viewer. It is a highly visible performance of privacy – after all, a shared moment cannot be truly intimate when it has been woven into the making of a theatre piece in this way. Thus, in a similar manner to pieces such as *Kontakthof*, the viewer becomes an unwitting part of the action. At the same time, the police dogs provide a visceral reminder that the dancers are trapped on stage. They cannot escape, though they may temporarily enter the realm of the audience. Accordingly, power play forms a significant theme in *Nelken*. While violent imagery is not overtly explicit in this piece, it materialises in the increasing force necessary for creating the boundaries of power and control. This implication of violence throws further into question the barrier that separates performer from audience.

In one unnerving sequence, four stunt men (their professional skills unknown to the viewer) scale the scaffold at the back wall of the stage before leaping off from a great height. They are watched by a dancer who tries in vain to draw her companions' attention to the possible disaster that is unfolding. When she is ignored by the other members of the company, she turns to the audience, seemingly hysterical and begging for help. Here, the stunt men not only put themselves quite genuinely at risk of physical injury but, in doing so, shake the audience from their passive enjoyment of the performance and startle the police dogs at the corners of the stage. Again, Bausch is inconsistent in her manipulation of the fourth wall, leaving the audience uncertain of how real the violence being played out onstage might actually be. This ambiguity regarding the veracity of pain is, Lehmann tells us, a latent tendency in postdramatic theatre, which can become problematic for the viewer, and further blurs the distinction between truth and artifice:

> Postdramatic theatre, however, is above all familiar with 'mimesis to pain' ('Mimesis an den Schmerz' – Adorno): when the stage is becoming like life, when people really fall or really get hit on stage, the spectators start to fear for the players. The novelty resides in the fact that there is a transition from represented pain to pain experienced in representation ... While the dramatic theatre conceals the process of the body in the role, postdramatic theatre aims at the public exhibition of the body, its deterioration in an act that does not allow for a clear separation of art and reality.[7]

Throughout this work, the dancers continually commit minor acts of masochism. A woman tickles a man's feet until he is nearly hysterical, another dancer frantically chops up an enormous pile of onions that he subsequently rubs into his eyes, which Servos compares to the theatrical technique of using onions to generate false tears.[8] This small but unpleasant gesture represents another facet of Bausch's tendency to reveal the mechanical elements of theatre, asking the audience to decide what is 'real' and what is merely performed.

Discomfort is a recurring feature of *Nelken*. As in preceding works, the spectatorial gaze is turned back on the audience but, in this case, the viewer is directly challenged for their unrealistic expectations of the cast of professional dancers. This is most explicitly addressed when Dominique Mercy enters the stage wearing a sundress, shouting at his colleagues to get out of his way. He then turns his attention on the audience, furiously confronting them as a result of their supposed expectation of him to perform balletic 'tricks'. Obliging this unspoken request, he performs a progressively complex sequence of ballet steps, asking repeatedly, 'What else do you want?' Mercy's engagement with the audience becomes increasingly aggressive as the pattern repeats, reflecting an Artaudian approach in the deliberate and direct challenge he issues to the unsuspecting viewer: the everyday cruelties associated with the dance world become the audience's responsibility when Mercy confronts us with his frustration as a dancer who seemingly cannot live up to our expectations. As Mercy reaches the end of his ballet offerings, the master of ceremonies enters and demands to see his passport, barking the order that he should 'put some proper clothes on'. The appearance of the master of ceremonies interrupts

Mercy's dialogue with the audience, resituating him in the confined world of the stage, and returning him to the role of a comic character.

The scene is significant, as it connects two seemingly disparate concepts – namely, authoritarian surveillance and the demands of a professional dance career. However, in examining the recurring motifs of Bausch's mature *oeuvre*, it becomes clear that ballet is almost inevitably associated with cruelty and tyranny. Her directorship of what was originally the Wuppertal Opera Ballet altered the framework of the company into a radically different format. The company's rebranding as Tanztheater Wuppertal reflects a change at the deepest level and a clear statement on the role of ballet in its organisation. Classical dance rarely features in any of her choreographies. When ballet is invoked, it is often represented in a mocking manner: she either pokes fun at the absurdities of the form, or reveals its underlying cruelties. This perhaps reflects, as Susan Broadhurst has claimed, a left-wing sentiment that rejected the formalism of ballet in favour of new methods of working.[9] Significantly, however, this correlation between classical dance and oppression in Bausch's *oeuvre* parallels Artaud's difficult relationship with the theatrical text, the sanctity of which he dismantles through his writings on cruelty.

Ballet represents the rigorous training that is a collective experience for Bausch and her performers. Its emphasis on illusionism, aesthetic beauty and technical perfection is completely reversed in her *Tanztheater*, and Bausch's work affords the dancers an opportunity to disassemble and openly critique the art form. This represents a continuation of the unmasking process that characterises her mature period: by revealing the quotidian and incessantly repetitive mechanics of ballet training, Bausch renders impossible the audience's suspension of disbelief. Bausch returns to the invocation of balletic cruelty repeatedly throughout this period. In *Walzer*, for example, the bathing-suited and stiletto-clad dancer shrieks at the audience, 'Look at this back! I worked years and years and years for this back!' In doing so, she reminds us of the painful (and, we assume, unrewarding) efforts that helped to form the body she is presenting. As the pieces produced through the *Stichworte* method move further away from linear structure and plot, the use of choreography is similarly transformed. Ballet and modern techniques were clearly visible in the early phase of her work but, in the mature era, these forms are broken down into exercises or individual actions, fragmented for comic or grotesque effect. Eventually, ballet steps are singled out for critical analysis, thus revealing the working processes that lie behind not only making a piece of choreography, but the formation of a professional dancer. This form of specifically bal-letic unmasking is achieved through provocative audience address, and the significance of confrontation between artist and audience is similarly prevalent in Artaud's writings. While Bausch retains the separation of performance space and audience with the proscenium stage, however, Artaud advocates a complete amalgamation of the two with what he calls 'a kind of single, undivided locale'.[10] It is this reformatting of the theatrical environment that facilitates interaction between the performers and the audience, though the importance of direct address is emphasised throughout his writings on the Theatre of Cruelty.

As is evident throughout her 'unmasked' works, Bausch refers to ordinary, routine occurrences as constant motifs. The conventions of classical ballet are frequently revisited and given the same treatment, in this case, signalling a form of artistic protest against classical dance. The ballet class itself falls into the category of the more general 'everyday' experience that Bausch distorts as, for professional dancers, class is an indispensable daily ritual. Consider, for instance, the infamous pointe shoe sequence in her 1986 work, *Viktor*. A dancer enters the stage holding a package of meat, a stool and a pair of satin pointe shoes. She barks at the audience, 'Das ist Kalbfleisch!' ('This is veal!'), before stuffing her shoes with slices of meat. The woman proceeds to dance *en pointe* for an uncomfortably extended period of time. The effort is evident, as her heavy breathing is audible despite the swelling soundtrack of Tchaikovsky's *Pathétique*. A significant marker of the everyday ballet routine – in this case, the pointe shoe – is made ludicrous by the deconstruction of its use. Instead of traditional lambswool padding, here the dancer wraps her feet in bloody veal steaks, an overt allusion to the pain and disfigurement a classical dancer must suffer for the beauty of her art. At the same time, the audience is tacitly involved in the act: addressed directly by the dancer, the spectator is forced to reconsider any preconceived notions regarding the illusionism of classical ballet. Here, Bausch transcends the Artaudian model into an increasingly postdramatic Theatre of Cruelty in her efforts to undermine and destabilise the relationship between audience and spectator; Lehmann suggests that, 'when the real asserts itself against the staged on stage, then this is mirrored in the auditorium'.[11]

Bandoneon (1981), a work that takes place in a similarly desolate dance hall to *Kontakthof*, exposes the rigorous processes behind the making of dance through a series of absurd yet unsettling vignettes. *Bandoneon* advances the unmasking of theatrical space seen in works such as *Arien* and *Walzer* (in which the lighting rigs and firewalls were visible to the audience), and shatters the illusionism of classical dance as the performers openly discuss the monotony and occasional misery of training. The piece returns repeatedly to the concept of artifice. At one point, a team of stage hands enter and begin to clear the set, a jarring distancing effect that derives from actual events that occurred during rehearsals. The technicians' street clothes stand in sharp contrast to Cito's elegant costumes for the dancers and lead the audience to question the authenticity of this scene. As is always the case in Bausch's work, however, nothing is improvised on stage. The break lasts for around fifteen minutes, in which time the action onstage has come to a complete halt. It is a stark distancing device: moments such as these, where Bausch permits lengthy pauses to interrupt her cyclical patterns, jolt the audience from their passivity, their false reality, and serve as a firm reminder of the inauthenticity of the spectacle.

As was the case in *Walzer*, where the bare stage resembled the rehearsal studio, in *Bandoneon* the dancers perform for one another as well as the audience: a woman dramatically (and enthusiastically) sucks a lemon while her peers applaud her efforts. Constant bursts of applause break out on stage, undermining any residual sense of theatrical authenticity.[12] There is a desire to make clear to the audience the integral processes that lie behind a dance production, perhaps refuting the accusation that her highly trained dancers rarely dance. When the performers recite anecdotes of cruelties inflicted during their training, the spectator is met with the result of their expectations. Tales emerge of being forced into painful exercises which are then put into practice before our eyes as the dancers stand on each other's knees to push the stretch further. A woman is forced to maintain her stage smile even when her head is dunked into a bucket of water: 'Smile. Learn to smile. Train yourself to smile. A ballet teacher says, "if you don't smile on stage, you are not a dancer."'[13] A woman chases another with a pair of scissors, swiping at her legs – her target regales the audience with stories of another sadistic childhood ballet teacher who would wield scissors at her young charges if she felt their legs were not sufficiently turned out. A man tells of his teacher's habit of holding a lit cigarette under his students' legs to force their extensions higher: 'Look, madam, it goes up – doch.' These anecdotes take on a more unsettling edge when one considers most of these events will have occurred in childhood or the teenage years.

Viewed collectively, however, this recurring association between ballet and suffering seems to offer two interpretations. In light of critical responses to Bausch's mature work, such open declaration of the sadistic expectations forced upon dancers acts as an explanation for the lack of recognisable dance technique in her productions. As Servos puts it, 'theatre is revealed to be a grotesque show of strength, a display of muscles, an expertise, behind which the genuine needs and desires must stay hidden'.[14] While any dance student would hardly baulk at the exercises enacted in these scenes, it is the unmasking of balletic artifice for the average theatregoer which precipitates an Artaudian jolt. An alternative reading might suggest that, rather than illustrating a derisive riposte to the dance world in these works, ballet in fact serves as an effective metaphor for authoritarianism more broadly. In Bausch's work, the spectator constitutes an important facet of this implied tyranny: in *Nelken*, the performers may be trapped by the police dogs at the corners of the stage, but they also demonstrate evident frustration with the weight of audience expectation.

Mercy's outburst thus rails not only against the scathing words of Bausch's critics, but also confronts the audience with the private thoughts of the dancer.

Jennings has described *Nelken* as '[a] flower-strewn battlefield of human misunderstanding'.[15] Childish playfulness and a humorous exploration of the dance world are overshadowed by a darker edge of authoritarianism that is ever present in the recesses of the stage. This contrast is perhaps most conclusively illustrated when one female dancer runs back and forward across the stage, screaming hysterically. Her shrieks permeate the accompanying soundtrack, an excerpt from Schubert's String Quartet No. 14 (*Death and the Maiden*). This uncomfortable sequence comes to an abrupt halt as another dancer enters the stage to address the audience directly with the words, 'I just wanted to say how wonderful it is that you're all here tonight.' Bausch transgresses the fourth wall once more, on this occasion, however, in order to thank the audience for its participation.

The damaged bodies of Bausch's company display their suffering with pride and defiance. In a 2005 review of *Nelken* and *Palermo Palermo*, Macauley observed that, 'Bausch's human beings choose to wreck not only their world but, above all, themselves.' Significantly, however, he acknowledges the fluid relationship between truth and fiction in her *Tanztheater*, pointing out that, 'no man or woman in Bausch theatre experiences genuine suffering – it's all manipulative. Sometimes this is the point.'[16] The unveiling process that emerges in her mature era enables the dancers to confront the audience with their complicity – the ticket-buying patron is faced with the unmasked reality of ballet training and technique. Ballet is presented as a cruel master, an aesthetically pleasing art form that injures and breaks bodies. Corporeality is shown in its brutal reality. However, Gilpin has theorised that one reason Bausch plays such theatrical games with the concept of authenticity comes as a direct result of her identity, that is, her generation's implicit desire to locate truth in everyday language and behaviour that had become tainted by the fascist past.[17] Thus, the unmasking of ballet serves a dual function: as ballet makes a useful cipher for tyranny, the authoritarian control exerted over the dance studio is symbolic of the creeping anxieties around social control that gain particular currency in the context of postwar, divided Germany.

Addressing the Past: *Auf dem Gebirge hat man ein Geschrei gehört*

Charting even the most basic history of the twentieth century reveals a period punctuated by episodes of extreme upheaval, violence and tragedy. The collective effect of two world wars, the formation and collapse of the Soviet Union, as well as genocides, famines and dictatorships the world over, has created a patchwork of traumatic memory that transcends cultural and political boundaries. As Cathy Caruth has intimated, 'trauma itself may provide the very link between cultures'.[18] In an age of rapid technological development, the seemingly limitless capacity for mass communication, and the expansion of photographic and filmic capabilities, we are more closely connected to our historical past than humanity has been at any other point in time. In the context of this constantly shifting landscape, it is unsurprising that such a significant proportion of visual culture has been concerned with addressing, commemorating and coming to terms with the relatively recent past.

In postwar German theatre practice, trauma is often born of particularly loaded and familiar experience. Heiner Müller's father was consigned to a concentration camp as a result of his political affiliation with communism, for example, and Müller witnessed his brutal beating by SS officers in their own home.[19] Much of his literary work directly responds to difficult aspects of his cultural history: *Germania Tod in Berlin* (*Germania Death in Berlin*) was a 1971 play that proposed Germans had not fully recognised their complicity in the events of the fascist era. Ann Stamp Miller suggests that, in works such as this, 'Müller refused to allow Germans to forget about the past; he confronted them with their history and guilt.'[20] Stamp Miller draws a comparison here with Brecht, who similarly refused to allow theatre to function as a pure form of entertainment. Thus, theatre becomes a space for reflection, a mirror of society and a space to contemplate our role in it. In the dark phase of Bausch's *Tanztheater*, her stages become similarly reflective surfaces, inviting audiences to acknowledge themselves in the performance of everyday rituals and inter-personal cruelties. In this era of her work, however, Bausch's methodology becomes more closely aligned with an Artaudian than a Brechtian model: distancing effects are frequently generated through shock, using the insinu-ation of violence to shatter audience expectation and theatrical illusionism. In this respect, Bausch's dark period can be seen as a further extension of the unmasking process already at play in her mature work.

Memory is a central facet of Bausch's *oeuvre*. It is one of her most frequently invoked themes, explored through a multifaceted array of gestures, signs and stories. Yet memory is also a deeply loaded aspect of her work. Rather than simply forming an archaeology of her dancers' childhoods and romantic his-tories, Bausch's productions emerge from a critical geopolitical context, that of German society in the wake of absolute devastation. The generation born during the Second World War came to maturity in an age indelibly coloured by the scars of global conflict and the otherwise unimaginable horrors of the Holocaust. Bausch belongs to the same postwar German generation that constantly questioned its parents' role in recent history. Bearing the weight of this difficult inheritance, her *Tanztheater* can be situated in a broader collective unconscious of artists responding to the recent past. This legacy is literally embodied by her dancers, who personify and exhibit trauma through their pluralistic movement language. Such communal embodiment is also indicative of postdramatic practice:

The physical body, whose gestic vocabulary in the eighteenth century could still be read and interpreted virtually like a text, in postdramatic theatre has become its own reality which does not 'tell' this or that emotion but through its presence *manifests* itself as the site of inscription of collective history.[21]

In his essay on the artist Anselm Kiefer, Andreas Huyssen observed that, 'West German culture remains haunted by the past', a concept the 1986 *Historikerstreit* debate rather controversially attempted to address through 'normalisation'.[22] As German artists working in the postwar period, Bausch and Kiefer share in a tradition of memorialising aspects of a problematic history which is often invoked in a confrontational manner. Consider Kiefer's *Heroische Sinnbilder* project (*Heroic Symbols*, 1969), a series of self-portraits set in various bleak landscapes or backgrounds, dressed in military garb and making the *Sieg Heil* salute (which was, by this point, banned in Germany). Yet where Kiefer addressed his nation's troubled past directly, and often shockingly, I suggest that Bausch explores similar themes of German 'haunting', or the concept of *Vergangenheitsbewältigung* (coming to terms with the past) through her exploration of performed violence. The legacy of the Second World War is memorialised through the repetition of violent imagery, a factor that has come to characterise Bausch's work in this period. Numerous critics have alluded to this: in her analysis of the darker aspects of Bausch's *oeuvre*, Mulrooney asks, 'can the *Tanztheater Wuppertal* be seen to be cleaning the psychic wound left in the aftermath of post-holocaust urban decay?'[23] Similarly, Felciano quotes an American dancer's germane observation on working in the climate of postwar Germany:

> Another former dancer, Meryl Tankard ... remembers that as an outsider she was impressed by Germany as a source of violence in Bausch's work. 'When I was there I could feel it, [the weight] of history in that country. But then it's not really surprising, considering what they have gone through. The angst [in Bausch's work] comes from the culture.'[24]

Such comments bear witness to an unavoidably political dimension in Bausch's work, and highlight the significance of embodied cultural trauma. Suffering becomes a recurring motif in her mature period, and is most explicitly invoked in the pieces produced between 1982 and 1989. Initially most frequently associated with the rigors and rituals of classical ballet, the complex works of the 1980s appear to connect images of pain and suffering with broader issues of societal and political cruelty. Although this forms an obvious thematic link with Artaud in light of the fact that suffering underpins a significant proportion of his writings,[25] Sörgel indicates a more nuanced association between Bausch and Artaud through 'how she emphasizes experience and mobilizes our affective memory and emotions'.[26] Sörgel's proposition can be developed here by suggesting that, in order to fully interpret this challenging aspect of Bausch's *Tanztheater*, it is necessary to consider the wider geopolitical environment in which is it made.

On 13 May 1984, *Auf dem Gebirge hat man ein Geschrei gehört* (*On the mountain a cry was heard*) was premiered at the Schauspielhaus in Wuppertal, the first new production unveiled by Bausch for almost two years. The title is derived from J. S. Bach's *St. Matthew Passion*, and is a fragment from a section that references Herod's massacre of the innocents (the full passage from which the title is derived reads: 'On the mountain a cry was heard, much lamentation and wailing; Rachel was weeping for her children and would not be comforted; for that was the end of them.'). That the title draws such an explicit allusion to mass slaughter seems to provide the viewer with a key to unlocking its content. Perhaps the most challenging work in her *oeuvre* – certainly one of her darkest pieces – *Gebirge* marks a dramatic departure from its predecessor, *Nelken*. The stage is covered in a thick layer of soil, providing an immediate reference to her landmark *Sacre*. As thick clouds of dry ice drift out into the realm of the audience, however, the setting appears significantly bleaker than in previous works. In the wake of Borzik's death, Bausch continued to experiment with the use of organic material alongside Pabst, with whom she had first collaborated on *1980*. Where in that piece, however, the image of freshly cut grass conjured a nostalgic impression of childhood summers, in *Gebirge*, it is an odour of soil and artificially generated smoke that fills the auditorium. The colour and vitality of nature evoked previously is now burnt out, replaced by a grim vision of a post-apocalyptic wilderness.

In this work, Bausch moves beyond the limitations of her distancing devices in favour of a more confrontational methodology. She crafts a contained environment in which her audience is able to negotiate the recent past and address the issue of humanity's inherent cruelty. Thus, building on a framework of modernist allusions Bausch creates increasingly complex, provocative work. Confronting the audience with images of violence and abuse, she manipulates the boundaries of an uncertain relationship between performer and spectator. While Bausch's *Tanztheater* is not overly political in content, works such as *Gebirge* cannot be divorced from events of the recent past. With these durational pieces, she creates an ambiguous space in which the past exists in traces and memories, where fact and fiction are intertwined, and cruelty is a constant and endlessly recurring reference point.

However, Bausch adopts an inconsistent and perpetually shifting attitude towards the theatrical devices employed in the making of her *Tanztheater*. For example, she portrays recurring motifs of alienation or estrangement, allowing her performers to address the audience directly, and shattering the illusion of the performance as immersive event. At the same time, her works

Figure 4.2 *Auf dem Gebirge hat man ein Geschrei Gehört*, Laszlo Szito

are composed of collective personal memories, and her dancers often address one another by their real names. There is simultaneously a distancing effect and a provocative aesthetic explored in these experimental works, a conflation of Artaud and Brecht's supposedly opposing conceptions of radical theatre. By the end of these pieces, after the audience has been met with a barrage of difficult and emotionally draining images, a space is left for the spectator to reflect on the nature of Bausch's brutality. In doing so, she does not induce the audience to identify or sympathise with identifiable characters, but instead aims to elucidate the wrongdoings of society more generally.

Although several of Bausch's earlier works are ultimately hopeful in their interpretations of human relationships, *Gebirge* (Figure 4.2) is almost relentlessly dark, its atmosphere oppressively heavy. The piece begins with a single man standing in the empty stage space wearing goggles and a pair of extremely tight swimming trunks. Curiously, many gestures in this piece relate to the action of swimming, yet the setting is utterly barren – in a reiteration of the design for *Sacre*, the floor is covered in thick soil, but the stage walls are left bare. In this desolate landscape, the hulking figure of the swimmer slowly blows up a balloon, and the audience braces itself for the inevitable explosion. The silence in the theatre is shattered by the bursting rubber. The swimmer picks up another flaccid balloon from the floor, and repeats the action multiple times. Despite his ridiculous appearance, there is a palpable sense of unease that surrounds the swimmer's action. He remains impassive throughout this sequence, which, as with many of Bausch's repetitions, quickly becomes uncomfortable to observe. As the piece progresses, it becomes clear that the swimmer forms a constant threat to the other performers – he is at once a torturer, a warden, an abusive partner and a violent thug. Almost all of his interactions with the dancers are violent and aggressive, but particularly so in relation to women.

Violence forms a constant reference point in *Gebirge*, from its opening scenes through to the conclusion. The swimmer is the main perpetrator of sexualised violence in this piece. A constant reminder of danger and incongruous dark humour, he is, as Servos has hinted, a Brechtian *Verfremdungseffekt* figure.[27] Notwithstanding his ludicrous appearance, he represents an ominous and threatening presence throughout. Various men drag individuals out from huddled groups of fearful women in order to abuse them, the swimmer slaps one dancer, another screams at his victim to 'Say uncle' while he assaults her: this invocation of the childish command to submit during a wrestling match contrasts unnervingly with the physical disparity between the man and woman. This character subsequently announces – in the midst of a fit of hysterical weeping – that he wants 'to rape and kill all women and children'. A woman performs a repeated action in which she shuffles forward, pulls her long dress over her head in order to expose her bare back and legs, and prostrates herself for the swimmer to slash red lipstick across her skin. As he does so, she hides her face behind her long hair, and flinches as though being whipped. The swimmer continues his campaign of intimidation, slashing a wooden table with a knife, terrifying another female dancer who races around the stage screaming. Throughout, the audience adopts the role of passive conspirator, observing the action without interrupting the abuse, as in the uncomfortable closing sequence of *Kontakthof*.

Gebirge is characterised by violent interactions: dancers are knocked to the floor, apparently unconscious; they are dragged or wrenched across the stage, pulling each other's hair; a man and a woman are grabbed by the group, manhandled and forced to kiss one another. Frantic group scenes, in which dancers run without direction around the dim, filthy stage setting, screaming and pushing each other, resemble a vision of hell on earth. *Gebirge* marks a sharp transition from absurdist dance theatre to the realm of Artaudian chaos and brutality. Bausch's recurring fascination with social niceties and everyday action is distorted to provide a view of a new world in which social order has been upended entirely. If *Sacre* explored a fertility ritual, and the verdant setting of *1980* proposed a gentle exploration of the cycle of life, *Gebirge* demonstrates the aftermath of a catastrophe and the resultant breakdown of society. Communication is often reduced to unintelligible shrieks or barked commands. We can ascertain here another important commonality with

absurdist theatre, in which language is fragmented down into nonsensical babbling. Artaud's Theatre of Cruelty similarly attempts to free the unconscious
mind, and suggests that language is not able to give voice to unconscious
desires. Language in Artaud's conception becomes primal, reduced to grunts
and animalistic noises, and linear plot is lost as a result: he claims that, 'to
make metaphysics out of spoken language is to make language convey what it
does not normally convey. That is to use it in a new, exceptional and unusual
way, to give it its full, physical shock potential.'[28]

Throughout *Gebirge*, the dancers appear almost constantly afraid and seem
unable to trust one another. They peer over their shoulders for hidden danger
and, on occasion, erupt into mass panic, barrelling across the stage in collective
terror. Even ostensibly loving gestures are given a dark reimagining, as when
a terrified-looking couple is forced to kiss by the manhandling of several male
dancers. Birringer tells us that, 'there are quiet moments when individuals or
couples cry out for help and affection and when their vulnerability becomes
a positive force. But these moments of longing are overwhelmed by uncondi-
tional violence'.[29] Repeatedly, gestures of tenderness give way to aggression,
the 'affectionate violence and violent affection' Servos has identified in her
work. An undercurrent of dread runs throughout this production, where the
misery of Pabst's stage design implies the aftermath of a battle, reminiscent of
a makeshift mass grave set into a burnt-out landscape. The dry ice pumped
into the stage setting reinforces this idea of a scorched wasteland, clouding
the audience's vision, and heightening the overall chaos of the scene. In one
scene, the swimmer shepherds a group of anxious women onto the stage, all
of whom are staring at the floor, their faces betraying evident fear. Parallels
with the muddied dancers of Bausch's *Sacre* are evident in their 'flocking'
configuration, as the women are crushed together, indistinguishable from one
another in their dowdy, stained dresses. This recurring image of a faceless,
suffering mass, soiled and constantly abused, is grimly reminiscent of images
of the concentration camps. This dark phase of *Tanztheater* demonstrates an
Artaudian streak in its refusal to grant the viewer a reprieve from discomfort,
reflected even in the barrenness of the setting. Instead, *Gebirge* confronts the
audience with a literalisation of their fears, which in this context takes the
shape of wartime imagery.

In her limited discussion of her own work, Bausch refused to discuss in
specific terms how her *Tanztheater* pieces ought to be interpreted, electing
instead to leave responsibility in the hands of her audience. Although there are
very few overt references to political issues or the recent past within the wider
context of her choreography, *Gebirge* marks an exception. In his description of
Gebirge, Servos highlights a sequence in which a dancer runs across the stage
singing the words, ''s brennt, brider, 's brennt',[30] ('it's burning, brother, it's
burning'). These lyrics seem to be derived from Mordecai Gebirtig's Yiddish

song, Undser Shtetl Brennt (Our Village is Burning), a commemoration of the 1936 Jewish pogrom in the Polish town of Przytyk; the song was later to become a popular marker of resistance in Nazi concentration camps.[31] In the context of Bausch's legacy, this fragmentary moment constitutes the most overt reference to Germany's troubled past, and provides a transient answer to the question of the otherwise unspecified location.

Indeed, it is difficult to interpret the blank and ambiguous setting of *Gebirge* without visualising the apocalyptic images of the Second World War and its atrocities. Yet these impressions of abuse, suffering and humiliation are not unique to the postwar experience, but exemplify a generalised embodiment of cruelty that is as unspecified and timeless as the stage design suggests. Bausch's choice of soundtrack suggests from the very beginning that *Gebirge* speaks of a wider problem in humanity – following the protracted silence of the opening balloon scene, Billie Holiday's Strange Fruit drifts across the speakers:

> Pastoral scene of the gallant south,
> The bulging eyes and the twisted mouth,
> Scent of magnolias, sweet and fresh,
> Then the sudden smell of burning flesh.

This iconic, haunting account of a lynching provides an immediate cross-cultural parallel. It is a striking reference to racial hatred and racially motivated murder, and sets the tone of unease that characterises the piece as a whole. *Gebirge*'s musical fragments, read alongside the work's title, can be pieced together as a thematic puzzle – the result provides us with a multi-layered impression of the consequences of man's capacity for violence.

In this distressing vision of a scorched wasteland, Bausch's approach aligns more closely with Artaud's Theatre of Cruelty than at any other point in her *oeuvre*. The setting of *Gebirge* invites comparison with the kind of post-traumatic images that are now wrought into collective consciousness, reminiscent of a deserted battlefield, a bombed city or the terrible, sprawling landscapes of the death camps. The fog that clouds the audience's view of the stage also chokes the performers at various points. Towards the end, the music is amplified to an almost deafening level, and the collective hysteria of the dancers is heightened further as they race across the stage in panic. Yet it is Bausch's deliberate ambiguity that makes *Gebirge* so effective, as her reference points remain largely unspecified. She invokes timeless images of human catastrophe. As in her *Sacre*, the soil-covered floor contributes to the otherworldliness of the setting. Here, however, she draws on significantly more shocking imagery to elicit a profound emotional response from the spectator. Presenting us with a range of impressions of humanity's potential for brutality, Artaud's conception of confrontational theatre is called to mind:

A headlong fall into the flesh, deprived of calling cruelty permanent, either cruelty of freedom.

Theatre is the *scaffold*, the gibbet, the trenches, the crematorium or the madhouse.

Cruelty, *massacred* bodies.[32]

During particularly vicious acts, the rest of *Gebirge*'s cast serve as a mirror for the audience, passive spectators who do nothing to halt the cycle of abuse. Bausch extends the scope of action into the intermission. Shortly before the end of the first act, a male dancer slowly dusts his female partner's hair with chalk until her head is completely covered in white powder. He exits the scene, leaving the woman standing centre stage, alone, silently weeping. At this point, another dancer enters the stage to announce the beginning of the intermission, although the crying woman remains in her place as the audience makes its way out of the theatre space. Fernandes recalled her experience as an observer of this scene:

> As the music stops, [Beatrice] Libonati's silence is invaded by the audi-ence's tumultuous voices as it begins leaving the theater. One viewer asks, 'Is it alright if I stand up right now?' It is embarrassing to leave while dancers are still 'representing,' but the intermission was announced! . . . Throughout intermission, Libonati stays onstage with tears rolling down from her eyes. When she finally leaves the stage during the beginning of the second act, she receives a great deal of applause from the audience.[33]

Thus, even the interval of Bausch's spectacle permits the audience no respite from discomfort and uncertainty. The audience is faced with a dilemma, whether to accept that the weeping woman is part of the performance or to intervene. This is the challenge of Bausch's *Tanztheater* of Cruelty – in these events where genuine memories are invoked and dancers refer to one another by their real names, a pervading doubt lingers over the divide between fact and fiction.

Gebirge is surely the most nightmarish production in Bausch's repertoire. In this work, she simultaneously confronts the viewer with unnerving imagery while estranging them from the action through innovative use of set design and direct address. The resulting spectacle is ambitious in scale and challenging in terms of its structure, forming a space in which the spectator is compelled to reflect on the darker side of humanity. The audience is bombarded with sounds, images and actions, and the chaotic assemblage does not let up for the lengthy duration of the piece. Meanwhile, the dancers' attempts to communicate with one another are thwarted by their inability to articulate their thoughts or needs, a failure that only results in further violence. As the non-narrative reaches its conclusion, the fragmentation of speech seems to underscore the ineffectiveness of language in the wake of atrocity – how can words alone sufficiently articulate the terror of humanity's innate capacity for (mass) destruction? That her work unflinchingly draws upon such themes presents an insurmountable obstacle for some viewers, as Anita Finkel has highlighted:

> Bausch will not allow us to deny nature, and we respond with anger. There are those who stay completely away from Bausch's theater because the spectacle of real flesh is too painful to bear, and they're right to absent themselves – once inside, Bausch's sense of the body as vulnerable is inescapable.[34]

Throughout this period, Bausch's dance theatre does not transform into a naturalistic model, but maintains the unmasking process already established in productions such as *Kontakthof* and *Walzer*. By this stage in the evolution of her *Tanztheater*, elements of multiple theatrical approaches can be discerned in her work: Brechtian distancing, absurdist word play and Artaudian cruelty are combined in her recurring patterns of everyday behaviour and movement. Nonetheless, a crucial distinction from Artaud is that, while his approach ultimately seeks to provide a form of catharsis for the audience, resolution is never provided in Bausch's dance theatre. In this respect, the enduring relationship with absurdism recurs in the productions of this phase. While Artaud's Theatre of Cruelty is not fully realised in Bausch's work, its theoretical underpinnings are evident throughout the dark period of her mature *Tanztheater*. Violence is not literally employed – even in uncomfortable moments, such as *Gebirge*'s swimmer slashing at one of the cowering women, the red marks left on her skin come only from a lipstick clenched in his fist. Instead, shock is employed as a means of disrupting audience passivity in a similar manner to the irregular fourth wall breaks of previous works. Christine Kiebuzinska suggests that, for Artaud, 'violence is seen as a symptom of the psychical distortions breaking out as the expressive behaviour patterns imposed by society become unbearable'.[35] In Bausch's dark dance theatre, a mirror is held up not only to reflect society's inherent cruelties, but also to demonstrate our own inescapable role in these cyclical and deeply embedded patterns.

ENGENDERING TROUBLE: *TWO CIGARETTES IN THE DARK*

The works created in Bausch's dark period reflect a climate of fear, suspicion and violence that is especially suggestive of Germany's difficult legacy: Mulrooney has argued that, 'Bausch's work itself is a carnivalesque ritual of post-war urban decay and of its society as a whole.'[36] Yet her evocation of violent imagery also connects Bausch's *Tanztheater* to a broader global legacy in performance practice. Violence as a motif recurs with increasing frequency in the aesthetics of avant-garde art and performance in the decades following the end of the war. Images of post-apocalyptic chaos, destruction and violence are equally visible and persistent themes in the performance traditions of the other defeated nations of the Second World War: the dramatic performances of early Japanese Butoh dance aesthetically and thematically anticipated the confrontational events of Viennese Actionism.[37] In the wider performance landscape, the portrayal of sado-masochistic violence and self-harm became characteristic of body art throughout the 1960s and 1970s, perhaps most famously exemplified in the work of Marina Abramović, Chris Burden and Gina Pane.[38] While many of these artists subjected themselves to genuine physical suffering, however, in Bausch's work, cruelty is predominantly a metaphorical device. The evocation or performance of violence is employed as a tool for confronting the audience, shaking them from their passive enjoyment of the spectacle. Important political reference points link these seemingly disparate elements across cultures, manifested through the recurring themes of fragmentation, distortion and violence.

Despite these considerable precedents in confrontational performance practice, viewers of Bausch's *Tanztheater* were still frequently shocked by its visceral content. While the critical reception to Bausch's aesthetic began to soften throughout the 1980s, controversy would greet the company's arrival in the United States in 1984. Here, pieces such as *Blaubart* were once again poorly received by audiences that seemingly could not comprehend Bausch's style. Some particularly memorable reviews included comments such as Alan Kriegsman's that, 'it's a . . . specifically Teutonic attraction to the powers of darkness, to an alliance of art, disease and malevolence';[39] Arlene Croce's now infamous remark that, 'she keeps referring us to the act of brutalization and humiliation – to the pornography of pain' and, '[Bausch is] an entrepreneuse who fills theatres with projections of herself and her self-pity';[40] and Donna Perlmutter's dismissal of the whole form as, 'obsessive, mindless self-flagellation [that] takes over in this psychiatric back ward'.[41] Croce went so far as to call her a 'theatre terrorist'.[42] Bausch's reputation spread quickly and gained a degree of notoriety outside Germany, though over time positive reviews began to outnumber the furious critics – Burt acknowledges that 'audiences come to performances by her company . . . prepared to endure a harrowing experience and then give the dancers a standing ovation'.[43] Critics who supported Bausch's work also challenged such negativity; Birringer, for instance, questioned the motivation behind this widespread disapproval:

> Since most American audiences were outraged by the violence portrayed in the performance, one might ask why they responded to the violence and not to the sharply focussed process of recognition that leads from the pathos of self-absorbed sexual obsession to the much larger patterns of mechanical evasion that a guilt-ridden society resorts to when it prefers to deny the consequences of its continuing aggression.[44]

On the occasions Bausch consented to interviews, she often expressed a weariness towards the reputation she had garnered and the effect such critical reviews had on the audience's ability to read her work: speaking with Christopher Bowen in 1997, she claimed that, 'people see [violence] all the time, even when it is not there'. Yet in the same breath, Bausch also made clear the necessity of including such difficult imagery, asking, 'how can you make clear on stage the feelings if we don't see why there is suffering, or anger?'[45]

Even in contemporary writing on Bausch's *Tanztheater*, certain issues continue to rankle, and it is perhaps the depiction of power dynamics that remains most controversial. Her repertoire is riddled with uncomfortable instances of gender conflict. Men often manipulate or exert control over women, a tendency that is revisited in earnest throughout Bausch's mature works. In *Gebirge*, women cower in terror from the constant threat of violence exuded by the swimmer and submit to the various punishments meted out with little resistance. Even innocuous moments are often imbued with a darker edge: while two women perform cartwheels, the looming presence of a silent, staring male spectator shifts the tone of what is otherwise a fairly innocent, almost naïve sequence. Like children unaware of the predatory potential of unknown strangers, they continue to perform, both for him and for the audience, revealing their underwear as they tumble across the filthy stage in an impromptu gymnastics display.

Gender violence is a difficult and often emotive issue in criticism of Bausch's *Tanztheater*, where her staged female characters are frequently the subjects of violent behaviour, always enacted by men. Goldberg comments that, 'Bausch walks a fine line between spectacular exploitation of the victimized woman and consciousness-raising',[46] while Siegel states quite plainly that 'she isn't pro anything, except the dramatization of sexual despair'.[47] In works such as *Sacre* and *Orpheus*, Bausch's dancers adopt the role of literal victims, whereas in *Blaubart* and *Die sieben Todsünden* they allude to the violence inflicted on women within the confines of a romantic relationship. Yet Bausch's depiction of 'victimhood' is not necessarily an indication of an inherently feminine weakness, as some critics seems to suggest: rather, her suffering women represent a broad cross-section of cruelty in society.

In this final case study of Bausch's dark period, I wish to propose that the gender violence is deployed for Artaudian shock, rather than necessarily making either feminist or anti-feminist statements. Given the depressingly universal reality of domestic brutality, Bausch's images provoke both an immediate, visceral and personal reaction from the spectator, yet the framing of the production engenders a space in which viewers are drawn in more intimately than mimetic theatre. Bausch's dark works, in this respect, rely upon specific movement and image to jolt the spectator, encroaching into the realm of the audience and, in effect, forcing the viewer to reflect upon the nature of cruelty and its myriad manifestations in interpersonal interactions. These are all fundamentally Artaudian practices. The spectator's silence in witnessing gender violence in Bausch's productions, stressed further through the narrowing of the gap between stage and spectator, suggests complicity in the act and is arguably at the root of the negative criticism her work accrued in this period. Bausch frequently reiterated that she was not a provocateur however, claiming 'I am terrified of violence, but I wanted to understand the person doing violence.'[48] I contend that Bausch is not the 'pornographer of pain' that she is made out to be, as her approach can actually be seen as a haven for unorthodox performers rather than perpetuating the cruelties of the professional dance world. Ironically, as we shall shortly see, the cruelty in this phase is perpetrated primarily by her critics.

Less than a year after the premiere of *Gebirge*, Bausch produced another lengthy, challenging work, this time comprised of a relatively small cast (eleven performers in total). *Two Cigarettes in the Dark* (1985) derives its name from Bing Crosby's ballad on loneliness and broken hearts, and revolves around a series of dream-like social gatherings and cocktail parties inhabited by bored, forlorn and isolated characters. Once again, references to the natural world are included in Pabst's stage design but, this time, it is enclosed within glass. The set is comprised of a stark plastic expanse, and surrounding the clinical white walls that encase the performers are three huge tanks, one an enormous goldfish bowl, another filled with rich plant life, and the third a desert scene complete with cacti. This containment stands in sharp contrast to the presentation of organic works such as *1980*, where the grassy setting is lush and seemingly alive. The sterile whiteness of the walls reinforces a sense of detachment that runs throughout this strange and unsettling work. It is unclear whether the action is taking place inside a museum or within a surreal impression of a scientific laboratory. Referring to Bausch's motif of enclosing the natural world in her sets, Cody has remarked that, 'the function of this bottled naturalism is hauntingly commemorative. Nature is artificially (and some might argue, morbidly) preserved in these lush wastelands'.[49] In *Two Cigarettes,* this is quite literally the case.

Ambiguity is a significant feature of Bausch's work, both in terms of physical location as suggested by stage design, and in the relationship established between Bausch's dancers and their audience. The interactions between performer and spectator in these productions are often inconsistent in tone, switching between an affectionate and seemingly genuine desire to connect (consider a sequence in her 2003 work, *Nefés*, in which the dancers approach audience members with their family photographs, sharing private memories with complete strangers), and confrontational, at times even aggressive, exchanges. In the dark phase of Bausch's *Tanztheater*, performers transgress the invisible boundary of the fourth wall to question, flirt, argue and plead with the audience, doing so with increasing regularity throughout this period. Indeed, the opening sequence of *Two Cigarettes* is an arresting example of this technique. From the back of the sterile white stage, a door opens and Großmann strides to the very edge of the stage. Resplendent in a cream and gold evening gown, she grins at the audience. Opening her arms, she proclaims, 'Please, come in. My husband is at war.' Without waiting for a response, she turns on her heel and exits the stage in silence.

The immediacy of this connection destabilises the sanctity of the audience's supposedly private space, and simultaneously transforms the proscenium stage into a domestic environment. In doing so, the gap between performer and spectator is narrowed, and the viewer is drawn into an uncomfortably intimate shared space. Bausch's reorganisation of the performance setting resonates with Artaud: in his first manifesto of cruel theatre, he underlines the importance of altering the physical environment of the production, and advocates a total integration of performance and audience space.[50] Artaud seeks to narrow the gap between viewer and actor in order to unsettle the spectator and disrupt the passivity that is an inevitable consequence of the traditional narrative framework. While this reconstruction of the theatre itself is not literally realised in Bausch's work, it is implicit in her repeated and overt disturbances of the fourth wall. Significantly, *Two Cigarettes* represents the first occasion in which the spectator is invited into the realm of the dancers. By reframing the stage as a domestic environment and beckoning the audience in, by implication we are made complicit in the actions that follow. This is a continuation of a theme established in *Kontakthof* and, as in that piece, the characters are trapped in similar cycles of interpersonal cruelty. They are encased by their unhappiness – this time, however, they openly acknowledge the audience as their guests, no longer simply passive observers.

Bausch's *Tanztheater* exists in the margins of theatre convention, shifting the confines of the stage space throughout the duration of each piece. As her dancers interrupt their own performances, they serve a sharp reminder to the audience that these dreamlike landscapes are temporary and fictional spaces. In one such moment in *Gebirge*, a male dancer pauses amid the action, turns to the audience and asks directly, 'Why are you looking at us?' Still more unsettling are the moments in which Bausch's performers simply make eye contact with the spectators, drawing them, most likely unwillingly, into the alternative world that they inhabit. Approximately halfway through the events of *Two Cigarettes*, two women approach the front of the stage and, in French and German, point to different parts of their bodies indicating the relevant price (in marks and francs respectively). Receiving no response, they proceed to stare intently at individual members of the audience in complete silence. This continues for several minutes on an otherwise empty stage – the other performers have departed the set by this point. The connection is finally disrupted when one of the women shrugs, smiles and announces that the intermission has already begun. There is a burst of self-conscious laughter from the audience as they rise from their seats and begin to exit the theatre. Nonetheless, the two women remain on stage, silent once again, still looking out at their spectators. In Bausch's *Tanztheater*, this reversal of the gaze is another recurring motif, a device that throws the recognisable hierarchy and structure of theatre convention into flux.

However, this scene also returns to Bausch's central problematic tendency, namely the representation of women on her stage. This particular fourth wall break is a comic take on the commodification of the female body, with both women seeking to directly communicate or barter with the audience. Read alongside works such as *Viktor* (in which dancers are paraded at the front of the stage in order to be auctioned off), we might interpret this as further sly commentary on the contractual relationship that exists between spectator and performer, where money is exchanged for the promise of entertainment. In the context of *Two Cigarettes* as a whole, however, the flippancy of this moment becomes rather more complex. Women are almost used as stage props throughout the piece, hauled around the space by their male counterparts. The issue of authoritarianism is ever present, and is at times deeply uncomfortable to watch – when a drink is spilled and, as a result, a female dancer is suspected of urinating in a corner of the stage, a man forces her head to the floor and rubs her nose in it, as one might chastise an untrained puppy.

With its reduced cast of dancers, *Two Cigarettes* might be classed as a Bauschian chamber piece. This concentration of the action casts a stronger spotlight on specific 'characters' than in the case of larger-scale and more chaotic works such as *Nelken* and *Gebirge* (my use of the term here is loose, however, as Bausch's method deliberately avoids the creation of singular or identifiable character roles). Helena Pikon is a readily distinguishable member of the ensemble, not least because of her striking on-stage resemblance to Bausch herself. In this work, her role functions as a theatrical foil to Großmann's hostess. Pikon enters the stage immediately after Großmann's opening address. Clad in one of the trademark *Tanztheater* evening gowns, her breasts are continually exposed to the audience by her deliberately ill-fitting dress. Accompanied by a soundtrack of Monteverdi, Pikon throws herself around the stage in an agonising solo, with a look of genuine suffering etched across her face. A male dancer enters the stage, slaps her and orders her to stop crying. The scene ends with him violently beating her. The contrast between these two women is striking: Großmann's overt self-assurance while her unwitting husband is involved in some unspecified war (as ever, Bausch leaves us uncertain of any specific location in time or space), versus Pikon's lonely, near-hysterical torment, slapped back into sense by an unidentified man. Later in the performance, Großmann appears on stage with her breasts bared, a cigarette hanging out of her mouth and an impassive expression across her

Figure 4.3 *Two Cigarettes in the Dark*, Laszlo Szito

face. Nudity is a device used in this work to reflect juxtaposing impressions of femininity, with Großmann acting as a repudiation to the critics' accusations of Bausch's women as weak and helpless.

However, while Großmann embodies a hyper-confident sexuality in this work, her female counterparts are largely silent, with several appearing fearful of the men sharing their stage. Costume plays a significant role in this: Bausch's performers are usually exquisitely dressed, and in *Two Cigarettes* the clothing is designed to conjure an image of the decadent parties of a bygone era (Figure 4.3). Yet the contrast between costume and setting is stark, and it is clear that the guests at Bausch's party are locked in the surreal world of their own unhappiness and introspection. Women are picked up and carried around the set by their male counterparts, and manipulated like dolls. At one point, a man changes a woman's dress for her, tugging the fabric over her exposed body as one might dress a child. There is a roughness to the gesture that is unsettling and, as is typical of Bausch's works, the glimpses and flashes of nudity are never titillating, but serve to reinforce the fragility of the human condition.

These doll-like manifestations belong to a line of continuity that leads back to *Blaubart*: dressing is a recurring gesture of Bausch's *Tanztheater*, and is often enacted to a deliberately grotesque effect. This marks another area of critical ire, as several writers have identified problematic gender stereotyping in the costuming of her dancers.

Goldberg, for example, highlights the manifestation of cross-dressing in Bausch's work, arguing that it is used almost exclusively for comic effect.[51] Like the complaint that Bausch's explorations of romance centre on heteronormative relationships, there is justification behind this critique. Nonetheless, this almost inevitable focus on issues of sexual politics has a propensity to deviate from uncovering the range of ulterior meanings in Bausch's choreography. Viewed alongside some of the commentary that emerges in negative reviews of the work in this period, her depiction of women is rather more subversive than her detractors suggest.

The dance world, and the realm of classical ballet in particular, espouses an obsession with perfection and projects a specific conception of femininity and grace, one that is almost impossible to achieve (and maintain) in reality. Bausch's company has never been uniform in its makeup, and is comprised of dancers that represent a wide range of nationalities, ages and body types. Endicott recalls joining the company after having given up a career in classical ballet, and that she was out of shape and 'a little fat' when Bausch asked her to dance in Wuppertal. Ditta Miranda Jasjfi, an Indonesian dancer who joined the company in 2000, was originally rejected at her audition on the grounds of her height, and had already abandoned classical dance due to her tiny stature. Bausch soon changed her mind, however, and asked Jasjfi to take on the role of the sacrificial victim in *Sacre*.[52]

Critical reviews of Bausch's *Tanztheater* in this dark period often return to the dancers themselves, and there is a notable fixation on physicality and body shape. Croce's notorious 1984 review of the company's first engagement in New York ('Bausch's Theatre of Dejection') is an especially cruel example, one that is littered with sharp comments regarding the bodies of Bausch's dancers. She refers to them as 'little fat girls', and 'sad sacks', before claiming that, 'when they strip they have nothing to show us', and finally stating that Bausch is responsible for 'having made women look worse on the stage than any misogynist ever has'.[53] Others have taken issue with the flimsy nature of the costumes in works such as *Sacre* and the resulting exposure of female bodies. Reviewing *Die sieben Todsünden* at the Brooklyn Academy of Music, Ellen Donkin and Rhonda Blair wrote that, 'the women repeatedly were seen in glad rags with breasts exposed, and were manhandled not only by the male dancers but also by our gaze as audience'.[54] Heathfield too has observed that:

> The female figures in Bausch's work seem to reside in some perpetual condition of dishevelled night-time reverie, their silken slips barely lodged across exposed backs, their bodies just one step away from sleep, from a movement that would fully inhabit the life of the unconscious. Bausch's reconstitution of ballet's grace took the feminine form, but marked it as fallen: the female body was seen as torn, always already ruptured.[55]

While Heathfield's remarks suggest a more sensual reading of the display of female bodies in Bausch's *oeuvre*, this common focus on corporeality betrays an underlying discomfort with the frankness of Bausch's theatrical framing. She does not shy away from displaying bodies in their actual, unaugmented form, and the exposure of breasts or other body parts is never employed to garner a cheap thrill. Equally, drag is often used less as a tool of mockery, but rather to create a specific aesthetic effect. Indeed, the comic element of her drag scenes is usually derived from the ridiculous efforts men and women must subject themselves to in order to conform to socially constructed norms. Bausch does not torment or humiliate her dancers, instead she creates a surreal and inclusive dream world in which our most intimate, humorous and dark thoughts are reflected and endlessly recycled. Her performers turn the gaze back on the spectator, breaking the illusionism of the fourth wall and redefining the limits of the theatre.

In the works that emerged from this provocative period in Bausch's career, the almost relentless sequences of violence stand for a larger problem than gender inequality alone. Consequently, Bausch's frequent reiteration of gender violence functions as a totem, symbolising human cruelty in a more general sense by drawing on an emotive and controversial image. Bausch's *Tanztheater* is designed to function and translate across cultural boundaries, and perhaps the most enduring and universal reflection of cruelty lies within human relationships and the often-thwarted search for intimacy. Something similar is at play in Artaud's work: Robert Vork tells us, 'Artaud seems to be suggesting that his play [*Les Cenci*, 1935] reveals emotions and experiences that we all attempt to proscribe and are unwilling to acknowledge, but which nevertheless occur.'[56] It is this same universality that challenges the audience, compelling them to accept some form of complicity in the everyday cruelties enacted on stage. Bausch's dark period shares in many of the objectives of Artaud's conception. Her blended approach presents us with uncomfortable spectacles that turn the gaze back on the viewer. As in the case of *Kontakthof*, where the spectator must contend with their reluctance to intervene, Bausch's dark works propose a broad, cross-cultural complicity in cruelty. Her *Tanztheater* is less concerned with commenting on gender inequality than highlighting a universal social anxiety, exploring the relationships between people more generally, rather than forming an explicit statement on gender and sexual roles.

It would be straightforward to read the often brutal or manipulative interactions between men and women in these works as reflective of a desire to draw attention to issues of gender violence specifically. I interpret Bausch's evocations of power dynamics differently: instead, we may understand these unpleasant interventions between men and women as referring to overarching power structures and authoritarianism, a contentious and relevant theme in postwar German society. These violent interactions represent a method of

addressing the past by acknowledging the darker features of the human condition, accepting that man is inherently capable of violence and deep cruelty.
Bausch visits this theme in various ways, exploring the search for love as a
basic need of the human condition. In the dark era of her *Tanztheater*, she portrays the most negative aspects of humanity, but at the same time refers to the
existence of a deep and underlying vulnerability. That these productions were
so negatively received by many critics is not especially surprising, and reflects
the fact that Bausch's movement vocabulary is capable of touching nerves as
easily as it breaks hearts. Birringer has adopted a similar stance, arguing that:

> Bausch's repetitive masochistic rituals and the struggle for love and
> recognition that her male and female dancers perform on each other
> with aggressive affection can only be considered offensive to the eye if
> one completely misunderstands the implied social critique. In order to
> see art as a form of cultural intervention, one must remember the specific
> German theater, opera and ballet tradition whose classics have always
> dominated the repertories of the state-subsidized theaters. It is this
> cultural repertory, with its social/political implications, that the women
> choreographers – the true heirs of Brecht's epic theatre – rebelled against
> with the full rage of a generation of daughters that witnessed the success-
> ful reconstruction of the old patriarchal regime, shortly after the horrors
> of fascism had arisen from Western civilization.[57]

In these dark pieces, Bausch retains a link to her earlier work. Indeed,
Gebirge and *Two Cigarettes* are self-referential in nature, revisiting themes
first explored in well-received works such as *Sacre*, *Kontakhof* and *Nelken*.
Physical exhaustion is a motif that emerges frequently. Dancers repeat actions
until they are visibly fatigued, with some appearing to be on the verge of
collapse. Other moments are similarly recognisable in light of Bausch's wider
oeuvre, for example, when a seemingly hypnotised figure runs across the
stage, he is attended to by a dancer who clears tables and chairs from his path;
surely a self-referential nod to *Café Müller*. In these works, the underlying
desire remains the search for intimacy and human connection, something that
remains perpetually just out of reach. However, the kindness of this gesture
is indicative of another important point, that even within the confines of this
oppressive netherworld, there is still tenderness, and with it, a vestige of hope.

*

Despite a tendency for depicting brutality on stage, Bausch's works are
rarely explicitly political in nature. Instead, the responsibility lies with the
audience to form their own interpretation of her challenging choreographies.
Speaking in Anne Linsel's 2006 documentary, Bausch described one particular
audience's reaction to *Nelken* while touring with the company in the former

Soviet Union. She claimed that many had read the piece as an allegory of the Holocaust, specifically referring to one scene in which a pair of dancers repeatedly, and ritualistically, pour sand over themselves. This action was interpreted as a kind of self-burial, where the sand was seen to represent the ashes of the gas chambers.[58] In this version of events, the Elysian Fields imagery of the stage covered in fresh carnations was read as a symbol of a mass grave, the performers haunted by the ghosts of their collective past. While the Soviet audience related *Nelken*'s themes to the challenges of their own cultural experience, at least one contemporary critic has related its world of lost souls to the migrant crisis provoked by conflicts in the Middle East, calling the piece 'fortuitously resonant'.[59] Thus, multiple interpretations of Bausch's dark works are possible, reflecting not only the ubiquity of violence and human cruelty but interpretative perspectivism.

The ambitious scale of her productions extends beyond the invisible border designed to separate performers from spectators – even when her dancers speak, they transcend a central theatrical boundary by addressing the audience directly, or leaving the stage in order to interact with their viewers. Fictional characters are conflated with the dancers' real names and life experiences. Accordingly, in these often-surreal landscapes, nothing is quite certain. In Pabst's sets, elements of ordinary life are often out of place: plastic flowers form a carpet that is bounded on all sides by police dogs, a barren, smouldering landscape is eventually covered in felled pine trees and a sterile, claustrophobic room is decorated with literal still lifes contained within gigantic fish tanks.

In the works surveyed here, Bausch presents a broad vision of her own Theatre of Cruelty, one that is not always easy or pleasant to observe. Heiner Müller once commented that, in Bausch's work, 'the image is a thorn in our eye'.[60] However, there is a universality present in these traces of past trauma: reference points such as Billie Holiday's song remind us that man's capacity for violence transcends all cultural boundaries. There are striking parallels in Bausch's approach with Artaud's conception, a reimagining of the stage in which the audience is confronted by the extreme actions of the performers in order to become aware and responsive to the workings of the subconscious. Nonetheless, Bausch's *Tanztheater* defies straightforward identification with standardised theatrical convention. While there are a multiplicity of modernist reference points located in her approach to choreography, she evolved a technique that was uniquely her own and transcended the limitations of Artaud and Brecht's particular models. Epic in scale and setting, with the dramatic inclusion of organic matter on the proscenium stage, these durational works approach the concept of the *Gesamtkunstwerk*, encompassing the natural world and artifice, fact and fiction, narrative and abstraction, violence and tenderness. Bausch's *Tanztheater* works are living pieces of theatre, performances that explore some of humanity's most primal tendencies. In these productions,

Bausch explores human relationships and their potential for cruelty, as well as the desire for intimacy and connection. At the same time, these are perhaps her most melancholic pieces as, in the end, there seems little resolution beyond the certainty of death.

In recent years, the negative reviews that characterised Bausch's early career have given way to critical acclaim, and the difficulties of the experimental period have been consigned to history. Much of Bausch's middle period draws on stark and uncomfortable reminders of the recent past, playing on recurring motifs of violence and cruelty. Elements of Bausch's aesthetic and driving themes are clearly influenced by her life experience in postwar Germany, and it is vital to understand the significance of German identity in the work. Nonetheless, her *Tanztheater* does not solely refer to a uniquely German experience. Instead, Bausch evolved a method in which violence and traumatic memory remind audiences that humanity is capable of great cruelty, but also, on occasion, humour and compassion.

Notes

1. Sturm, 'Illustrated talk on the work of Pina Bausch'.
2. Benjamin, 'The Storyteller', in Benjamin, *Illuminations*, p. 86.
3. Martin, 'Theatre of Cruelty', pp. 52–3.
4. Artaud, 'Theatre and Cruelty', *Collected Works*, p. 64.
5. Morfee, *Antonin Artaud's Writing Bodies*, p. 40.
6. Artaud, 'No More Masterpieces', *Collected Works*, p. 63.
7. Lehmann, *Postdramatic Theatre*, p. 166
8. Servos, *Pina Bausch*, pp. 100–1.
9. Broadhurst, 'Pina', in Broadhurst and Machon (eds), *Identity, Performance and Technology*, p. 94.
10. Artaud, 'The Theatre of Cruelty: First Manifesto', *Collected Works*, pp. 73–4.
11. Lehmann, *Postdramatic Theatre*, pp. 103–4.
12. Fernandes, *Pina Bausch and the Wuppertal Dance Theatre*, p. 65.
13. Hoghe, *Bandoneon*, p. 31.
14. Servos, *Pina Bausch*, p. 90.
15. Jennings, 'Obituary'.
16. Macauley, 'Meat and Veg', p. 16.
17. Gilpin, 'Amputation, Dismembered Identities, and the Rhythms of Elimination', in Jankowsky and Love (eds), *Other Germanies*, pp. 175–6.
18. Caruth, 'Trauma and Experience', *Trauma*, p. 11.
19. Müller, *Krieg ohne Schlacht*, pp. 18–19.
20. Stamp Miller, *The Cultural Politics of the German Democratic Republic*, p. 139.
21. Lehmann, *Postdramatic Theatre*, p. 97.
22. Huyssen, *Twilight Memories*, p. 212.
23. Mulrooney, *Orientalism, Orientation, and the Nomadic Work of Pina Bausch*, p. 276.
24. Felciano, 'Pina Bausch', p. 68.
25. Jannarone, *Artaud and his Doubles*, pp. 8–10.
26. Sörgel, *Dance and the Body in Western Theatre*, p. 123.
27. Servos, *Pina Bausch*, p. 105.
28. Artaud, 'Production and Metaphysics', *Collected Works*, p. 32.

29. Birringer, 'Pina Bausch', p. 93.
30. Servos, *Pina Bausch*, p. 107.
31. Goldfarb, 'Theatrical Activities in Nazi Concentration Camps', p. 4.
32. Cited in Finter and Griffin, 'Antonin Artaud and the Impossible Theatre', p. 16.
33. Fernandes, *Pina Bausch and the Wuppertal Dance Theatre*, p. 40.
34. Finkel, 'Gunsmoke', in Climenhaga (ed.) *The Pina Bausch Sourcebook*, pp. 162–3.
35. Kiebuzinska, *Revolutionaries in the Theater*, p. 115.
36. Mulrooney, *Orientalism, Orientation, and the Nomadic Work of Pina Bausch*, p. 22.
37. Weir, 'Abject Modernism'.
38. Langston, *Visions of Violence*; Nelson, *The Art of Cruelty*.
39. Croce et al., 'Pina Bausch in America', p. 18.
40. Croce, 'Bausch's Theatre of Dejection', in Climenhaga (ed.), *The Pina Bausch Sourcebook*, pp. 193–4.
41. Perlmutter, 'Reviews: *Café Müller'*, pp. 34–5.
42. Croce, 'Bausch's Theatre of Dejection', in Climenhaga (ed.), *The Pina Bausch Sourcebook*, p. 195.
43. Burt, 'Genealogy and Dance History' in Lepecki (ed.), *On the Presence of the Body*, p. 39.
44. Birringer, 'Pina Bausch', p. 91.
45. Bausch, quoted in Bowen, 'Every Day a Discovery', in Climenhaga (ed.), *The Pina Bausch Sourcebook*, p. 102.
46. Goldberg, 'Artifice and Authenticity', p. 111.
47. Siegel, 'Carabosse in a Cocktail Dress', p. 110.
48. Jennings, 'Tanztheater Wuppertal Pina Bausch'.
49. Cody, 'Woman, Man, Dog, Tree', p. 116.
50. Artaud, 'The Theatre of Cruelty: First Manifesto', *Collected Works*, pp. 73–4.
51. Goldberg, 'Artifice and Authenticity', pp. 108–9.
52. Mariani, 'Dancing and Making it in the World'.
53. Croce, 'Bausch's Theatre of Dejection', in Climenhaga (ed.), *The Pina Bausch Sourcebook*, p. 194–5.
54. Donkin and Blair, 'The Seven Deadly Sins', p. 116.
55. Heathfield 'Dance-Theatre and Dance-Performance', in Kelleher and Ridout (eds), *Contemporary Theatres in Europe*, p. 197.
56. Vork, 'The Things No One Can Say', p. 311.
57. Birringer, 'Pina Bausch', p. 96.
58. Linsel, *Pina Bausch*.
59. Cheng, 'Carnations on Shaky Ground'.
60. Müller, *Rotwelsch*, p. 103.

5

TRANSIENT *TANZTHEATER*: THE CO-PRODUCTION MODEL

In 1981, Bausch made a brief creative diversion from the all-encompassing realm of her dance theatre to work with the celebrated director Federico Fellini. In an unusual move for the otherwise intensely private choreographer, she accepted a starring role as the ghostly Princess Lherimia in Fellini's film, *E la nave va* (*The Ship Sails On*, 1983). Speaking after their collaboration, Fellini described Bausch as 'an exiled queen'. Despite its flippancy, this remark from an admiring fellow artist provides an accurate portrait of Bausch's evolving creative practice. In the next phase of her career, Bausch significantly expanded the touring remit of her company. From working intensely with a group of international dancers in West Germany's industrial heartland, the ensemble would take their experimental collaborative process on the road, spending a significant proportion of the year roaming between locations.

By the late 1980s, Bausch's career had survived the negative reviews that characterised her years of experimentation. International touring became standard practice for the company, which had itself diversified to include dancers from a range of performance backgrounds and a wide array of countries. In Bausch's 'global' period, she and her ensemble became increasingly nomadic, though Wuppertal would remain an enduring homeland.[1] Their appearances in theatres across the world drew ever greater audiences and significantly broadened the reach of her stylistic influence, with Bauschian trademarks becoming a regular feature on contemporary dance stages. In her obituary for the choreographer, Susan Manning asserts that the company's extensive touring schedule impacted significantly upon the development of modern dance both in Europe and in the United States. Manning goes so far as to call her 'one of, if not *the* most influential choreographer of late-20th-century globalization'.[2]

This pattern of influence is not one-sided, however. Throughout her career, Bausch's reference points have expanded to encompass a broad geopolitical landscape. Even in the early years of her directorship, when Bausch's work relied upon a formalised vocabulary of dance, her movement vocabulary drew upon her bilingual training, synthesising American modern techniques with aspects of German *Ausdruckstanz*. This period represents the first indicator of Bausch's desire to create a universal language of performance, one that could transcend national and cultural boundaries. In her experimental and mature phases, her approach undergoes a radical shift in form and methodology. The resulting dance theatre pieces of this era reference a range of European theatre sources, including the writings of Brecht, Beckett and Artaud. The development of her practice in the mature era produced a recognisable structural framework for her work, and audiences were increasingly well-versed in its recurring themes and motifs. In looking at her subsequent work, however, a further shift in style becomes apparent. This period, extending from the late 1980s into the twenty-first century, is characterised by a sense of migration. The peripatetic nature of these productions mirrors a significant change in creative practice, marked by Bausch's collaborations with international institutions. In the final chapters of this volume, I explore how Bausch's latent itinerancy has come to typify her later work, casting an influence over two decades worth of material.

EXCAVATING THE ETERNAL CITY: *VIKTOR*

Bausch's co-productions comprised fifteen productions devised in collaboration with international cultural agencies, based on residencies held in specific locations. These pieces tend to be overlooked in discussion of her radical approach to dance, as if they fall outside a period of genuine innovation. The co-productions, conceived as Bausch was rising to greater prominence in the last decades of the twentieth century, began to include more explicitly a patchwork of elements from the cross-cultural dialogue which informed her early choreographies. In each case, Bausch and her dancers would undertake a short period of intensive research in the chosen location (usually three to four weeks), before returning to Wuppertal where they would continue to shape and refine the piece through the *Stichworte* method. Accordingly, the co-productions are not works 'about' a location, nor do they attempt to frame a narrative around the cultural context: instead, as Elswit proposes, 'they were not performances made for a given place, but by and through exchanges with it'.[3] Rituals of everyday behaviour still dominate these pieces and, stylistically, the early co-productions maintain the form and structure of Bausch's mature *Tanztheater*. This chapter's analysis of three co-productions spans a period of fifteen years, forming a bridge between her dark period (exemplified by *Viktor*) and signalling a turn into a new era of optimism.

The first international co-production was unveiled on 14 May 1986. Made in conjunction with the Teatro Argentina in Rome, *Viktor* was based on a short period of research and development in the Italian capital. However, the resulting performance is not a vision of the city that would be immediately recognisable to the average tourist. Instead, Bausch evokes a shadowy impression of Rome. The stage design again forms an impressive spectacle of organic matter contained within the proscenium arch, as the stage walls are flanked by twenty-foot-high banks of soil. Like *Sacre, 1980* and *Gebirge*, *Viktor* is an 'earth' piece, though the visual impression is stark and more overtly funereal than its predecessors: as if to reinforce this point, a gravedigger hovers over proceedings, shovelling earth into the stage space and on top of the cast members throughout the duration.

In considering the relationship between *Viktor* and its cultural context, however, the precise meaning of the set design becomes less certain. Perhaps, rather than gazing directly into a grave site, the piece is in fact taking place within the confines of an archaeological excavation. This alternative reading constitutes a less-than-oblique reference to Rome's legacy as an ancient city and the seat of a global empire. It is curiously appropriate that the first piece of Bausch's nomadic collaborative works would be set in Rome, the seat of an itinerant (if colonising) ancient civilisation. However, the unknowing spectator of *Viktor* would likely find their expectations dashed by the lack of overt references to the city itself. The precise location of the cast's absurdist action is never made clear, and while glimpses of Italian culture and its associated stereotypes do materialise, the connection with Rome is never explicitly proclaimed. This remains a constant throughout the co-production model: the resulting works do not centre around a location, but evoke its culture in gestures ranging from the obscure to the comic. The *Stichworte* method remains Bausch's primary tool in constructing these works, blending queries relating to the location and the dancers' experience during their short residencies with more general prompts. According to the programme, the preliminary *Stichworte* query that initiated rehearsals on *Viktor* was, simply, 'was ich in Rom heute sah' ('what I saw in Rome today'), while other queries included, 'Tell the story from the point of view of a mouse', 'How not to use a knife', 'Veal', 'Do something with a lifeless corpse' and 'What do you like about Rome?'[4]

The central themes of *Viktor* revolve around interpersonal interactions, displays of sexuality, and frustration. The dancers parade around their earthy environs clad in stylish gowns, fur coats and sunglasses. A woman performs a solo in which she reveals her cleavage to the audience and announces, 'I want to touch you.' The effect is comical, however, as her performance of feminine wiles is so ludicrously exaggerated. Similarly humorous in its hyperbolic account of the Latin temperament is a café sequence in which ill-tempered waitresses sit drinking and smoking while their ignored customer looks on in bemusement. Later, two dancers sit at individual tables, applying butter and jam to huge piles of bread rolls. When several of the cast leave the stage and enter the auditorium, they offer the sweet treats to individual audience members. This type of fourth wall break becomes a recurring feature of the co-productions, where audience members are regularly offered food or drink by the performers.

In *Viktor*, Rome is evoked as a site of opulence, humour and sensuality, but at the edges of this notion lies a darker impression. As the gravedigger shovels soil onto the stage for the duration of the piece, we are reminded of sand passing through an hourglass, perhaps an ominous portent of time irrevocably passing. Death and sex form the underlying themes of the first co-production, which is permeated with characteristically black humour. *Viktor* opens with the entrance of a lone woman wearing a bright red dress (Figure 5.1). She stands centre stage, smiling at the audience. Disconcertingly, however, she appears to have no arms. Her broad grin does not falter as she stands before the audience for an extended period, while a waltz plays loudly over the speakers. Thus *Viktor* opens with another Bauschian fourth wall break, using an extended period of inaction and direct eye contact with the audience to begin the piece. As the woman gazes placidly at her audience, a man eventually enters the scene, places a coat upon her shoulders, and leads her offstage. Her vulnerability is uncomfortable to observe as she silently acknowledges the eyes of the audience upon her seemingly fragmented body (throughout the sequence, her hands are firmly clasped behind her back). Her missing arms are immediately reminiscent of the incomplete remains of classical sculpture: as an opening statement, Bausch has opted for a rather morbid animation of a static form, connecting bodily dismemberment with classical art. Fragmentation is the primary characteristic of *Viktor*, from this display of damaged bodies to its overarching disjointed structure. Kisselgoff, reviewing the piece in 1988, states:

> The disparate episodes were deliberately nonintegrated. And yet, as a visiting architect noted, the same kind of nonintegration is found in new architecture today. In 'Victor,' the parts were more important than the sum, but recurring motifs dealt very much with the way people submit to each other.[5]

As the armless woman exits, her body now hidden from view, two dancers rush into the space and fall to the ground as though they have dropped dead.

Figure 5.1 *Viktor*, Laszlo Szito

The first man returns and begins to adjust their bodies like dolls. He conducts a surreal marriage rite while they lie sprawled on the floor, and physically nods their heads for them at the crucial moment. At the end of the ceremony, he manipulates them to kiss. Once again, intimacy is presented in Bausch's *Tanztheater* as an impossible goal. The opening sequences suggest a revival of the absurdist black humour of Bausch's mature work, especially in the recurring motif of disembodiment. She identifies at once with the broken antiquities of Rome and the fragmented bodies, minds and voices of modernist theatre.

Viktor forms a bridge between Bausch's dark period and the era of co-productions that, as time progressed, would become gradually more light-hearted in tone. In this piece, however, it is difficult to escape the oppressive atmosphere conjured by the presence of the gravedigger and the bursts of tormented action that occur onstage. A woman performs a convulsive solo dance while seated in a chair. Clad in black, she frantically wraps her arms around her body, lurching forward to grind the chair towards the front of the stage. She briefly addresses the audience before a man drags her chair back, only for her to begin the solo once more. *Viktor*'s pessimism thus returns to the themes of Bausch's theatres of absurdity and cruelty. Direct address is employed to confront or plead with the audience, and attempts at tender interactions either fail or are refused outright, as when a man and a woman attempt to kiss without taking the cigarettes out of their mouths. The stage design can be read as a further development of the earth imagery I charted in Chapter 4: *Viktor* digs beneath the surface, locating its performers – and, by extension, the audience – subterraneously.

Visually and thematically, the theme of burial also recalls Beckett's *Happy Days*. In this work, Beckett literalises the sense of entrapment suggested in *Endgame* and *Godot*, burying his protagonist in sand for the duration. In the first act, Winnie is submerged to the waist but, in the second, the level of sand has risen to her neck. She refuses to acknowledge her encasement, breathlessly chattering about past events and memories while her worn husband (also buried in the sand) quietly fades away. She seeks to maintain a façade of middle-class mores, continually peppering her stories with the proclamation that 'this *is* a happy day', despite all appearances to the contrary. Michael Beausang, in this respect, has referred to her performance as 'feigned optimism'.[6] *Happy Days* depicts a dreamlike, or perhaps more appropriately, nightmarish scenario, and its surrealist imagery is strikingly reminiscent of the closing scene of Luis Buñuel and Salvador Dalí's *Un Chien Andalou* (1929). Beckett's conflation of physical entrapment with obsessively revisiting the past – Winnie steadfastly refuses to concede to her plight, choosing instead to remain ensconced in her stories – alludes to the innately constricting nature of personal history. In *Viktor*, Bausch appears to draw upon a similar metaphor: the relentless digging at the sides of the stage never permits the performers respite and threatens to trap them further in their surroundings, akin to Winnie's progressive confinement in the sand. In this similarly hostile environment, the performers simply carry on with their activities, ostensibly never noticing – or refusing to notice – the circumstances that are enclosing them. Whereas Beckett provides some sense of resolution, however (Winnie eventually dies in the sun), we leave Bausch's characters trapped inside their burial plot, the earth still ominously raining down on them, with no end in sight.

As in her absurdist productions, *Viktor* also features many surreally comic vignettes: a woman continually puts the skirt of her dress over a seated man's head; men carry women across the stage like mannequins. A mock auction of the dancers takes place, and ends abruptly when one of the men sweeps the auctioneer into a passionate embrace. Later, a woman barters her belongings in exchange for two (live) sheep. Yet even in its lighter moments, there are frequent references to death, as when an ostensibly dead man is laid out on a table like a mortuary slab before abruptly coming to life when he tries to turn off an alarm clock. Sexuality is a constant undercurrent but, as with the depiction of *Viktor*'s location, it is a murkier side of the theme that Bausch explores here, and a sense of loss and loneliness permeates the piece. Various men try to fix the straps of a dancer's dress and she remains passive, almost childlike, while they adjust her. A woman repeatedly performs handstands while a man first supports her, then inspects her thighs, and finally spanks her. A woman in a hat and sequinned dress scrubs the stage floor with a tiny cloth while a male dancer attends to a woman as though she were a horse, brushing her hair roughly and 'shoeing' her. Next to them, a male dancer cuts planks of wood with a table saw. As in the case of her dark works, it is this pessimistic sensibility that would continue to divide audiences. In her analysis of gender in Bausch's work, Goldberg has argued that:

> The women strain despite their relentless smiles; they flinch only a little after repeating the passionate onrush. These women are trapped in an oppressive Hollywood version of romance that prevents any true flights of passion. For an American audience, nihilism is the greatest foreignness in Bausch's work.[7]

The vision of Rome suggested in *Viktor* conflates glamour and sexuality with acts of absurdity and cruelty. Men and women are in constant conflict throughout the piece, using one another's bodies as props. A man fills up a woman's mouth with water and washes his hands in it as she spits the water out. The sequence repeats until two men begin bathing from the stream of water she spits out. As a woman joins them in their bathing, one of the men repeatedly burns the sole of her foot with a lighter. The performers continually seek the approval of others, presenting themselves for inspection or consumption. When the female dancers stand on a row of chairs and pull their skirts up to allow a man to measure their legs, a Beckettian theme of bodily fragmentation is evoked once more. Yet the gender disparity is striking here in the women's passive offering of themselves as objects for measurement, displaying their muscular legs for analysis to their male counterpart, as well as the audience.

Numerous scenes are repeated throughout the duration of this work, several forming intertextual references to earlier pieces. The recurring theme of physical exhaustion is one such example. A woman describes her family while skipping around the stage, slowing down in evident fatigue as the repetitions continue. The motif is, by this stage in Bausch's work, immediately familiar, and almost identical to a sequence in *1980*. In that case, a female dancer runs around the perimeter of the stage fifty times while repeatedly chanting, 'I'm tired.' When she eventually collapses, a man picks her up and forces her to continue running around the stage. These recursive scenes emphasise the physical limitations of the dancers' bodies, and remind the audience of the strains they undertake in the name of entertainment. *Viktor* similarly references the invocation of balletic authoritarianism that persists throughout her dark works: a seated woman wrapped in a fur coat affects a bored manner while calling out ballet steps to another female dancer. The irrationality of the situation is emphasised both by her disaffected tone, and by the fact her 'student' obediently performs pliés and tendus while wearing an evening dress and high heels. As she attempts to extend her leg into arabesque, a male dancer pokes and prods her body, before strapping her into the cords hanging from the side of the stage. Physicality is woven into the striking visual material of Bausch's *Viktor*, not least in its oft-cited sequence in which several women clad in flowing ball gowns swing suspended from gymnastic rings. As The Way You Look Tonight plays over the sound system, the women smile benignly at their audience, their faces never betraying the physical effort required for this scene and its use of men's gymnastic equipment. It is a reversal of the *Kalbfleisch* episode, where bodily suffering is played out in an overly exaggerated manner.

The undercurrents of cruelty that run through the first co-production are also implicitly referenced in its ambiguous title. In the first act, a disembodied female voice announces, 'My name is Viktor, I'm back.' The juxtaposition of gender recalls Bausch's first work for the company, *Fritz*, and, as in the case of *Renate*, the titular character never physically materialises. However, it is Mulrooney's analysis of the piece, based upon research conducted during company rehearsals, that has unearthed the title's unexpected origins in the music collection of one of the company's dancers. Her notes read: '"VIKTOR": anonymous fascist march, cassette brought by dancer Urs Kaufmann. "Not one I would have in my collection" (musical collaborator Mathias Burkert).'[8] That the march would be selected for inclusion in the accompanying score is not surprising, but that it would form the title of the work itself is striking. This subtle invocation of the fascist past illustrates further parallels with Bausch's dark productions, such as *Gebirge*: in the transition towards the co-production model, vestiges of recent history still find their way into the fabric of her work.

Viktor ends with a recapitulation of its opening motifs. This is a recurring tendency in Bausch's work, in which linear narrative is replaced with a cyclical structure, and beginnings and endings are gradually merged together. In the context of *Viktor* specifically, with its emphasis on the passage of time and the gravedigger hovering overhead, there is a suggestion of the pointlessness of its mundane rituals and petty squabbles. As in characteristic of Bausch's mature *Tanztheater*, it is an unsettling and unresolved piece that re-examines many existing tropes in her *oeuvre*: sex, death and surrealism. Despite recurring instances of black humour, *Viktor* strikes a macabre note by de-romanticising its location, and situating its interpretation of Rome within a mass grave. Barbara Confino, reviewing the work after its US premiere in 1988, stated: 'Here, even more than in her formal and technical aspects, Pina Bausch is the quintessential German expressionist, dark, brooding, uncompromising: someone for whom nothing escapes the taint of universal despair.'[9] This piece marks an important transition between two distinct phases in Bausch's *oeuvre*. As the first co-production, it heralds the beginning of a new working method that would lead Bausch away from the 'Teutonic darkness' critics found so challenging in her mature period. At the same time, its form and content share many commonalities with the sombre themes of this preceding era. *Viktor*, like Bausch's *oeuvre* more broadly, sits somewhere in the margins.

CIRCUMVENTING ORIENTALISM? THE CO-PRODUCTION MODEL

The theme of itinerancy is not confined to this period of Bausch's *oeuvre*. In fact, *Walzer* was the first to play with the theme of travel and nomadism (and arguably constitutes the first co-production, as the piece was made in conjunction with the 1982 Holland Festival). Similarly, *Bandoneon* was devised as a direct result of global touring, emerging from the aftermath of the company's 1980 tour of South America.[10] Yet, where *Walzer* took place in the liminal zone of international travel, and *Bandoneon* played out inside an old-fashioned dance hall to the accompaniment of Latin rhythms, neither piece explicitly drew upon the cultural associations of these locations. Instead, both invited audiences to look beyond theatrical artifice and presented unmasked stage settings.

Bausch's co-productions represent a further evolution of her working method, charting a progression from the theatres of absurdity and cruelty that dominated her mature period towards an increasingly light-hearted outlook. Judging by the considerable increase in favourable reviews, one might ascertain that this shift in register is at least partly responsible for her work reaching more diverse audiences. Certain themes remain a constant throughout her *oeuvre*, such as sexuality and the search for intimacy, recursion and childish games. However, the co-productions integrate oblique and dreamlike ciphers of their individual locations into the cyclical framework of each piece. They respond to the research environments through indirect means, just as the *Stichworte* questions allow Bausch and her dancers to explore human quirks and frailties through subtle or obscure theatrical imagery.

The early co-productions are among the most ambiguous in terms of the relationship with their city of origin. Initially, these partnerships were exclusively European, with *Nur Du* (*Only You*, 1996) representing the company's first transatlantic venture. The early years of the co-production model also demonstrate clear thematic parallels with the dark period of Bausch's mature *oeuvre*. *Viktor* was followed by *Palermo Palermo* (1989), another Italian collaboration based on a residency in Sicily. Taken together, these works bridge the period between Bausch's dark period and her later work, standing in marked contrast to the international, intercultural pieces in which Bausch's dancers revel in more joyful aspects of human existence. *Palermo*, for example, opens with the collapse of an immense brick wall that fills the stage space. Throughout the action that follows, the dancers gingerly pick their way through the rubble of this theatrical wasteland. Only a few weeks prior to its premiere, the Berlin Wall was brought down, signalling a new era in European history. The opening motif of Bausch's piece thus accrued an eerily prescient yet unintentional symbolism – the set design had been devised well before the events of 9 November, and was purely coincidental.

Following the success of the *Viktor* experiment, Bausch accepted propositions for subsequent co-productions across a wide range of locations. She continued to create her work through the *Stichworte* method, but the company transformed into a fundamentally nomadic one. Bausch took her international troupe of dancers from Spain (*Tanzabend II*, 1991) and the United States (*Nur Du*) to the Far East (*Der Fensterputzer* [*The Window Cleaner*, 1997]), making new choreographic works across continents and touring more widely. Bausch's co-productions reveal a deeply embedded fascination with other cultures and the possibilities they afford creative expression. This migratory approach resonates with a lengthy continuity of intercultural exchange in performance, reflecting patterns of movement that have increased exponentially from the twentieth into the twenty-first century.

The enduring legacy of foreign inspiration on the evolution of modernist performance – what we might term the Orientalist 'Other', following Edward Said's framing – is evident across disciplines, with visual artists, dancers, theatre-makers and writers mining non-Western sources of inspiration throughout the twentieth century. Olga Taxidou has argued that Far Eastern theatre traditions helped to shape the development of modernist theatre in the West, and that these cross-cultural dialogues remain 'central to the whole process of redefinition and retheatricalisation of the theatre'.[11] The influence of the exotic Other casts a lengthy shadow across the radical developments in modernist literature and drama: William Butler Yeats was introduced to Noh theatre by Ezra Pound and Ernest Fenellosa, writing two plays – *At the Hawk's Well* (1917) and *The Death of Cuchlain* (1939) – that were inspired by his study of the minimalist form. Brecht also looked to this archaic Japanese form in creating his *Lehrstücke* works: *Der Jasager* (*The Yes-Sayer*, 1930) was almost a direct translation of the Noh play *Taniko*, and his use of masks in *Der Kaukasische Kreidekreis* (*The Caucasian Chalk Circle*, 1944) mirrored Noh masking technique (Noh masks are designed to reveal part of the actor's face, thus breaking the illusion of the actor having been subsumed into his character, and serving as a reminder to the audience that they are watching a work of fiction).[12] Meanwhile, Kiebuzinska identifies Helene Weigel's 'silent scream' in *Mutter Courage und ihre Kinder* (*Mother Courage and her Children*, 1939) as a Western borrowing of Kabuki *mie*, poses designed to halt the onstage action temporarily.[13] Following in Brecht's wake, Grotowski maintained a deep interest in non-Western dramatic practice, including Indian and Japanese performance, and Artaud was heavily influenced by Balinese theatre, which forms the subject of several essays in *The Theatre and its Double*. Orientalist appropriation can equally be discerned throughout the different strands of early modern dance, from Laban and Wigman's ritualistic events to Ruth St Denis and Isadora Duncan's highly exotic choreographies. Wigman's experiences at the Zurich Dada venues introduced her to the creative potential of masked dances. However, where Marcel Janco's grotesque distortions of elongated, animalistic faces were inspired by an Africanist conception of the primitive form, Wigman developed a specific interest in the use of Noh masks. Her adoption of the mask similarly sought to alienate the audience from the performer, creating a barrier of obvious artifice that would disrupt the fourth wall.

Non-Western theatre is central to the evolution of modernist performance practice, emerging from a problematic but fashionable association with 'primitive' cultures uncorrupted by commercialism and the ills of modern society. This common thread of influence represents a facet of the modernist legacy in visual culture, a unique intercultural exchange of aesthetic principles that has ultimately led to the development of some of the most innovative performance methods of the twentieth century. Said's *Orientalism* asserts that the Orient of Western thought and language is an artificial construction, and argues that these inaccurate, romanticised versions of the Orient – what he terms 'latent Orientalism' – are, in fact, harmful rather than innocuous tropes. Said states: 'The Orient is not only adjacent to Europe; it is also . . . one of its deepest and most recurring images of the Other.'[14] The Other has both stereotypical positive and negative attributes: it is both the exoticised (and indeed, frequently sexualised) Orient of literature and the imagination, and at the same time a mysterious and potentially threatening force.

Said posits that the Oriental world is inevitably read as inferior to the West, in need of education and general 'improvement' by the superior worldview.[15] Maintaining a distinction between the Western and Eastern worlds has been an important facet in upholding this illusion of superiority; that is, underlining the otherness of the Other indicates a necessity for translation, for 'bettering' the unrecognised. One particular key term of distinction between the Western and Orientalised worlds is 'rationalism'. This extends into the realm of 'primitivism', an assumption that Western, educated, or 'First-World' philosophy is dominated by rational thought, whereas the Oriental world is inherently irrational, by implication backwards, primitive in both nature and attitude. Thus, inspiration drawn from the primitive or Orientalist 'Other' stands for a desire to purify aesthetics, to strip them of traditionalist Western readings and look into a new and exotic trajectory. Carlo Severini posits that the concept itself is something that informs 'a morphology of cultural exchange'.[16]

In considering the emergence of Bausch's migratory co-production model, the question arises whether her own cultural explorations might constitute a contemporary embodiment of this lengthy history of Orientalist borrowings. Earlier Western interpretations of Eastern art forms are unfortunately tainted by the colonialist fascination with the Saidian Other and its attempts to 'contain' and 'refine' the practices of primitive cultures in order to serve the needs of a Western audience. Yet Bausch does not attempt to rationalise the Other in her creative wanderings, and Mulrooney states quite clearly that Bausch 'does not colonise the cities'.[17] Rather, in this era, I propose that Bausch approaches a form of universal theatre, seeking a movement vocabulary with the capacity to translate across cultures. Where an Orientalist approach constitutes an Othering, estranging practice that suggests an essential distance between spectator and performer, Bausch's co-production model largely absolves her of this accusation due to its explicitly collaborative nature.

Interculturalism is a recurring concern of much postmodern theatre practice, though the term has undergone various redefinitions since its introduction in the field of performance studies by Richard Schechner.[18] A significant proportion of scholarly analysis focuses on the work of Peter Brook, and the problematic relationship between interculturalism and cultural appropriation. Brook is also regularly cited as an important precursor to Bausch's own migratory practice. Like Bausch, Brook moved away from naturalistic theatre in the late 1960s as a result of a growing fascination with ritual. Early works such as *King Lear* (1962) hint at a Beckettian influence in terms of its minimalism and absurdity. However, heavily influenced by Artaud's Theatre of Cruelty and Grotowski's poor theatre, Brook's most enduring contribution to theatrical theory lies in his notion of empty space, in which 'any bare space' can be transformed into an active stage.[19] Like Grotowski's idea of 'via negativa', what Brook terms 'pruning away' enables the transformation of the stage space. Works such as *La Tragédie de Carmen* (1981) demonstrate this pared-back approach, reducing the complexity of Bizet's opera to a cast of four and reframing the text to include spoken word as well as song (despite often being framed as a beneficiary of Brook's innovations, Bausch's Macbeth Project seems to anticipate the structure and format of this adaptation). Most significantly, however, Brook's notion of blankness also enables the director to strip cultural associations, ciphers and stereotypes from the action itself, allowing them to work, interculturally, in a vacuum.

Since establishing the International Centre for Theatre Research (CIRT) in Paris in 1971 with Micheline Rozan, Brook's subsequent experimentations have attempted to create a universal theatrical language in conjunction with an international assemblage of performers. This territory is, of course, fraught, as much 'universal' theatre experimentation occurs on Western stages and is framed by Western directors. For example, Brook's ambitious *Mahabharata* (1985) synthesised his theories around intercultural theatre practice, utilising this conception of empty space to permit the required shifts of location to fantastical and terrestrial realms integral to the narrative. Critics were deeply polarised, however, with Una Chaudhuri asking, 'Is this kind of interculturalism a sophisticated disguise for another installment of Orientalism or worse, of cultural rape?'[20]

Parallels can be certainly identified between Brook's working practice and that of Bausch: Mulrooney draws on this connection, observing that 'Brook and Bausch broke away from Orientalist Western theatre where the "other", the "Orient" remains firmly "other", firmly "Oriental", camouflaged behind an alienating clamour of babbling clichés'.[21] Yet despite formal similarities between their respective theatres, Bausch's co-production model functions quite differently to Brook's intercultural method. Their respective *oeuvres* are thematically quite distinct, not least because Bausch abandons the notion of theatrical adaptation after the Macbeth Project. What particularly distinguishes Bausch from Brook's more controversial approach is the collaborative, democratic process afforded by the *Stichworte* method. Her pieces are the result of a collective creative effort, made in conjunction with the dancers of her diverse company (thoroughly international from its conception in the 1970s onwards). The co-productions function as a three-way collaboration, a partnership shared by Bausch, her company and the chosen location. The *Stichworte* method is itself meandering and unfixed, relying upon a patchwork of simple prompts, questions and observations. It also functions as a collaborative approach that works especially effectively in such a diverse co-operative as Tanztheater Wuppertal. The *Stichworte* system aids in transcending the inevitable language barriers that can inhibit the development stage of a new work, and enables the dancers to work in a deeper somatic method, where movement can be understood on a level beyond language. Bauschian prompts, whether individual words or short questions, are played with, and worked on, by her dancers, and subsequently refashioned into their 'final', yet multifarious, forms. These, in turn, engender interpretations as varied as the company itself. This approach is indicative of Bausch's refusal to give instructions on how to read her works: privileging multiplicity over singularity enables interpretations to migrate as freely as her ensemble does.

This is not to suggest that the co-production model is entirely unproblematic, of course. Creating artwork that purports to draw upon aspects of an unfamiliar culture has a lengthy and complex history. At the same time, intercultural theatre practice is a product of the rapidly changing changing global landscape, and in particular, the relentless growth of cities.[22] Globalisation is inextricably linked to the development of intercultural theatre and the increasingly universal manifestations of culture. In this peripatetic period, Bausch reduces her use of estranging devices in favour of pursuing a more inclusive and interpretable dance theatre. Her co-productions are designed to translate across cultures rather than merely appropriating elements of their exotic Otherness. Accordingly, her work forms an imagistic response to the locations rather than constituting an attempt to inhabit or creatively colonise the space.

FINDING A UNIVERSAL LANGUAGE: *MASURCA FOGO*

As her method evolved through these collaborative productions, the content of Bausch's work began to shift from the almost relentless darkness of the mid-1980s to a more serene approach. Beginning in the early 1990s, we can discern distinct changes in the form and content of her *Tanztheater*, signalling a celebration of the range of cultures encompassed by her company and experienced during their extensive touring. At the same time, the prevalence of choreography within these works suggests a renewed appreciation of the possibilities of pure dance. While frustrated desire and absurd humour still form recurring themes, the cruelty of her previous work gradually lessens through the development of the co-production model. In this analysis of one of Bausch's 'mid-period' co-productions, I wish to highlight the resulting transformation of her *Tanztheater* practice through the evolution of recurring themes such as quotidian activity, interpersonal relationships, direct address and set design.

Bausch premiered *Masurca Fogo* (*Fiery Mazurka*) in 1998 in conjunction with the Lisbon World Exposition. Its setting is minimalist, consisting of a large rock formation at the back of an otherwise bare, white expanse. The stage narrows towards this dark, volcanic landmass, creating a false sense of perspective. In this respect, *Masurca* amalgamates the austere blankness of *Two Cigarettes* with the incongruity of monumental (and artificial) markers of the natural world, as seen in floral works such as *Nelken* and *Der*

Fensterputzer, or the towering cacti of *Ahnen* (*Ancestors*, 1987). In this later phase of Bausch's *Tanztheater*, Pabst's complex stage design also moves in a new direction, stripping away elaborate, organic settings in favour of singular statement props (such as *Masurca*'s rock formation, or the whale's tail fin in the 2004 Japan co-production). In *Masurca*, the blankness of the stage canvas also shows a commonality with Brook's notion of empty space, as the setting undergoes multiple configurations over the duration of the piece. Where the large-scale organic works such as the earth and water pieces are ultimately 'fixed' in their construction (the stage design cannot be altered during the performance), in the era of the co-productions, Bausch and Pabst begin to consider stage design as a mutative entity.

Masurca opens with a male dancer performing a frantic solo that is identifiably Bauschian in its freely undulating use of the arms and upper body – this routine will constitute the first recurring motif of the piece. He flees the stage and the booming music fades to k. d. lang's Hain't it Funny, while a woman wearing a flowing floral dress sighs heavily into a microphone. As she does so, a group of men enter the stage and lie down in a row. She climbs onto their waiting arms and they pass her overhead while she continues gasping into the microphone, the sound now significantly amplified (Figure 5.2). The tone is unmistakably sexual, her groans increasingly orgasmic as she is passed from man to man, and lang's lyrics augment the charged undercurrent of this scene.

The woman is handed around like an object, the physical exchanges

Figure 5.2 *Masurca Fogo*, Laszlo Szito

reminiscent of trust-building exercises as the men pass her body weight to one another. The tension of this sequence builds when she climbs onto a man's shoulders and pitches forward into the arms of the rest of the group. There is, it would appear, quite genuine risk involved here, in a manner similar to the stunt men of *Nelken* throwing themselves off the scaffold – the audience watches her fall from a significant height before being caught close to the stage floor. Periodically gasping into the microphone throughout, she drifts from one man to the next somnambulistically. She then lowers herself onto a chair, which one of the men picks up and spins her around at considerable speed. Her orgasmic gasps change to hysterical screaming here, and, in the intertextual world of Bausch's *Tanztheater*, the encounter recalls the women of *Blaubart* being swung wildly around the stage encased in white sheets.

Sexuality is the fundamental theme, but rather than evoking a battle between the sexes, *Masurca* demonstrates passages of tenderness, pleasure and, for once, instances of actual connection. A man enters the stage wearing a floor-length strapless dress and solemnly arranges women into pairs of dance partners. Another attempts to charm various women in the audience with effusive compliments, only for one of his female colleagues to kick his hat off his head. A group of women return to the stage wearing brightly coloured swimming costumes and splay themselves on the rock formation at the back of the stage, 'sunbathing' in the white cube that forms the stage design. The dancers alternately luxuriate in this theme of sensuality or use it as fertile comic material: a woman comes to the front of the stage, eager to tell the audience of her grandmother's ability to attract male attention, which she illustrates by acting out the scene repeatedly with the bemused men on stage. *Masurca* is an exploration of sexuality, romance and nostalgia that, rather than reiterating patterns of failed intimacy or missed connections, depicts a more plausible impression of the joys and tribulations between lovers.

Accordingly, instances of failed intimacy counteract scenes of romantic bliss. A couple slow dance while the male partner reads a paperback novel over the woman's shoulder. Later, when the sequence is repeated, the distracting element is a television set, which serves to engross both partners. Another couple mime an argument, during which the woman continually turns to the audience with a sly smile. Each time, her partner grabs her face to turn her attention back on him. While estrangement is implied in these sequences, the cruelty and suggestion of violence seen in previous work is largely absent, though flashes of Bausch's darker work do arise. A man attacks a red dress with a pair of scissors, then attempts to throw himself from a chair, and burn himself with a lighter. A woman enters the stage clad only in underwear, a pair of high heels, nipple tassels, and strategically placed balloons. She regales the audience with a story about a cruel teacher while the men of the company gather around her. She obligingly lights their cigarettes, which they use to burst her balloons, leaving her shrieking and attempting to cover herself. Later, a man forces the same woman to dunk for apples, holding her by the hair and forcing her head into the water, pinning her arms back. Still, these are rare instances of cruelty in a piece that otherwise appears to revel in the possibilities of romance.

Indeed, the mood of *Masurca* is considerably more playful than that of preceding works: Servos has called the piece 'a generous homage to life', while Climenhaga has described it as 'buoyantly gleeful'.[23] The everyday is evoked here through costume, choreography and thematic content, but with less cynicism than is usually seen on Bausch's stage. Many scenes revolve around motifs of socialising, eating and drinking. The movement vocabulary is comprised of flirtatious gestures, and moments of competitive behaviour and nonsensical exchanges run through the piece. Reviewing the piece in 2001, Kisselgoff stated that, 'this absurdity is rooted in reality: the key to a Bausch work is the familiar made strange'.[24] In fact, in the work of this period, the reverse is true, as Bauschian estrangement gives way to familiarity. The women are clad in colourful floral dresses rather than the satin eveningwear of most previous productions, lending a more casual air to the proceedings. Water forms a central motif: a woman washes her long hair in a bucket, and a group of dancers construct a water slide from a sheet of plastic at the back of the stage, sliding down it joyfully, acting like children. A woman is even wheeled onstage in a bubble bath, where she is revealed to be washing dishes. Later, a man attempts to teach several of the women how to swim on top of the rocky outcrop, though his instructions become increasingly surreal as he insists they act like mermaids. Indeed, comic scenes often veer into absurd territory, as when a woman enters the stage carrying a live chicken. Stroking the bird to keep it calm, she feeds it the remains of a smashed watermelon on the floor. The artificial creatures of Bausch's earlier works – *Arien*'s hippopotamus, *Ahnen*'s walrus, the plastic deer of *1980* – gradually transform into living animals, with dogs featuring most frequently (*Nelken*, *Palermo*, *Two Cigarettes*). Their brief appearances are always a surprise for the audience, such is the incongruity of seeing live animals on a theatrical stage, and especially within Bausch's otherworldly environments. Their tangibility is abruptly juxtaposed with the artificiality of her *Tanztheater* landscapes.

Direct address features once more, though in this case, spoken word is less frequently invoked, and movement often takes precedence over language. When the dancers do speak to the audience, they occasionally climb down from the stage to interact with individual spectators more intimately, with some going so far as to sit on audience members' laps. A woman introduces herself to people seated in the front row, asking each one, 'Where do you come from?' One significant instance of a fourth wall break sees a male member of the company tell an account of his childhood in Venezuela. In this era, Bausch increasingly gives voice to her international cast and permits a more intimate connection between performer and spectator. The dancers tell stories from their childhoods, talk about their home countries, or teach the audience words in their native tongue. In this respect, the shift that takes place in the era of the co-productions is not solely the result of the company's increasingly itinerant status, but a new level of self-awareness in relation to the international cast of performers. While the *Stichworte* method has always involved the creative input of the dancers, it is in this new phase of Bausch's work that the director herself becomes less visible, allowing her company members to present themselves as individuals to their global audiences. Themes that are already universally recognisable, such as the quest for intimacy, are afforded a new depth when the audience can identify, and identify with, company members rather than fictional characters.

In *Masurca*, the Venezuelan monologue is indicative of the other underlying theme of the work, namely its depiction of Latin culture. Portuguese fado music plays at regular intervals, and the volcanic ridge at the back of the stage is suggestive of a coastline, a transformation enabled by the recurring soundtrack of crashing waves. When asked to explain the thematic content of this piece, dancer Michael Whaites replied that, 'it reflects Lisbon's seafaring past, its adventurers and explorers'.[25] Another interpretation of this statement might suggest the piece is an exploration of the country's colonial heritage and, indeed, references are made throughout to Portugal's former territories: even the title is a reference to a popular dance style in Cape Verde. Brazilian salsa and traditional Cape Verdean music form part of the collagist soundtrack. During the interval, a film is projected onto the white cube stage showing footage of a 1996 Cape Verde ballroom dancing competition. In the second act, the dancers construct a shaky wooden shack onstage and pile inside to dance wildly to samba music. The image is immediately reminiscent of a Brazilian favela, artificially constructed in front of the audience's very eyes inside the tight space of Pabst's set.

A malleable definition of 'Lisbon' is explored in this work, where Portugal is hybridised with aspects of Brazilian and Cape Verdean culture. This loose categorisation of Latin culture coalesces with the underlying theme of sexuality, and the characters that emerge from *Masurca*'s landscape are depicted as elegantly corporeal and passionate, even during the occasional frenzied argument: Kisselgoff has suggested that *Masurca* represents a particularly northern European vision of 'Latin sensuality'.[26] This framing marks another sharp change of direction from preceding co-productions such as *Viktor* and *Palermo*, both of which depicted Italy through images of brutality, destruction and decay amidst a sense of waning glamour. The racial diversity of her company is also explored more overtly here: in one sequence, a white dancer with thick, curly hair uses her hands to fluff it up to full-sized proportions. As she proudly presents herself to the audience, Regina Advento (a black Brazilian dancer who joined the company in 1993) glides across the stage, her own hair now backcombed into an impressive Afro. Later, Advento addresses the audience directly in order to teach them words for different parts of the body in Portuguese, a sequence that demonstrates the embodiment of cultural identity.

In Bausch's *Tanztheater*, culture and identity are fluid concepts, and this becomes a defining feature of the co-production period. There is no suggestion of a singular experience or a unique cultural identity: rather, *Masurca* illustrates what will become a common feature of the co-productions, centring on the cross-cultural miscellany of experience. The indefinite nature of cultural identity in Bausch's work is a further reflection of its inherent liminality: at (and on) every stage, her dance theatre resists classification. In the era of the international co-productions, its shape-shifting form emerges from a territory reminiscent of Homi Bhabha's Third Space – that is, in refusing to evoke a direct impression of an individual location, these works exist in the interstices between cultures. Bhabha proposes that hybridity emerges from a similarly liminal zone, and that 'the process ... gives rise to something different, something new and unrecognizable, a new area of negotiation of meaning and representation'.[27] It is the undefined and indefinite nature of Bausch's hybridic work that allows a new form to emerge. Parallels may also be identified in the company's increasingly nomadic status: Tanztheater Wuppertal is a diverse collective of international artists that, in this era, spends a significant proportion of time in the process of travelling, taking up temporary residency in constantly changing locations. Wuppertal becomes a home for the multinational ensemble, as, each time, the entire company return to the city to construct and, in most cases, premiere the works resulting from the new method. Yet where Bhabha's liminal zone represents a site of potential conflict – Jenni Ramone suggests that the 'tension' aroused through Bhabha's model is necessary 'to create a crisis for systems of authority which depend upon their ability to ascribe a kind of sense to colonialism' – Bausch's *Tanztheater* is not overtly politicised.[28] The hybridity suggested by her co-production serves the same purpose as her ritualised depiction of everyday behaviour and routines. Her dance theatre seeks to evoke an oneiric impression of universal experience, allowing audiences across an array of cultural, social and educational backgrounds to construct their own individual reading of, and identification with, the resulting work.

Masurca reaches its conclusion through now-established patterns of repetition and mirroring. The musical accompaniment is gradually drowned out by the sound of the sea as a projection of crashing waves fills the stage walls. The opening sequence is reiterated, with the lone woman sighing heavily into the microphone. By this stage in Bausch's *oeuvre*, circularity has become a choreographic constant, providing the audience with a set of signifiers to understand the work has reached its conclusion, rather than providing a resolved narrative. In pairs, the cast dance a shuffling step seen earlier in the performance, then lie down on the stage while embracing one another. The sound of waves increases in volume as the lights dim, and projections of flowers fill the stage walls. The inference of sexuality is at its most explicit in this final scene, with the stage awash with nuzzling couples and magnified, time-lapse imagery of brightly coloured flowers lubriciously opening their petals.

Film is used to much stronger effect than in previous works and becomes an integral facet of the production. The use of digital technology as an aspect of set design also emerges as a defining feature of the co-production era. Where film is originally used to create a distancing effect, such as the screenings in *Kontakthof* and *Walzer*, it serves an entirely different purpose in *Masurca*. Bausch's use of 'empty space' allows the innovative use of film projection to continually transform the stage, conjuring an array of locations within the course of a single piece, and drawing the audience into a series of other realms. This new mutability in design reflects the increasingly itinerant nature of the company itself: just as the company can pack their belongings and enact these productions on stages the world over, so too can the stage be condensed and transported through the medium of film. The transformative potential of filmic projection also enhances the sense of audience immersion in these works, as the spectator's imaginative effort is significantly reduced. In the case of the organic pieces, the set design remains static and encases the performers within a specific environment. Their actions are juxtaposed with the stage setting, as in the case of *1980*'s talent contest, *Arien*'s dinner party and *Viktor*'s café scenes. Incongruity dominates these works, and the audience is constantly reminded of theatrical artifice. The increasingly bare stages of the co-production phase are readily transformed, encouraging the audience to willingly suspend disbelief and join the dancers on their transcultural voyages. In *Masurca*, the accompanying soundtrack undergoes a similar transition, with recordings of waves blending into the non-diegetic musical collage. Sound and film are used together to transform the meaning and location of the stage space, transporting the audience to different locations just as the cast attempt to do with their construction of the favela party shack. Babak Ebrahimian frames this new approach to set design as both 'textural' and 'surreal'.[29] Bausch and Pabst's layered approach to stage design thus seeks to evoke the exoticism of the cultural reference points through innovative new processes.

Masurca is an innovative, experimental marker of Bausch's co-production period, signifying crucial changes in form and thematic content. The harshness of her mature work is softened through these pieces, and established devices such as direct address no longer stoke confrontation between viewer and performer. Though the pieces are produced through institutional collaborations – sponsorship is usually derived from a theatre, festival or cultural agency –

they do not constitute straightforward readings of individual locations. These are not theatrical tourist postcards. Instead, works such as *Masurca* occur within similarly liminal spaces to the productions of Bausch's experimental and mature stages, but are tied to individual locations through the creative process. As a result, the intangible, transient locations of onstage action reflect her company's increasingly peripatetic status and diverse composition. In an era of transience and transformation, Bausch's directorial gaze remains the primary constant.

'DANCE IS THE ONLY TRUE LANGUAGE': *ÁGUA*

The co-production model, initiated in *Viktor* and developed over the following two decades, illustrates Bausch's growing desire to formulate a universal theatrical language with her *Tanztheater*. Widespread international touring would become a new norm for the company, and Bausch's work reached more diverse audiences than at any other point in her career. With this development in working method comes a further evolution in the aesthetic of her dance theatre: throughout the period of the co-productions, Bausch increasingly reintroduces lengthier passages of recognisable dance into her work, shifting ever further from the darkness and absurdity of the mature pieces.

Bausch's later co-productions represent a more primal form of dance theatre. Repeating patterns of movement begin to replace prolonged spoken word passages, and the gradual reduction of language reflects a new outward-looking tendency in Bausch's *oeuvre*. The oppressive atmospheres and wordy narratives that alluded to European playwrights such as Brecht and Beckett are replaced with increasingly joyful and emphatically aesthetic works. In this phase, her desire to formulate a *Tanztheater* that translates across cultures is unambiguous. The emphasis lies on gesture and image, utilising a broadening movement vocabulary in place of verbal language: Mulrooney, in this respect, has called Bausch's co-productions 'deliberately orphaned by words', and this is a tendency that becomes more explicit in the later years of her career.[30]

The late co-productions exemplify key characteristics of what I have identified as the final stage of Bausch's *Tanztheater*. These works demonstrate the beginning of a return to pure dance, a facet of her early work that is nearly abandoned in the mature period. It is a reversal that begins to make sense when viewed in light of Bausch's observation that 'dance is the only true language'.[31] Graham famously made a similar proclamation when she claimed that 'dance is the hidden language of the soul, of the body'.[32] In the search to create theatrical images that can be universally understood, dance lies at the heart of Bausch's increasingly accessible and international work.

While this marks the beginning of a new era in Bausch's *oeuvre*, the prominence of visual material in her co-production model exhibits significant parallels with the working method of Robert Wilson. Their careers follow a strikingly similar trajectory, not least in their shared roots in dance practice. Wilson's formative years in New York City exposed him to the modernist dance of Graham and her celebrated student, Merce Cunningham; Roger Copeland has argued that Cunningham's influence can be discerned in Wilson's 'decentralised' set design and his 'separation of "image" and "sound track."'[33] Balanchine's neoclassical revision of ballet technique also had a strong effect on the young artist, as Wilson would later claim Balanchine was 'the first major influence' on his work.[34] Wilson established a dance company – the Byrd Hoffman School of Byrds – which included several non-professional performers, and collaborated extensively with postmodern dance artists such as Lucinda Childs and Meredith Monk. Interviewed in 1977, Wilson insisted that, 'everything I do can be seen as dance'.[35] Indeed, the body is central to Wilson's theatre, and his unique dramaturgical approach is closely related to Bausch's conception of dance theatre. Their respective works exist in the liminal zone between choreography and dramaturgy, and as individuals they also share a nomadic status. Bonnie Marranca states:

> He inhabits the cosmopolitan's kind of homelessness, the capacity to live anywhere and nowhere. The natural state of his work is translation. If the idea of the 'dispersed' describes the lives of texts, Wilson's own manner of working only stylizes this general condition of literature.[36]

Wilson's theatre emphasises the importance of aesthetics over spoken word: Marranca first labelled Wilson's work a 'theatre of images', while Stefan Brecht has similarly defined it as a 'theatre of visions'. Lehmann has classified Wilson as a 'scenographer' rather than a playwright, a term Katherine Arens indicates is in fact more closely linked to choreographic practice than traditional theatre making.[37] Lehmann identifies Wilson as a defining figure in his framing of postdramatic theatre for his multifaceted, genre-defying dramaturgical style: indeed, Wilson's theatre is a composite of sound, image and, to a lesser degree, text. Following his early experimentation in postmodern choreography, Wilson's next identifiable phase centred on the fragmentation of language, a direct result of his interest in, and interactions with, disabled children and adults. His work with Raymond Andrews, a deaf teenager, led to the creation of such renowned plays as *Deafman Glance* (1970). In this phase, recognisable language is greatly reduced in favour of arresting imagery and slow, ritualistic choreography. Pedestrian movement and everyday activity are cornerstones of his choreographic vocabulary – Lehmann credits him with creating 'a theatre of slowness'.[38]

A key commonality between Bausch and Wilson lies in the intensity of their working processes. Both favour an internalised, somatic method, requesting that the performers attempt to explore creative prompts and instructions on an almost unconscious level. Bausch often kept details of accompanying soundtracks and set design from her dancers during the development period. Wilson similarly asks his actors to separate the action of the rehearsal space from any preconceived interpretation, and devises separate visual and audio 'scores', which, David Bathrick tells us, 'are initially developed independently of each other and then brought together, but never synthesized, during rehearsal'.[39] Wilson's unconventional approach can present a challenge to actors unfamiliar with his method, something Darryl Pinckney recalls in his account of *The Forest*, a collaboration with Heiner Müller staged in Berlin in 1988:

> When the interpreter for the deaf American actor who was playing Enkidu asked for notes, Bob told him to tell him that the only motivation an actor needed was the will and intelligence not to die on stage. 'Keep it internal,' said the oppressor who made everyone stay in place until the technicians' union said they had to be allowed to go home.[40]

Like Bausch, Wilson's sets are often complex and expansive, and conventional logic and linear time are suspended in these all-encompassing environments. Rather than building new material sets for every production, many of his works utilise film projection onto the walls of the stage, with the performers situated in front of the screening. The physical presence of the performer is often dwarfed by these surroundings: Fischer-Lichte claims that these projected backdrops can have the effect of 'dissolving the actor's corporeality in the flatness of the image', and that 'the actor's body threatens to vanish entirely in the process'.[41] Lehmann too observes that: 'In Wilson's work the phenomenon has priority over the narrative, the effect of the image precedence over the individual actor, and contemplation over interpretation. Therefore, his theatre creates a time of the gaze ... Human beings turn into *gestic sculptures*.'[42] Bausch's late *Tanztheater* similarly privileges spectacle over storytelling, character development and spoken word. Like Wilson, her onstage landscapes are shifting, transient settings that, in this phase particularly, are revealed to be of equal importance as the dancers themselves. Grotowski's legacy is clear to see in both creative approaches, as neither director encourages their actors to formulate (or identify with) individual characters. This results in what Lehmann terms 'a de-hierarchization of theatrical means', where narrative, character development and even a coherent sense of physical location is suspended.[43] Lehmann claims that Wilson's actors become 'incomprehensible emblems' – surely the same theory can be applied to the multiple personalities of Bausch's dancers.

Interculturalism is a recurring motif of Wilson's nomadic *oeuvre*. His 1993 staging of *Madama Butterfly* based its movement vocabulary on the aesthetics of modern Butoh, while *I La Galigo* (2004) reinterpreted the creation myth of the Bugis people, an ethnic group of South Sulawesi – the ambitious scale of the latter work might draw comparison with Brook's controversial *Mahabharata*. In both productions, narrative is directed primarily by movement and gesture, in an effort to more easily 'translate' the material. Indeed, silence is a defining feature of Wilson's *oeuvre*: Ionesco claimed that:

> Beckett succeeded in creating a few minutes of silence on stage … while Robert Wilson was able to bring about a silence that lasted for four hours. He surpassed Beckett in this: Wilson being richer and more complex. His silence is a silence that speaks.[44]

In both Wilson's and Bausch's theatres, conventional language and choreography are excluded, just as defined markers of cultural identity are blurred around the peripheries. Audience expectation is continually confounded, narrative is fractured or non-existent and, above all, the image takes precedence. The spectator is left to interpret the content and shape their own narrative from the visual material presented on stage. Bausch's late co-productions place a renewed emphasis on visual imagery and choreography, and this aesthetic phase of her *Tanztheater* demonstrates some of the most apparent parallels with Wilson's theatre of images; indeed, Lehmann's description of Wilson's 'theatre of metamorphoses' might just as easily describe Bausch's late *Tanztheater*.[45] Finkel, for example, has stated that, 'so imaginatively, richly and confidently is Bausch able to explore this imagery that she is able to let go of her earlier methods – to become, in the process, more of a "painter" and less of a "dancer"'.[46] Equally, Confino identifies Bausch as 'a dazzling exponent of the theatre of images and the direct inheritor of the German expressionist tradition'.[47] In the final years of her career, Bausch's method exemplifies a change of direction through the use of dance chorography, featuring lengthy passages of movement for the sake of aesthetic impact.

Água (2001) is one such emphatically visual example of Bausch's late co-production model. Bausch returned to a Lusophone theme, producing the work in collaboration with the Goethe-Institut São Paolo. Critics have not always been kind to this work, which, in terms of content, is perhaps more easily classified as a 'touristic' co-production than earlier works such as *Viktor* and *Palermo*. This is compounded by the fact the company seemingly spent a total of five days researching and developing the piece on location at the end of a tour in Brazil.[48] In formal terms, however, *Água* demonstrates a significant transition in stage design and choreographic structure that heralds the beginning of a distinct phase in Bausch's work. It is another of her 'white' pieces, set in a brightly lit, expansive, blank space like that of *Two Cigarettes* and *Masurca*. The reduction of set design develops further here, as the walls are unadorned and the stage largely empty. Where its Portuguese predecessor took place within an encased cube, *Água* is played out on a semi-circular platform devoid of organic matter or any external reference points. Again, however, the bare walls enable the stage to become a *tabula rasa* for her exotic and otherworldly theatrical images. Throughout, footage of lush rainforest and Amazonian vegetation is projected onto the stage walls. The gradual transition in stage design from organic matter (both genuine and synthetic) to such two-dimensional depictions of nature suggests a reiteration of Bausch's interest in theatrical unmasking. At the same time, it functions as a new way of 'containing' the natural world: instead of filling the stage with soil, water, grass or flowers, Pabst's projections contain a multiplicity of natural environments which can change the location of the action at will. In this late phase of the co-production period, even Bausch's established signifiers translate to adopt new meanings: the prevalence of water both on stage and in the work's title suggests that *Água* can be grouped under the same elemental class that includes the Macbeth Project and *Arien*. Where water takes on loaded symbolism in these preceding works, alluding to guilt and cleansing in the case of Macbeth, for example, in *Água* its allegorical relationship is connected to bathing and playfulness.

The piece begins with a single woman entering the stage. Behind her, swaying palm trees are screened onto the stage walls. She begins to peel an orange, sucks the juice from the fruit, and eats the pulp slowly. Throughout, another dancer holds a microphone in front of her which only further exaggerates the pleasurable noises she emits throughout the process. Thus, *Água* opens with the stark reframing of an otherwise unremarkable everyday activity – eating an orange is re-presented as a source of near-orgasmic pleasure. The viewer might read this as a reference to the opening of *Masurca*, a piece with which *Água* shares multiple formal and thematic similarities. The woman goes on to describe an experience of waking up in the middle of the night with a cramp in her leg, explaining that this was in fact a joyful occurrence, as it allowed her to look at the night sky illuminated by stars. Pain is introduced not as an inevitability of romantic love, its standard correlation in Bausch's dance theatre, but as a transformative experience. Certainly, transformation is the primary recurring motif in this piece, which appears to abandon the modernist theatrical impulses that characterised her earlier work.

Scene and location changes are marked throughout by the film projections. The woman is initially joined on stage by several other dancers performing solo or duo passages of choreography, all within the tropical landscape of palm trees. As they build towards an ensemble dance, the background image changes, now depicting a group of Brazilian musicians drumming. The accompanying music, however, has not altered, and this creates a discontinuity between image, onstage action and soundtrack. The disjuncture is solved by Bausch's choreography as it quickly becomes apparent that the dancers' movements are responding to the fast-flowing hands and arms of the projected drummers. Set design, score and movement are amalgamated in an entirely unexpected manner, and the resulting visual effect is arresting. The complexity of interaction between stage design and movement indicates an extension of choreography into the wider component parts of the production. Wilson achieves a similar effect through his innovative use of lighting, which works in tandem with the movement of bodies on his stage.[49]

The absurdity and humour of preceding periods continues in *Água*, and themes of love and loss recur, as do her endless repetitions, but references to Beckett and Brecht are largely absent. Language is reduced even further in this work, a factor that is underscored by its lengthy choreographic passages. Dance dominates the opening scenes, though gradually solos and ensemble sequences give way to a second occasion of direct address. In a manner reminiscent of Bausch's mature, unmasked dance theatre, a woman enters the stage and provides the audience with a rambling explanation of why she does not want to perform her own 'turn'. She lists the activities she would rather take part in, such as sawing the legs off a table and burning them, smashing a glass, or dressing up beautifully before throwing away all her clothes. Confronted with the depths of her reluctance to perform, the progressive exaggeration of this scene elicits laughter from the audience. Yet, as Servos has observed, 'the apparent rejection of the theatre is itself a theatrical moment'.[50] The correspondence with more confrontational pieces such as *Walzer* is evident here, though in her later works, direct address is rarely provocative.

Água signals a further development in Bausch's interest in physicality and the body. Where in previous works the dancer's body is presented as a site or recipient of cruelty, in *Água*, the body is elevated for appreciation. The punishing demands of productions such as *Sacre* or *Gebirge* give way here to lengthy passages of slow movement or leisure, as in the case of a drawn-out sunbathing scene, or in the recurring motif of the Bauschian cocktail party. Interactions between men and women do not descend into patterns of brutality or suffering, and the air is permeated by a gentle sense of whimsy – her sun-worshippers even ensure they apply protective lotion, and are watched over by attentive lifeguards. The brightly coloured costumes of the dancers further reflect this newfound lightness in Bausch's approach. In one of the most visually striking sections, Advento enters the stage clad in an electrified dress comprised of light bulbs. The effect of the brightly burning bulbs is boldly reminiscent of the Japanese Gutai artist Atsuko Tanaka's 1956 work, *Electric Dress*: Bausch's reference points are amalgamated into a cross-cultural melange once more.

Glamour and aesthetic beauty are central to Bausch's late works, though this tendency is reflected in the costume design of her female dancers throughout a significant proportion of her *oeuvre*. When questioned about this characteristic motif, Bausch responded:

> They look beautiful, that's all. People don't dress up any more – me also; I don't dress up. But on stage you can dress up and I think that's a very

beautiful style. I like the way they walk; I like the way their legs look. I like colour; I like materials; I enjoy all that. It's everything we don't see outside there [she gestured to the window] – in Wuppertal, at least.[51]

Bausch thus exoticises her own dancers, while using their physicality to remind the audience of the cruelties of societal expectation. In *Água*, hair becomes a recurring motif: a woman addresses the audience to tell them about a white hair she has found, another dancer allows a man to slowly brush her hair, while a third becomes increasingly incensed by the state of her hair, which she insists is too dry. Two women perform neurotic turns as they seek out and then reject compliments from admirers onstage. The humour of Bausch's *Tanztheater* is considerably lighter in this work, where the cast formulate jokes from their insecurities (a theme that runs throughout the gamut of her *oeuvre*). Allusions to unrealistic standards of physical beauty are literalised in a comic sequence that sees the dancers playing with beach towels, their fabric imprinted with cartoonish images of rippling muscular torsos and voluptuous curves. They toy with the stereotyped image of Brazilian beach-dwellers using another internationally recognisable symbol: the language of sexuality. At the same time, the fact that this parodic scene is performed by a cast of professional dancers, their toned, muscular bodies clad in swimwear, somewhat undermines its apparent purpose.

Água is a deeply aesthetic production. The dancers are presented as exotic creatures within a continually shifting landscape, and spoken word is increasingly translated into gesture, mime and choreography. As a result of this new emphasis on the visual, a clearer link is established to its location of origin. Brazilian culture is clearly referenced throughout the piece, but is most explicitly invoked in a short capoeira sequence and the samba and bossa nova songs woven into its accompanying score. Pabst's set design accentuates the cultural connection further. His video footage brings the Brazilian landscape into the theatrical space, transporting the audience to palm groves, rainforests and, in the final scenes, waterfalls. The stage design thus constitutes a visceral tour through the Brazilian landscape, but the sheer scale of the projections and their transformative effect on the stage suggests the possibility of nature threatening to engulf civilisation. Amidst the party games and playful interactions between the dancers, the immersive force of the natural world is overwhelming and, in its grand scale, touches on the Romantic notion of the sublime. This is most evident in the closing scenes of *Água*, where the dancers engage in a water fight, but are dwarfed by projected footage of the Iguaçu Falls. The sheer scale of the waterfall enhances the sense of dramatic irony here, highlighting the insignificance of the dancers' infantile games. In this late phase of the co-production model, however, the shift from organic matter to filmed imagery has a curiously distancing effect: when the stage is fully lit and the austerity of

Figure 5.3 *Água*, Laszlo Szito

the setting revealed once more, the image of dancers sunbathing or lounging by an imaginary poolside seem far removed from their intended location. Incongruity thus features once more in the bare, almost clinical setting of Pabst's open-plan stage. Artifice, a recurring concern in the experimental and mature stages of Bausch's *oeuvre*, is reintroduced through this new form of set design.

Servos refutes the critical response that the piece is without much content or meaning, stating, 'This piece does not seek to be read as a document of classic dance theatre but as a piece of pure choreography, obeying solely the laws of contracting and expanding energie.'[52] With its lengthy passages of solo movement, *Água* signifies an important transitional point into Bausch's late dance works. Servos' observation extends also to the set design, which transforms the stage from day to night and transports the location of action from urban centre to rural jungle (Figure 5.3). Pabst's projections are constantly moving, forming a visual dialogue with the dancers throughout the duration of the piece. Accordingly, *Água* becomes a fully choreographed spectacle and, rather than representing a period of creative stagnation in Bausch's *oeuvre*, symbolises a new interest in transformation and universally comprehensible action.

In his analysis of the collaborative relationship between Wilson and Heiner Müller, Bathrick argues that both artists are linked by their desire to separate 'preordained referential meaning' from their work. He refers to the distinction between gesture and interpretation that, in the case of Wilson's work specifically, is intended to readily translate across borders and cultures.[53] Bausch's late co-productions demonstrate an important commonality with Wilson's theatre of images in their conversion of language into movement. The visual impact is reminiscent of dream imagery, not least in the sweeping set changes afforded by Pabst's film projections. Yet whereas Wilson's intercultural explorations are often shaped by direct reference points or derive from existing texts, as in the case of *I Galigo*, Bausch's co-productions are less clearly defined. Instead, her oneiric dance theatre works, devised in conjunction with and performed by a diverse cast of dancers, reject clear categorisations of identity, nationality or culture. Favouring action over spoken word, the late international pieces blur boundaries between locations, and further underline the liminality of Bausch's dance theatre more broadly.

*

In 2012, ten of Bausch's co-productions were selected for London's Cultural Olympiad. Over the course of four weeks, and at significant financial cost (£1.8 million, or $2.8 million, as reported by *The New York Times*), the company performed a feat of endurance even by the exhaustive standards set by Bausch. The works ranged from *Viktor* to her last complete piece, '. . . *como el musquito en la piedra, ay si, si, si* . . .' (*Like moss on a stone*, 2009), a Chilean collaboration, and this broad span demonstrated the striking change her work underwent in the later years of her career. As Elswit has indicated, the lack of detailed analysis of the co-productions (with the exception of Mulrooney's important study) is likely a consequence of the fact that they are rarely seen collectively, but are usually mixed with work from all periods in the company touring schedule (though she also acknowledges that this was largely due to funding availability than a desire to 'curate' Bausch's city works in isolation).[54] Nonetheless, the international collaborative works signal the formation of a distinct period in Bausch's evolving *Tanztheater* and, with it, an increasingly positive outlook.

Bausch's interest in intercultural theatre is not, it appears, politicised. She does not use her (increasingly visible) platform to make direct statements about the state of the world, to rail against inequality or protest injustice. Her hybridic, experimental co-production model is thoroughly institutionalised, with each work receiving generous funding in conjunction with international cultural organisations and enacted upon proscenium stages. There is no suggestion of artistic or anti-establishment protest embodied in these works. Instead, Bausch's intercultural period demonstrates a common aim with Wilson's experimental process, namely the desire to liberate performance from its reliance on language, using movement in place of words.

At the same time, labelling the co-productions as Bausch's 'city works' is not an entirely accurate categorisation. These pieces are not performed versions of the cities from which they derive, and rarely make explicit reference to their location. Nor do they follow in the Orientalist appropriations of predecessors such as Wigman or Graham: Sturm, for example, has claimed that Bausch had no interest in trying to imitate local or folk dances and culture. Rather, the co-production method is an investigation of the environment as experienced by the dancers themselves. The resulting pieces provide symbols and signifiers of each location, often using the city as a metaphor for a wider definition of cultural identity, and playing with the social dynamics of interpersonal interaction. Following Bausch's death, the process would be reversed with the release of Wim Wenders' feature film tribute: *Pina* (2011) helped bring her *Tanztheater* to a broader audience worldwide, and recreated scenes taken from a wide range of her works in locations across Wuppertal. Wenders' film returns the work to its point of origin, emphasising the centrality of this city in Bausch's *oeuvre*.

Bausch's *Tanztheater* has always existed in liminal zones, hovering in between established forms and creative approaches: works from *Sacre* onward occur in liminal spaces. In the phase of international co-production, cultural identity is afforded the same treatment. However, that she so unproblem-atically presents her audience with suggestions of a universal, amalgamated culture is itself problematic. By conflating cultures under this broad umbrella, co-productions such as *Masurca* are left open to sharp critique, not least in the context of a piece that makes multiple references to Portugal's colonial past. Interpreting Bausch's seemingly apolitical notion of hybridity also presents a challenge. Gabrielle Klein indicates that Bhabha's conception has 'become greatly overloaded', and indeed, it is challenging to examine Bausch's work using this particular language, as Bhabha makes clear that his theorisation of hybridity is intractably connected with issues of postcolonial power relations rather than identity politics.[55] Yet Bausch's *Tanztheater* does not consciously exoticise her encounters with the Other. Rather, the peripatetic existence and diverse makeup of her company begins to lead her away from inward-looking tendencies of her mature *oeuvre*, exemplified by darker works such as *Arien* or *Gebirge*. In so doing, Bausch's reference points move away from European modernist theatre practice, increasingly drawing upon the experiences of her thoroughly international ensemble.

Collaboration is central to Bausch's *Tanztheater*, a factor first established in her early works produced with Borzik and more fully developed in the *Stichworte* collagist method of questioning her dancers. The co-productions extend this collaborative face further, representing a reciprocal form of cultural exchange linking Bausch, her dancers and the nominated cities. Her dance theatre is symptomatic of a broader cross-cultural experience, and the resulting pieces continue to focus on interpersonal relationships and quotidian life, instead of drawing directly from existing texts, works of art or politicised debates. It is the emphasis on shared, lived experience that enables her work to be universally comprehensible. Like Wilson's 'vocabulary of gestures', Bausch's choreography approaches the concept of a danced Esperanto.[56] In moving further from the post-Brechtian estrangement of her earlier work, the co-productions are specifically designed to be read by audiences across cultures, age groups and social backgrounds. In this final phase of Bausch's *oeuvre*, dance itself becomes the key to translation.

NOTES

1. While, to date, detailed discussion of the co-production model has not been thoroughly explored in the literature on Bausch, Mulrooney's 2002 volume makes a significant contribution to the field. Based on extensive research conducted in Wuppertal, Mulrooney has charted the thematic development of what she terms Bausch's 'nomadic' practice, drawing upon Said's theorisation of Orientalism. I am indebted to her groundbreaking work on this important area, and to her generosity in our wider conversations around Bausch's *oeuvre*. More recently, Gabrielle Klein's research project ('Gestures of Dance, Dance of Gestures') takes the co-production model as its focus in exploring the 'translation' of culture through movement practice.
2. Manning, 'Pina Bausch', p. 11.
3. Elswit, 'Ten Evenings with Pina', p. 219.
4. Ibid., p. 219.
5. Kisselgoff, 'Pina Bausch Adds Humor to Her Palette'.
6. Beausang, 'Myth and Tragi-comedy in Beckett's Happy Days', p. 59.
7. Goldberg, 'Artifice and Authenticity', p. 106.
8. Mulrooney, *Orientalism, Orientation, and the Nomadic Work of Pina Bausch*, p. 60.
9. Confino, 'The Theatre of Images', in Climenhaga (ed.), *The Pina Bausch Sourcebook*, p. 48.
10. Mulrooney, *Orientalism, Orientation, and the Nomadic Work of Pina Bausch*, p. 134.
11. Taxidou, *Modernism and Performance*, p. 118.
12. Coldiron, *Trance and Transformation of the Actor in Japanese Noh and Balinese Masked Dance-Drama*, p. 129.
13. Kiebuzinska, *Revolutionaries in the Theater*, p. 32.
14. Said, *Orientalism*, p. 325.
15. Ibid., pp. 40–1.
16. Severini, 'Primitivist Empathy', p. 112.
17. Mulrooney, *Orientalism, Orientation, and the Nomadic Work of Pina Bausch*, p. 52.
18. See Schechner's keynote address at the Conference on the Indian Dance Tradition and Modern Theatre, Kala Mandir, Calcutta (January 1983).
19. Brook, *The Empty Space*, p. 11.
20. Chaudhuri, 'The Future of the Hyphen' in Marranca and Dasgupta (eds), *Interculturalism and Performance*, p. 193.
21. Mulrooney, *Orientalism, Orientation, and the Nomadic Work of Pina Bausch*, p. 46.
22. Schechner's recent writing on interculturalism reflects a further reinterpretation of the term in the contemporary context of globalisation – see *Performance Studies*, pp. 263–325.

23. Servos, *Pina Bausch*, p. 168; Climenhaga, *Pina Bausch*, p. 31.
24. Kisselgoff, 'Sun, Surf and Sexuality in a Pina Bausch Romp'.
25. Lawson, 'Pina, Queen of the Deep', in Climenhaga (ed.), *The Pina Bausch Sourcebook*, p. 223.
26. Kisselgoff, 'Sun, Surf and Sexuality in a Pina Bausch Romp'.
27. Rutherford, 'The Third Space', in *Identity*, p. 221.
28. Ramone, *Postcolonial Theories*, p. 112.
29. Ebrahimian, 'Mascura Fogo', p. 653.
30. Mulrooney, *Orientalism, Orientation, and the Nomadic Work of Pina Bausch*, p. 67.
31. Bausch, quoted in Servos, *Pina Bausch*, p. 232.
32. Graham, 'Martha Graham Reflects on her Art and a Life in Dance', in Bruckner (ed.), *The New York Times Guide to the Arts of the 20th Century*, p. 2735.
33. Copeland, *Merce Cunningham*, p. 7.
34. Wilson, quoted in Holmberg, *The Theatre of Robert Wilson*, p. 133.
35. Wilson, quoted in Lesschaeve, 'Robert Wilson', p. 224.
36. Marranca, 'The Forest as Archive', p. 38.
37. Arens, 'Robert Wilson', p. 15.
38. Lehmann, *Postdramatic Theatre*, p. 156.
39. Bathrick, 'Robert Wilson, Heiner Müller, and the Preideological', p. 67.
40. Pinckney, 'Tensions and Nostalgias', p. 151.
41. Fischer-Lichte, *The Transformative Power of Performance*, p. 85.
42. Lehmann, *Postdramatic Theatre*, p. 80.
43. Ibid., p. 79.
44. Ionesco, quoted in Holmberg, *The Theatre of Robert Wilson*, p. 52.
45. Lehmann, *Postdramatic Theatre*, p. 78.
46. Finkel, 'Gunsmoke', in Climenhaga (ed.), *The Pina Bausch Sourcebook*, p. 166.
47. Confino, 'The Theatre of Images', in Climenhaga (ed.), *The Pina Bausch Sourcebook*, p. 45.
48. Elswit, 'Ten Evenings with Pina', p. 229.
49. Holmberg, *The Theatre of Robert Wilson*, p. 142.
50. Servos, *Pina Bausch*, pp. 180–1.
51. Bausch, quoted in Brown, 'A Place Where Life Happens'.
52. Servos, *Pina Bausch*, p. 181.
53. Bathrick, 'Robert Wilson, Heiner Müller, and the Preideological', p. 65.
54. Elswit, 'Ten Evenings with Pina', p. 218.
55. Klein, 'Practices of Translating in the Work of Pina Bausch and the Tanztheater Wuppertal', in Wagenbach (ed.) *Inheriting Dance*, p. 29; Bhabha, *The Location of Culture*, p. 56.
56. Pinckney, 'Tensions and Nostalgias', p. 153.

6

'I ONLY TRIED TO SPEAK ABOUT US'

At the turn of the twenty-first century, Bausch's influence had grown considerably, and this tendency would continue in the years following her death, with originally dissenting critics writing effusive obituaries celebrating the radicalism of her creative method. The co-production model doubtless aided in widening the reach of her *Tanztheater*, its less confrontational approach enabling audiences to more readily identify with signature themes established throughout her career. In this same period, Bausch's dance theatre underwent another stylistic evolution, one that emerges from these international collaborations. The increasing visibility of choreography signifies a new phase in her work, with lengthier sections of pure dance gradually replacing verbal exchanges and monologues. Despite this evident shift in creative approach, however, the productions of Bausch's final years are rarely discussed, and critical analysis of her *oeuvre* often ends with the co-production model.

Throughout this volume, I have charted the evolution of Bausch's dance theatre by delineating and interpreting distinct phases of its form and content. In doing so, I suggest that her work ought not to be considered as a homogenous entity, but as an evolving and constantly shifting medium. Bausch's hybridity positions her on the cusp of modernism and the postdramatic, and in the liminal zone that separates dance from theatre. Over the course of four decades, her *oeuvre* draws upon a wide range of theatrical influences in evolving a palimpsestic creative methodology, but examining Bausch's work across the span of her directorship at Tanztheater Wuppertal reveals a cyclical progression in the evolution of her dance theatre. Her early works use the languages of German and American modern dance to recount familiar tales and myths of love and loss. In the experimental and mature periods that followed, dance is replaced with a theatrical language reminiscent of Beckett and Artaud, where narrative gives way to continually recurring patterns of physical behaviour. In the late works, Bausch reverts to her native tongue, with dance taking precedence over spoken word, and the cruelties of earlier works gradually replaced with a new level of optimism. Yet several writers have suggested that the emphasis on aestheticism in Bausch's late period represents a 'softening' of her approach. This is a problematic, yet persistent, reduction of what is in fact a distinct phase in the development of her approach: as Elswit has proposed, framing Bausch's late works in this manner misses the significance of their contribution to the canon.[1] My analysis of Bausch's final productions attempts to rectify this reading, challenging the notion that they are somehow 'lesser', and instead proposing that they represent a crucial new stage of creative evolution, albeit one that abruptly ends with her death.[2]

This chapter forms my final point of discussion, centring on the question of legacy. The intimate and intensive nature of Bausch's collaborative process presents unique challenges for the progression of her company, from passing on individual roles from one generation of dancers to the next, to authorising performances of entire productions with other dance companies. It is a weighty inheritance that raises difficult questions of authorship, ownership and transference.

EIN STÜCK VON PINA BAUSCH? PASSING ON THE WORK

Bausch as a performer is physically absent from almost every work in her repertoire. This is in sharp contrast to the inclinations of her predecessors: Wigman danced well into middle age and Graham into her seventies, for example, and, while Cunningham's career as a professional dancer did not last quite as long, he still found roles for himself in several of his own choreographies. In Bausch's case, however, for many years, *Café Müller* was the only production in which she continued to perform. At its premiere, the piece marked the first time she had appeared in her own work since dancing the title role in Boris Blacher's 1973 opera, *Yvonne, Prinzessin von Burgund*. In 1995, she created a small role for herself in *Danzón*, dancing on an empty stage in front of a film projection of a greatly magnified goldfish. Otherwise, Bausch's appearances on stage are more familial: in *Bandoneon*, one of the portraits lining the walls is of her own father, while in *Palermo Palermo*, her son made a cameo appearance, somersaulting across the set near the beginning of the piece.[3]

While Bausch does not often appear physically in her work, she does conspicuously materialise in print form. Each *Tanztheater* piece is usually titled with a colon, after which they are denoted as 'ein Stück von Pina Bausch'.

This might be read alternately as a Bauschian seal of approval or as an artist's signature. Yet authorship is a problematic issue in the context of her dance theatre. Despite this identification of a single 'author', Bausch's pieces are a composite of experiences, innovations and memories, many of which are drawn from the company members. Guy Delahaye, for example, has claimed that Bausch herself viewed the dancers as 'co-authors' of the works that they devised in collaborative practice.[4] The creation of these large-scale pieces necessitates a significant level of trust between choreographer and cast, and requires a demanding degree of engagement and sacrifice from the dancers. The *Stichworte* method allows Bausch to delve into their childhood memories and personal histories in order to form the building blocks of her productions, 'collecting' movements from responses to the questions and arranging them into the non-linear structure of the resulting work. Bausch thus adopts the role of a *monteur*: she becomes a collagist piecing together the efforts of the collective group and synthesising the movement into a more homogenous vocabulary. This quasi-aleatory process of questioning shapes the framework upon which each new piece is constructed. However, unlike Cunningham's choreographic experimentations, in Bausch's *Tanztheater*, chance is always tempered by choice. The dancers are posed the same questions and prompts, and respond individually while Bausch observes the entire process.

Many of her dancers have noted that, during the preliminary stages of making a new work, Bausch tended to remain expressionless, rarely inter-rupting the action of rehearsals, and almost never providing direct feedback. Speaking about her experience of working with Bausch in Wenders' film, Brazilian dancer Ruth Amarante recalled the choreographer only ever giving her one correction, telling her, 'You've just got to get crazier.' Instead of providing specific directions, the dancers are encouraged to find their own language of movement through the prompts of the *Stichworte* method. It is an open-ended, experimental approach: Raimund Hoghe states that, '[when] asked by a dancer whether a scene is meant to be with text or only with ambi-ance, she answers: "One has to try it out. I cannot tell theoretically."'[5] The developmental process leaves no room for the dancers to overanalyse their responses to Bausch's prompts, and it is imperative that they remain focused on the internal process while the work is still evolving. Mercy's description of the embryonic stage of making work emphasises its somatic nature:

> I think the most important thing is what you are doing in the moment. The period of time in which you develop something, these three months, in making a piece, that's the most important thing. You share something with each other, you live together, and what I now feel in the work with Pina is – I don't know if I can describe it – something that is becoming more and more valuable.[6]

This approach establishes a crucial distance between the choreographer and the events of each rehearsal, removing emotional responses from the equation, and allowing the dancers to formulate ideas without Bausch's direct input. It also represents a departure from traditional choreographic methodologies, as individuality is central and the dancers play a pivotal role in the creative development of a piece. The resulting work, compiled by Bausch, would not exist without the contributions of individual company members. The purpose of her process is not to produce choreography in the traditional sense, given that her *Tanztheater* productions are collages based on a framework of memory and experience. It is a time-consuming, intricate and deeply personal method, one that has a tendency to push the dancers to their physical and emotional limits. Even longstanding members of the ensemble have acknowledged that the process did not become any easier over time: Julie Shanahan, who joined the company in 1988, claimed that, 'it got more difficult because you've done so many things on stage, you've shown so much about yourself'.[7] Indeed, the unique challenges of working under Bausch are well known throughout the dance world – the renowned ballerina Sylvie Guillem infamously dismissed the idea of working for her by claiming, 'I think it's like joining a cult.'[8] Interviewed in 2010, Endicott has also suggested that the relationship between company members and their figurehead was, at times, uncomfortably co-dependent, and that it occasionally resulted in dancers leaving altogether. Many would return after a short spell away, however: Endicott claimed that, 'it was hard, that balance. There was Pina and there was real life . . . I could never quite get rid of her.'[9]

As an entity, Tanztheater Wuppertal is markedly distinct from many of its institutional peers. The structure is non-hierarchical, and company members are not ranked according to seniority or experience (as principal, soloist, corps de ballet and so on). The dancers act as collaborative partners in the creation of individual works, and take the responsibility for passing on their roles to new members. During her analysis of company rehearsals, Mulrooney observed that the dancers are not provided with scripts in the making of a new piece, but rather hand-write their own notes on their role and the corrections they receive. These transcripts are then used to pass on information about the individual role to newcomers, or during changes of cast.[10] From the 1980s onward, established company dancers have been tasked with this responsibility, a fact that further underlines the collective and collaborative effort that characterises Tanztheater Wuppertal. Endicott, Förster, Mercy and Pikon worked with Bausch from the early days of the company, and began to train new recruits relatively soon in the process. Even Bausch herself would eventually hand over her part in *Café Müller* to Pikon (the profound significance of which she discusses in Wenders' film).

Dance companies are not static, and the line-up of members tends to change frequently as a consequence of the physical exertions of the job. It is well known that the career of a professional dancer is not lengthy, especially in the world of classical ballet. Even in contemporary ensembles, the body can only endure an intense schedule of training, rehearsing and performing for so long before the dancer must step away from the stage – in the ordinary course of a company's touring schedule, roles are regularly handed down or substituted due to illness or injury, for instance. The variability inherent in the dance environment presents a particular challenge to Bausch's working method: how does one begin to restage a work created not only upon, but also in collaboration with, a specific cast? Similarly, how can a role be accurately portrayed by another dancer when its origins lie in personal memory or experience? In considering these enquiries around authorship and inheritance, it becomes clear that Bausch's dancers become not only co-authors of the work, but also rehearsal directors, and the custodians of an exclusive legacy.

In an average ballet or modern dance company, generations of dancers pass on choreography through different means. Traditionally, the duty lies with the company's roster of ballet masters, retired professionals who hold an intimate knowledge of the material and teach the steps to a new dancer through individual instruction. Dance notation, using a system such as Labanotation or Benesh Movement Notation, can provide a more accurate representation of choreography than relying on an individual's recollection of the steps, what dancers often refer to as 'muscle memory'. Notation strips away some of the subjectivity associated with this kind of pedagogy, as the movement can be recorded in a similar manner to a musical score. However, by no means are all dancers familiar with the language of dance notation, nor are all choreographies recorded in this form.

In the case of Bausch's *Tanztheater*, the hybrid language that characterises her work renders the use of dance notation all but impossible. Equally, while a theatrical script might aid in memorising lines of dialogue, the resulting productions cannot be accurately condensed into text alone. Mulrooney's written transcriptions of several co-productions provide a useful reference point for understanding the order of events in each piece, and help to give a sense of how specific roles are to be performed. Yet they do not fully convey the thematic atmosphere of the piece, and even rendering Bausch's enigmatic work on film cannot capture the nuances of her dancers' individual performances. Reprising older works and passing on individual roles can only be achieved through a combined effort, uniting the expertise of current and former dancers with less ephemeral choreographic traces, such as filmed footage and rehearsal notes. Accordingly, as the company evolves over time, the pieces must adapt in turn.[11]

The *Tanztheater* performer must offer a degree of adaptability that synthesises the approaches of a dancer and that of an actor. They must be equally capable of learning the physical steps of a role as well as embodying the inner motivation of that specific character. Several of Bausch's dancers have discussed the difficulties inherent in taking on roles devised for other members of the company, especially those pieces that derive from personal experience. Amarante states, for example, that:

> I joined in this piece [1980] long after it was completed. I mean, I'm doing someone else's role. So, in the beginning it is quite formal. You have to be in the right tempo, you have to take care not to get in people's way . . . After some time, you start relaxing and then getting the feeling: the thing starts having a life of its own.[12]

This conception of the role as a 'thing' that has 'a life of its own' bestows upon it a degree of animacy. In doing so, Amarante involuntarily extracts the part from its origins (having originally been part-created and danced by Anne Marie Benati) and transforms it into an object that can be inhabited. Referring to a scene in which Benati describes how her father would dress her as a child, Amarante explains that 'it is her history, but I take it for myself'. These two dancers shared the experience of having lost their fathers at a young age, which Amarante suggests made the role somewhat easier to adopt, though she acknowledges that this is not always the case in Bausch's *Tanztheater*, and that each piece 'works in a different way'.[13] There is a distinction between this process and substituting a role on a temporary basis (something Amarante describes later in the same interview), a common facet of life in a dance company. In these dance theatre works, the script may not necessarily change, but the dancer must adapt to embody and convincingly portray the role they have assumed.

In one of her rarely granted interviews, Bausch stated, 'my pieces grow from the inside outwards'.[14] By encapsulating her *Stichworte* method in this way, she unconsciously connects her approach to many choreographers who used similar language. Indeed, Bausch's phrasing is almost a direct quote from American modern dancer Doris Humphrey, who claimed that dance was a representation of 'moving from the inside out'.[15] Meanwhile, Graham called the soul 'an inner landscape' made visible through dance.[16] Semantically, these interpretations all refer to a transition from internalised to externalised movement, suggesting that the creative process begins somewhere within the unconscious. Thus, even when passing on a role that has been developed upon and devised in conjunction with a specific individual, there will always be underlying features of the part that a new performer can inhabit. Just as Bausch seeks to employ a universal theatrical language to translate across different audiences, her creative method is equally malleable when new generations of dancers enter the company.

There is no concrete sense of a beginning or ending to Bausch's productions. Rather, it is more appropriate to think of them as circular formations, or patterns of spirals. At their root, these are deeply subjective pieces: though there is a script upon which each piece is structured, the individual contributions of different dancers to each work marks a sharp distinction from restaging dance theatre pieces to, for instance, re-mounting a different choreography of a classical ballet. The collaborative method adds a layer of complexity to the process of archiving and reviving Bausch's works. This reflects Broadhurst's observation that Bausch's work is, in some respects, 'unresolved'.[17] She does not seek a straightforward conclusion, just as her works are not framed around a normative narrative. Instead, her process results in non-linear structures and incessant repetitions of individual gestures. It is with this complexity in mind that we return to the original notion of authorship and the question of how to reconcile *ein Stück von Pina Bausch* with this complex and collaborative approach to choreographic practice. I suggest that Bausch's artistic signature becomes a synecdoche, a part for the whole, embodying the company, the work and the collective's memories.

AGEING GRACEFULLY

Bausch's *Stichworte* working method presents numerous challenges when roles are passed on from their original cast to a new group of dancers. An added layer of difficulty arises when a work is revived from the recesses of her repertoire. The dancers must rely upon a combination of personal coaching and the use of recorded footage to restage the event. *Ahnen*, for example, was not performed for many years before being toured to London in 2015. Scott Jennings, a British dancer who joined the ensemble in 2012 (several years after Bausch's death), learned his role from former company member Mark Sieczkarek, on whom the part was originally created. Jennings explained that, in order to embody the role, it was necessary to blend his study of Sieczkarek's character with events in the dancer's own life around the time of *Ahnen*'s conception.[18] Evidently, the process of taking on an existing part in one of Bausch's productions goes beyond the practice of a character actor, requiring research not only into the role itself, but into the real-life memories and experiences of the original performer as well.

The issue of individual roles being handed down can also be extended to the fate of individual pieces. Throughout her lifetime, works created by Bausch via the *Stichworte* method were only performed by her company. Earlier choreographic pieces, however, were licensed for performance elsewhere. The Paris Opera Ballet was awarded the rights to *Orpheus* in 2005, having performed Bausch's *Sacre* since 1997. That Tanztheater Wuppertal continues to perform *Sacre* allows for direct comparison to be drawn between interpretations: viewing stagings by the Paris Opera, it is clear that Bausch's choreographed works take on a different form when performed by a classical company. Watching such emphatically classical dancers perform a work such as *Orpheus*, for example, underscores the innate musicality and intense lyricism of Bausch's early aesthetic. In these choreographed works, Bausch slackens her firm hand of authorship by allowing external companies to perform, if not fully reimagine, such pieces.

Bausch's theatrical aesthetic undergoes a process of constant evolution. In the later years of her directorship, she continued to seek new ways to renew her dramaturgical vocabulary, reflecting the shifting nature of the company itself. Physically demanding choreographies such as *Sacre* are no longer performed by older members of Tanztheater Wuppertal, for example, and casts of younger dancers have come to substitute the generation of its origins. Change is also evident in the new works produced in this period: at the dawning of the twenty-first century, the co-production model had become well established, and the sharpness of her mature period was increasingly replaced with celebratory impressions of the company's widespread touring remit. Nonetheless, it is in this late period that Bausch begins to more overtly explore the possibilities of reviving and reinterpreting older pieces. This is reflective of her deeply contemplative approach during the creative process: former dancer Barbara Kaufmann has claimed that, 'she liked to challenge herself by confronting her previous work. She was often curious to see things again.'[19]

Certainly intense criticality was an ingrained character trait in Bausch. Gabrielle Klein and Marc Wagenbach claim that she collected reviews of her own performances and choreographies from the 1950s onwards.[20] Her consistency in collating material and practice of rigorous note-keeping suggests an underlying understanding of the importance of legacy. Perhaps most importantly, she also created an unofficial living archive of each work in the bodies of her dancers.[21] In the late period, this tendency is perhaps afforded a new urgency as a result of working with a company of dancers spanning several generations. By the early 2000s, a number of new members would become embedded in the ensemble, learning existing roles and taking part in the creation of entirely new pieces.

Today, the company regularly revives and reworks older productions from its repertoire. For the fortieth anniversary of Tanztheater Wuppertal in the 2013–14 season, works such as *Renate* were performed for the first time in decades. Pieces brought out of obscurity will inevitably change over time. Each time one is performed, subtle changes occur, but as the gaps between stagings grow longer, the connection to its original script becomes less distinct. As the pieces have been devised through the collaborative method, restaging older works in Bausch's *Tanztheater* catalogue can be challenging. Choreographies such as *Sacre* and *Café Müller* are included in almost every touring season, and these regularly reprised examples remain essentially unaltered. Even so, the work sees changes emerge over time, and with each new cast member taken on, the effect alters further. This is reflected in Joshua Abrams description of watching *Café Müller* decades after its inception, in which he states that:

Thirty years after it was first created the piece carries not simply itself; it bears with it all of Bausch's history, as well as the field that she has created. She has redefined dance and produced an audience for much contemporary boundary-shifting work. We remember her remembering in a piece that may be less shocking than it once was, but is now more powerful for its own historical continuity.[22]

This notion of 'historical continuity' similarly recurs with each revival of Bausch's once-shocking, and now canonical, mature works. While experimental pieces such as *Blaubart* and the Macbeth Project have not been staged in many years, productions such as *1980*, *Nelken* and *Viktor* regularly tour internationally. Even as roles are passed to a new generation of performers, these frequently toured works are less susceptible to change.

In 2000, *Kontakthof*, one of Bausch's most successful productions, was staged for the first time by an entirely new cast. Bausch had expressed a desire to see the work performed by a group of people with greater 'life experience'.[23] Accordingly, auditions were held for Wuppertal locals over the age of 65, and a cast of non-dancers were assembled and taught the 'script' to perform, initially, as a one-off production. The result was so successful that the new version of *Kontakthof* would tour internationally and be recorded for the public domain. Eight years later, Bausch handed over the artistic directorship of this piece to Benedicte Billet and Endicott for a further restaging, this time mounting a production for a cast of local teenagers (the process was lovingly documented in Rainer Hoffmann's 2010 film, *Dancing Dreams*).

Kontakthof is one of Bausch's signature works, and an especially significant piece in the evolution of her individual vision of dance theatre. It marks the beginning of a defined period in which her experimental technique is effectively codified and, as a result, her reputation as an avant-garde innovator firmly established. The restaging also takes place at a point in time where she has moved into a markedly different aesthetic: contemporaneous pieces draw more upon the concept of a Wilsonian theatre of images than the Beckettian, estranging productions of *Kontakthof*'s era. The revisitations of *Kontakthof* can be interpreted as experiments in recreating Bausch's artistic vision without her direct involvement. Such restagings are pivotal given that they represent the first time she hands over the directorial reins, and involve the performative contributions of non-professionals. Such decisions are indicative of Bausch beginning to expand her artistic horizons and move in a new direction in this late period. We can see not only an expansion in terms of reach by moving away from the co-production model, but also a return to an earlier mode of production where she transitions from highly experimental and theatrical processes to more dance-focused methods.

The cast members in these versions, however, are not part of the *Stichworte*

Figure 6.1 *Kontakthof (Mit Damen und Herren ab 65)*, Laszlo Szito

creative process, but are taught the steps of an established production. Instead, they are used as symbols to make separate statements regarding youth and ageing. This is evidenced in Wenders' film, in which the opening sequence of *Kontakthof* is performed by all three casts – Bausch's own company, the teenagers, and the older ladies and gentlemen. Wenders' deft intercutting creates a *trompe l'oeil* effect, asking the spectator to assume the three different age groups represent the same character, envisaging that this particular casting call has been ongoing for decades. Time is sped up and rewound in a sequence that depicts an insatiable desire to continue performing and seeking validation.

Both non-professional casts have a powerful impact on the content of this specific work and how the viewer might interpret it. Observing *Kontakthof* performed by a collective of teenagers, the underlying theme of a battle between the sexes is brought to the surface with a newly sharpened focus: the painful self-consciousness expressed by the opening sequence is reiterated throughout with greater visibility. It is precisely this self-awareness and embarrassment we automatically associate with teenage years. Bausch's interpersonal cruelties also adopt a new layer of meaning as childish spitefulness is now played out by actual children. This further reminds us of the child-adults that people her work – in pieces such as *Arien*, *1980* and *Walzer*, we observe them during their childhood games, tormenting one another and, ultimately, mourning their lost youth. At the same time, however, scenes of sexualised intimacy enacted by awkward teenagers are increasingly uncomfortable to watch, not least the sequence in which a couple slowly undress for one another from opposite ends of the stage.

The older cast's interpretation is similarly loaded, though bears a more poignant relationship to Bausch's company. The vulnerability of the performers is highlighted by their amateur status – their performance is, unsurprisingly, less assured than Bausch's experienced, professionally trained dancers – but also by their advanced age (Figure 6.1). In pairing these two elements, Bausch displays the anxieties of her *oeuvre* anew, providing an even more penetrating gaze into the psyche. Her desire for a universal dance theatre is arguably most effectively realised in the amateur stagings of *Kontakthof*: childish games, the search for intimacy and the sorrow that accompanies rejection are as convincingly embodied by the non-professional casts as by the Tanztheater ensemble. Yet the display of elderly bodies on a dance stage has a more jarring effect than in the case of the younger cast, perhaps a result of the dance world's emphatic preference for youth. Once again, Bausch disrupts the normal order of the theatre space and confounds audience expectation, even when using the tested formula of an established and well-known production. In doing so, she affords a new reading of this piece.

In Chapter 3, I suggested that, in the midst of Bausch's liminal and intangible spaces, *Kontakthof* seems to evoke a clearer sense of time and space. When the cast is comprised of older bodies, the theme of memory and the passage of time is starkly brought to the fore. The dingy dance hall, outdated costumes and soundtrack of postwar popular music give new meaning to a piece now performed by an elderly cast. The theme of ageing is a recurring feature of Bausch's *oeuvre*, though it is often subtly invoked. In for example, *1980*, two versions of Somewhere over the Rainbow feature in the collagist soundtrack. The first is sung by a youthful, full-throated Judy Garland, while the second recording was produced much later in her career, the tremulous note in her voice underscoring the fragility we associate with the aged star. At the back of the stage, a pair of parallel bars serve as equipment for an elderly gymnast to enact the steps that would have characterised their childhood training. Watching the unnamed, silent older figure attempt feats usually associated with adolescent athletes, the audience is reminded of the loss of physical strength that accompanies the ageing process. An added sense of poignancy comes from the realisation that muscle memory is never lost.

For the professional dancer, the daily working routine is, generally speaking, a joyful activity that, after many years of training and its incessant repetitions, becomes effectively second nature. This degree of ingrained embodiment is reminiscent of Pierre Bourdieu's notion of 'habitus', a concept he defines as, 'a set of historical relations "deposited" within individual bodies in the form of mental and corporeal schemata of perception, appreciation and action'.[24] Indeed, Bourdieu has further described habitus as a kind of 'embodied history'.[25] However, as Steven Wainwright and Bryan Turner have suggested, the professional dancer's habitus can be 'fractured' by events like serious injuries and the effects of ageing on the body.[26] The dance world is uniquely cruel in this respect: just as the individual reaches the peak of their mental stamina and acquires a deep understanding of the body, the irreversible process of ageing and the intense competition of this environment must eventually put a halt to career progression. One dancer interviewed in Wainwright and Turner's study states that:

> There is something so sad that dancers' careers really are relatively short. Because just at that point when you are in your mid-thirties, I think, you just begin to understand so much more about the world, and yourself and life and other people and emotions. But you can no longer dance like you could when you were 25. So it's a cruel business. It has wonderful rewards for probably very few people to go on in the business in the way they'd like to.[27]

Bausch's *Tanztheater* acts as a mirror that reflects the cruelties of interpersonal relationships and the loneliness of modern life. For dancers, her work references more of a personal issue, specifically, the authoritarianism of the ballet world and the weight of audience expectation. Her hybridised format offers an alternative creative model to the restrictions of classical ballet. In turning away from the formalism of dance technique, Bausch suggests that an amalgamated blend of dance and theatre approaches offers a new creative vocabulary, one that embodies greater potential for translation across borders, cultures and life experiences. In the contemporary landscape of dance, choreographers continue her tradition of disrupting the boundaries of dance and unmasking its interior workings. Jérôme Bel, an artist significantly influenced by Bausch's work, exemplifies this aspect of her legacy. His work defies categorisation, though it has been termed *Konzepttanz* (conceptual dance) and, along with Xavier le Roy, his method has also been framed as 'non-dance', a concept Bel himself has rejected (Siegmund indicates, however, that this terminology is further complicated by the fact that the choreographers it describes do not apply such labels to their own work[28]). His experimental dance theatre questions the nature of dance and rejects the hierarchal structure of its classical forms. From the early years of Bel's career, his approach to choreography was unconventional, writing a kind of script which he would take into the studio to work around with the dancers.[29] His methodology is influenced by a wide array of interests, extending to philosophy as well as dance and theatre. From this emerge questions which Bel explores through choreography. Like Bausch, his is an inquisitorial method, one that, as in her mature *oeuvre*, interrogates the nature of the theatre and the relationship between performer and spectator.

A similarly critical examination of ballet and ageing in Bausch's work is at play in Bel's *Véronique Doisneau* (2004). In this piece, the eponymous Paris Opera dancer discusses her career as a *sujet* in the company, observing that she never rose to the rank of principal – in the Opera's hierarchy, an *étoile*, or 'star'. As in Bausch's dramaturgy, there is a palpable self-awareness that underlies Doisneau's performance. She recounts her favourite roles and the luminaries she worked under, including Cunningham and Rudolf Nureyev. However, she also outlines for her audience her age, salary and provides a list of injuries sustained in the line of duty. These memories are not selected at random, but emerge from a process of questioning initiated by Bel, which is then structured into a narrative arc that gradually exposes the frustrations and cruelties of the ballet world. Thus Bel utilises a parallel method to the *Stichworte* approach, and revives the unmasking tendency established in Bausch's mature work. In doing so, he leads the audience to question the authenticity of his documentary exploration of the dancer's life. When Doisneau turns her back on the audience to watch her favourite dancer perform Mats Ek's *Giselle* (1982), Bel invokes a Bauschian distancing effect, but imbues it with a new level of pathos: one feels profound empathy with the dancer as she transforms from the object of the audience's gaze to just another audience member. The piece alternates between fantasy and reality, synthesising the childhood dreams of a promising ballet student with the cruel realities of working life in a major company. Bel's canny, unflinching investigation of the dance world, constructed through a radically theatrical choreographic language, is clearly indebted to Bausch's legacy.

Bausch's working method around *Tanztheater* and her company presents a tacit acknowledgement of the cruelties associated with ballet habitus. Viewing her twenty-first-century revivals of *Kontakthof*, there is surely an underlying connection with Bausch's ensemble of dancers, many of whom continue to perform well beyond the average retirement age for their peers. The broad range of ages represented in her company constitutes another subversive rejection of classical ballet and its unforgiving treatment of the older dancer. As Lisa Schwaiger has observed, retirement from professional dance is often induced by factors more complex than the loss of high-level physical capacity: she suggests that competition for roles with younger dancers has a significant (and negative) psychological effect.[30] In this respect, Bausch does not 'cull' her dancers. Instead, she permits them to continue working without the ever-present threat of competition and replacement. Tanztheater Wuppertal is a kind of sanctuary for dancers of retirement age (although, compared to most other industries, this is young – most dancers retire in their early forties). Similarly, her working method affords many company members an easier transition from dancing life. Wainwright and Turner have suggested that coaching might offer a degree of compensation at the end of a performing career, what they term 'the loss of "the performing self"'.[31] In licensing works such as *Kontakthof* for performance by new casts, new pedagogical roles are thus established for Bausch's longstanding company members.

The restagings of *Kontakthof* brought renewed critical attention to a work emblematic of Bausch's radical rejection of choreographic tradition, drawing audiences back to what, for many, represents Bausch's signature style. Her mature work may have polarised audiences and critics, but it established Bausch's impact on the wider landscape of contemporary dance. Similarly, while the methodology behind her dance theatre is unusual, presents her dancers with significant challenges and, on occasion, might push them away from the company altogether, it enables Bausch and her ensemble to create and inhabit a world largely removed from the brutality of the classical dance environment. As her *Tanztheater* evolves through these final years, Bausch's authorial signature remains resolute, but the pieces shift in form and content once more, speaking to the 'knowing' spectator and permitting the dancers greater expressive freedom.

TURNING BACK TO DANCE: *VOLLMOND*

Though Bausch's late period is most immediately associated with her inter-national co-productions, she continued to create pieces outside the model of external institutional affiliation. The non-institutional pieces arguably demonstrate most clearly the characteristics of her late period, as they are neither coloured by their association with a precise location, nor are they commissioned by a cultural institution. In these final works, we can discern a continuing diminution of spectacle in favour of an almost cinematic aesthetic. Spoken word passages are replaced with lengthier sequences of movement and fully choreographed solos. Yet her last productions also exhibit a deepening sense of self-awareness and intertextuality, reiterating the themes and motifs of earlier work in an increasingly polished and self-assured theatrical backdrop. With these pieces, Bausch creates an inner landscape on stage, while making self-referential gestures to earlier works. In this respect, Bausch can be said to recycle her material.

Vollmond (*Full Moon*, 2006) is one such example of this choreographic recapitulation. Preceded by a series of co-productions based on residencies in Turkey, Japan and South Korea, it uses a reduced cast of dancers (only twelve performers in total) and minimalist set design to explore her eternally recurring queries around human relationships. While she draws upon familiar thematic reference points here, several features mark *Vollmond* as a distinctly late work. The soundtrack is a seamless montage of contemporary music, a more finessed and professionally mixed collage than the jarring breaks of her mature period. Similarly, the action onstage is smoothly directed and there is a sense of constant movement – even in moments of relative silence, the cast do not stop moving. When they are not performing, they exit the stage space, resulting in

Figure 6.2 *Vollmond*, Oliver Look

long periods where only a few dancers (or a single individual) inhabit the stage.

The black set is bare except for a large rock, its looming presence reminiscent of the volcanic formation in *Masurca*. *Vollmond* is another elemental piece, with water forming a constant reference point. A depression in the floor forms a shallow swimming pool that recalls the flooded stage front in the Macbeth Project. Where in that experimental work a garden hose ran incessantly throughout its duration, in *Vollmond*, water is manifested in an array of forms. The dancers pour it into glasses and over one another's heads. Throughout the performance, they are progressively soaked by water falling from the stage ceiling, an artificial rainfall that alternates between light mists and torrential downpours (Figure 6.2). As the piece progresses, the cast's clothing becomes soaked, marking another intertextual reference to Bausch's own work, specifically *Arien*. As in the case of the earlier piece, the dancers seem unaware that their elegant formalwear grows increasingly wet. Just as the flimsy dresses of *Sacre* reveal the bodies of the dancers, and the flooded stage soaks the eveningwear of the dancers in *Arien*, the cast of *Vollmond* are simultaneously clothed and unrobed by the water.

Water functions as a symbolic element, but also serves a visual and practical purpose. It interferes with the action onstage and disrupts our willing suspension of disbelief. Water further serves as a distancing effect throughout this piece: the natural world is invoked through rain, but its presence indoors is estranging and, when framed within a proscenium stage, clearly artificial. As is the case in almost all of Bausch's work, the time period and location of the actions are unspecified, and the overall effect is like a dream sequence, a watery interior peopled by a cast of characters clad in gradually more saturated formalwear. The water acts as a reflective surface, but it also represents a passageway, forming a conduit or prism that enables us to see into another world. Pabst's set is an otherworldly space that plumbs the depths of the collective unconscious of Bausch's company. It resembles the approximate version of reality that tends to emerge in dreams. The water pieces centre on unconscious desires played out within oneiric spaces where time is suspended. Water thus signifies the hazy, fluid demarcation between reality and the imaginary.

As in Bausch's earlier elemental pieces, water is presented as both a destructive and a nurturing force. The omnipresence of water connects to the work's title, suggesting the relationship between the moon and the tide. As one dancer advises, 'It's a full moon – don't get drunk.' However, the full moon is also a metaphor for madness, an appropriate reference point for a piece characterised by folly and the upending of social behaviours and norms. The cast are dressed in sumptuous formalwear once again, but their examination of social rituals and behaviours is played for increasingly comic effect. A woman dreamily addresses the audience while attempting to burn her hair with a lighter – at the crucial moment, she is interrupted by a man rushing past who inadvertently splashes her with water, extinguishing the flame. Later, the same dancer covers herself in the juice of a lemon, at first sensually, then with an air of desperation as she repeats the words, 'I wait, and wait and wait', followed by 'and then I cry and cry and cry', ending her monologue with an anguished scream. Throughout the piece, emotions are hyperbolic and the collective energy level borders on hysteria. Melanie Suchy has suggested that their movements are at times animalistic or amphibian: the dancers frequently drop to the floor and crawl across the stage, over the rock or through the watery trench.[32] A woman stalks across the stage on all fours smiling seductively at the audience – as she does so, she is draped in pink fabric by a male dancer who bathetically announces that she is the Pink Panther.

The moon also signifies a reference to femininity though; as is now an established tendency in Bausch's *oeuvre*, markers of gender are often greatly exaggerated. A female dancer summons her partner onstage to function as a human chair – he obediently obliges her. Later, another man chivalrously pours water into a woman's champagne glass, though it quickly overflows, and when he leaps onto her chair in excitement, he soaks her dress and causes her to flee the scene in fury. In the second act, a belligerent woman demands a man bring her various items, chastising him for failing to select the correct chair or jacket. A diminutive female dancer clings to a man's waist, her dreamy smile suggesting she has failed to notice his struggle to escape her grasp. The quest for intimacy again begins to break down into the 'affectionate violence' of Bausch's mature work, though the dancers' failures are increasingly presented as comic rather than tragic. A woman teaches two men how to take off a bra, challenging them to compete for speed. Any residual sensuality is negated by the woman's patronising, almost maternal, tone as she either congratulates or gently scolds the men. The scene contains a curiously overt fourth wall break as the woman looks over her shoulder into the audience and winks. Embodied in this mischievous gesture, Bausch's customarily fluid approach to the barrier between spectator and performer is presented as assumed knowledge on the part of the viewer.

Vollmond recapitulates many motifs of Bausch's earlier work. Indeed, its recursive framework suggests the piece might be interpreted as a reward for the experienced *Tanztheater* spectator. Sex is presented as a conflict zone once more, moving away from the optimism of *Água* to a familiar shift between anxiety, cruelty and comedy. In the opening sequences, a woman frantically kisses a man as he backs across the stage. Meyer reiterates the feral nature of the performers in this scene, comparing the woman's frenzied show of affection to that of 'a hungry bird'.[33] However, it is also a clear Bauschian reference point, a more energetic, even aggressive version of similar scenes in *Arien* and *Walzer* (both feature a recurring motif in which a man carries a woman across the stage, kissing without breaking their embrace). Moments where relationships break down or couples fail to make contact with one another recapitulate the failure motif established in works such as *Café Müller*. *Vollmond* continues the search for human connection that colours so much of Bausch's *oeuvre*: a couple play childishly romantic games with one another that rapidly deteriorate into spitefulness, with their embraces transforming into a struggle between holding on to and rejecting one another.

Intermittent acts of cruelty also refer to darker periods of Bausch's *Tanztheater*. Two men lie side by side upon the stage and throw a rock into the air, rolling out of its path at the last minute. Another dancer performs extravagant tricks to an indifferent audience on stage, and a woman punches herself in the stomach to demonstrate how one might force a fake laugh. In such moments, the unmasking of theatrical artifice that characterises the work of the 1980s is reimagined, as if the 'keep smiling' scene of *Bandoneon* has been reworked for an audience now thoroughly familiar with Bausch's desire to reveal the mechanics of the creative process.

However, it is the constant presence of water that serves as the most direct reference to Bausch's earlier work. Beyond its clear association with *Arien*, specific scenes draw upon motifs of other mature works: in one group sequence, the men enter the stage holding barge poles and push their way across the stage as though rowing gondolas. Later, several dancers appear from the edges of the stage and swim an awkward breast-stroke through the shallow trench. The swimming motif of *Walzer* is reimagined and literalised here, though ultimately it is still in vain. The same piece is referenced further when a man attempts to capture a woman by tracing her outline on the stage floor in chalk; equally, when a female dancer draws exaggerated circles around her own footsteps, the audience is reminded of *Walzer* and its chalk outlines of dance steps, as well as Endicott's attempt to leave her physical mark upon the stage.

Vollmond is a multidimensional piece in which Bausch and Pabst demonstrate the multiplicity of forms that water can adopt. In comparison, a work such as *Arien* seems static, exhibit-like, its performers essentially trapped within the flooded stage. *Vollmond* constitutes a response to the darkness of its predecessor as it explores the life-giving potential of water. Bausch uses Pabst's stage design to create a more expansive, all-encompassing set, one that closely evokes Wilson's highly artistic and sculptural installations. In fact, the rock is the only constant, a seemingly immovable object that, on the otherwise empty stage, looks as if it has come from another realm – Servos emphasises its mutability, calling it 'a bridge, a refuge, or a comet fallen from the sky'.[34] The opening sequence features an unusual use of stage prop and sound as two men swish their water bottles through the air. The resulting noise resembles that of a scythe cutting through the space – they smile gleefully at one another as though only just realising the evocative potential of their gesture. Moments such as this exemplify a tendency in Bausch's late work that approaches the notion of the *Gesamtkunstwerk*. It is a Wilsonian construction of material and content, playing with movement, stage, lighting and sound. *Vollmond*, as with the other works of Bausch's final decade, is an emphatically visual and physical piece of dance theatre.

The surreal action of *Vollmond* is repeatedly interrupted by lengthy sections of choreography. In this regard, the piece demonstrates a further evolution of the tendency established in *Água* towards rejecting language in favour of movement. Bausch's particular dance vocabulary does not place much importance on virtuosity or athletic prowess, but emphasises expression and individuality. Though a classically trained and gifted ballet dancer in her own right, Bausch owes her emphasis on expressivity to her German dance heritage: Wigman's 'absolute dance' was characterised by abstracted narratives and permitted the dancer to express their individuality. In terms of technique, Wigman's *Ausdruckstanz* made extensive use of the upper body, with swirling or rotating movements of the hands and arms becoming a defining characteristic. Bausch's *Tanztheater* is similarly concerned with the upper body, transferring the locus of movement from the legs and feet, as is characteristic of classical ballet.

In *Vollmond*, however, Bausch gives her cast the opportunity to dance for extended periods in their individual movement vocabularies. A male dancer's frantic solo in the opening scenes brings him to the point of evident physical exhaustion. He repeatedly swings his arms in wide arcs, a Bauschian tendency now significantly amplified. Yet the movement is also highly reminiscent of the swinging exercises in the *Ausdruckstanz* of Laban and Wigman, and especially of the swings and suspensions of José Limón's influential technique. Jasjfi, a dancer immediately recognisable for her diminutive frame, plays a significant role in this work. Her presence is keenly felt in a number of Bausch's late productions and, in *Vollmond*, her otherworldly, almost feral, solo blends aspects of Western techniques with the characteristics of East Asian dance forms. There is not one homogenous choreographic language used in the piece. Instead, it is an assemblage of solos and group dances in markedly different styles. This marks a further evolution from Bausch's earlier work – when dance does materialise in pieces such as *Kontakthof*, *Walzer* or *Nelken*, it is usually in the form of a choreographed ensemble sequence, or a reimagining of partnered social dance such as the tango or waltz.

Vollmond is simultaneously a celebration of Tanztheater Wuppertal's past and future. It revisits and reimagines motifs associated with earlier phases of Bausch's work that divided audiences and provoked sharp critique. At the same time, its lengthy stretches of choreography promote the physicality and creative potential of a new generation of dancers: Azusa Seyama, a Japanese dancer who joined the company in 2000, addresses the audience while rain lashes over her. She announces, 'I am young. My body is strong. My ears hear promise; my eyes see dreams.' Later, a male dancer strips to the waist and screams, 'This is me!' He turns his back to the audience, displaying his muscular physique, before performing a frantic, almost compulsive solo. Bausch's dancers demand to be seen, and she provides them with ample opportunity here to display their talents to the spectator.

In this at-times hysterical display of youthful competition, Nazareth Panadero and Dominique Mercy function as anchors. As two of Bausch's longest-serving company members, they drift in and out of the action like shadowy reminders of the Tanztheater's lengthy history. Mercy remains estranged from the other performers on stage, though at one point, he shares an intimate moment with a much younger dancer. A woman sits on a chair luxuriating in her long, thick hair. Mercy stops and watches her, and the two briefly kiss before he exits the scene. The contrast in age is explicit, and their fleeting contact seems to leave the older man with a sense of dejection as he helplessly looks on. His clothing is rumpled and unkempt, in marked contrast to the sleek gowns of the female dancers. Mercy acts alone throughout *Vollmond*, as though he is on the outside of this abstracted world looking in on the glamorous, frenzied animals that people the stage. Judith Mackrell has described his role as, 'some elderly Hamlet, reluctantly brought back to life'.[35] Towards the end of the piece, Mercy performs an extended solo that melds his clownish persona with the fluidity of his notable dance technique. In the midst of the sequence, however, he pauses in seeming exhaustion, sagging forward and panting, before slapping himself back into desperate action. His appearances on a stage otherwise dominated by youthful vigour remind the audience of the fragility that comes with age, and its particular poignancy for the older dancer.

Bausch's late works espouse a critical shift in movement quality. Her mature productions are notable for sequences structured around awkward, even ugly, movements, but in the late period this is translated into a more flowing, danced language. There is a decisive stylistic change as well as a shift in emotional content as, in this final phase, Bausch jettisons the darkness and violence of her mature works. Brought into being by the co-production model, the work produced in this period sees a further development of the choreography of spectacle. Bausch's last dance theatre productions celebrate beauty, sexuality and vulnerability, but also explore the contrast between youth and maturity, allowing the audience an intimate glance into the physical and emotional workings of the ageing performer.

ON NOT FORGETTING: 'SWEET MAMBO'

The term *Tanztheater* has undergone radical revisions across a multitude of forms since Laban's coinage in the first decades of the twentieth century. In the 1970s, Bausch and her German peers redefined the *Tanztheater* of their mentors, moving away from narrative-led productions into increasingly abstracted territory. Their practice emphasised the intensity of experience, using minimalist set design and simple, repetitive movements to foreground the body on stage. This form of dance theatre appeared to reject recognisable technique outright, abandoning narrative in favour of expressing inner emotional impulses. The resulting pieces remain a challenge to the spectator in their starkness and austerity.

Classification remains a point of contention in analysing Bausch's wide-ranging and constantly evolving *oeuvre*. Price suggests, however, that the hybridity of Bausch's work need not constitute a problem, and that it 'is *both* dance *and* theatre'.[36] Indeed, despite her apparent rejection of the form from the late 1970s onward, Bausch's work is never entirely devoid of choreography. The movement language of her dance operas (*Orpheus*, *Iphigenie*, *Sacre*) is based on an amalgamation of techniques that reflected the bilingual training she had received. Even in her experimental productions, Bausch replaces the formalism of ballet steps with other ways of reading movement. Meanwhile, her mature works continue to touch upon dance reference points, at times figuratively, as in the abstractions of ballet steps or references to its cruelty, and other times more directly. In her 1988 review of *Viktor*, for example, Kisselgoff observed:

The second half . . . begins with a woman making exactly the same arm-rotating gestures that William Forsythe uses in 'Steptext.' These are taken from the exercises and movement 'models' developed by the German modern-dance pioneer, Rudolf von Laban. Thus, what looks mysterious is not as meaningless or as secretly coded as it appears.[37]

Kisselgoff's informed reading of this scene illustrates a facet of Bausch's *Tanztheater* that is often overlooked. Her critique of ballet in this era is clear – Heathfield, for instance, has referred to 'the empty formalism of the dance against which she turned'.[38] However, she retained a love of classical dance and a fascination with ballet form and technique throughout her life. Bausch continued to take barre classes well after her own dancing career was over, and befriended such figures as Guillem, Forsythe and Carla Fracci. Even in the radical works of her mature period, dance is not rejected outright as a form of artistic protest, but as a result of creative experimentation. Förster, in this respect, states:

> When we started doing Arien, it looked like a dance piece. There were about ten movement phrases Pina gave us that we did for a long time over and over again. In the finished piece, they all concentrated into these two big dancing scenes, which I think are some of the most beautiful things we've choreographed in terms of movement . . . Pina always starts with a lot of movement, and during the process she finds out things that are much stronger. She always tries. It's not a conscious effort not to move.[39]

Bausch's *Tanztheater* espouses an ambiguous attitude to classical dance, though her last works connote a renewed admiration for pure movement. From her very first choreographic ventures with the company, she has consistently drawn upon the aesthetics and formal structures of other dance and theatre makers. As her career progresses, these reference points broaden to include a wider geographical and cultural range of experience. Her allusions extend beyond the universal themes of human emotion and interaction, reaching across the landscape of contemporary performance practice. This challenges any notion that her work occurs in isolation: rather, Bausch's hybrid form constantly mirrors the environment that surrounds it.

In the last years of her life, Bausch's approach undergoes a further transition that seems to emerge from the changing makeup of her company. With a new generation of dancers, she could explore the possibilities of choreography anew, exhibiting their diverse technical abilities. Years of extensive international travel had also introduced Bausch to a wide range of cultures and precipitated important collaborations: the celebrated Kuchipudi dancer Shantala Shivalingappa first worked with her in 1999 with *O Dido*, and would take on further roles, including restagings of *Sacre*, as well as the Indian co-production

Bamboo Blues (2007). The movement quality that emerges in Bausch's final dance theatre works draws upon this wide range of experience, referencing the bilingual training of her youth as well as more diverse forms of movement practice encountered during her company's rise to global celebrity. At the same time, a generation of established dancers forms the backbone of her ensemble, and the late *Tanztheater* works function as a celebration of both youth and experience. The restagings of *Kontakthof* exemplify this tendency most explicitly, though it recurs throughout her final choreographies. Where *Vollmond* provided a platform for the newer members of the company, Bausch's final creations shift the spotlight onto the minds and bodies of her older dancers.

'*Sweet Mambo*' (2008) is Bausch's penultimate work, completed a year before her death. Followed by '*como el musguito*', it is also the last piece made without an external institutional affiliation, and thus marks an appropriate end point to my analysis of Bausch's choreographic approach. Like *Vollmond*, it is a low-key production, made with an even smaller cast of dancers (nine in total), shorter in length than many of her co-productions and, unusually, uses the same set from the previous year's *Bamboo Blues*. The minimalist stage design consists of two billowing white curtains that drift across the space throughout the duration. In contrast to the 'fixed' large-scale and organic sets of her mature era, the curtains are notable for their intangibility, continually transforming the set from a theatrical space, to a luxurious interior, or invoking the realm of the unconscious. Servos has even interpreted the curtains as resembling 'an amniotic sac'.[40]

The relative blankness of the set enables Bausch to experiment with technology once more and, throughout the piece, a black-and-white German melodrama, *Der Blaufuchs* (*The Blue Fox*, 1938), is screened onto the back of the stage (Figure 6.3). The dancers' exploration of romance and nostalgia is thus reflected upon the walls of the stage, which transform into a cinema screen for the audience. This represents another self-referential acknowledgement of a Bauschian tendency, the penchant for drawing moving pictures into the theatre space. However, unlike the film screenings of *Kontakthof* and *Walzer*, the dancers do not notice the projection, which instead forms part of Pabst's set. As in the 'white' pieces, the mutability of the curtains function as a *tabula rasa*. At times, they appear almost animate, swelling into a form that dwarfs the dancers before evaporating into their role as background scenery. The women's costumes seem to be a further extension of the set, as the rippling curtains visibly complement Bausch's enduring fascination with silken evening gowns.

'*Sweet Mambo*' is a shape-shifting piece. In the context of a wider *oeuvre* that has consistently referred to the world of dreams and unrealised desires, it most closely realises this environment. It is one of her most expressionistic works, constructed around a layering of visual imagery and lengthy sections of choreographed movement. Again, there is no narrative to speak of, but the

Figure 6.3 *'Sweet Mambo'*, Murdo MacLeod

depiction of longing is unambiguous. The dancers quite literally plead with the audience not to be forgotten: 'My name is Regina. Not pronounced with a "g", but with a "sh"', Advento tells us, 'do not forget'. This becomes the first recurring motif of the piece, an appeal for remembrance, and to view the dancers as distinct entities rather than a collective ensemble. Though by this stage such overt fourth wall breaks have become an established trope of Bausch's *Tanztheater*, *'Sweet Mambo'* makes explicit the desire to be remembered, stripping away theatrical artifice to reveal the individual behind the role.

Vulnerability is the dominant sensation in this oneiric landscape. The force of the audience's gaze is intensified by the minimalist set and the reduced number of performers on stage. Extended passages of solo dancing take precedence over direct address, though when the dancers do speak to one another, or to the audience, it is usually with some form of request. A woman runs into the auditorium asking for someone to zip up her dress. Another chases a man around the stage, insisting that she wants to talk with him. Her initially strident tone gives way to helplessness as she modifies her demand – now, she wants to talk with him, but only if he wants to talk with her too. Her garbled delivery is comic, but the constant repetition, along with the pursuit of her uninterested partner, indicates that we have once again returned to Bausch's eternal quandary of loneliness. Desperation is invoked when a woman attempts to reach a voice offstage calling her name. Each time, she is lifted off the ground and carried back to her starting position by two men. When the sequence is reiterated, they use the physical barrier of a table to prevent the woman from reaching her unseen caller. Yet the cruelty that underpins works such as *Kontakthof* is largely absent. Instead, *'Sweet Mambo'* reveals the self-consciousness that belies the assumed confidence of a theatrical performer, or the assuredness of the glamorous woman at the centre of a cocktail party: this is literally played out when a woman explains to the audience how to simulate the perfect party smile, repeating the word 'brush' as a constant refrain. The dancers openly present their anxieties and fears to the audience, inviting the viewer to share in their confidences. It is another facet of Bausch's desire to evolve a universal language, this time narrowing the space between stage and spectator to suggest that we are all performing a version of ourselves, one that we ultimately wish to be remembered for.

With *'Sweet Mambo'*, Bausch's uncomfortably insightful gaze into human frailty is softened by passages of pure aestheticism, humour and intimacy. She allows her cast the opportunity to engage in occasionally sensual interactions with one another. The childhood games of earlier works are now replaced with more adult themes – the men kiss and stroke the exposed skin of three women who, in turn, close their eyes and smile in evident pleasure. A woman sits in her partner's lap, where her shuffling movements build into an apparent orgasm. The men often function as props in this work, and are notable for their relative absence – they are outnumbered, with six women in contrast to four male dancers. The women are afforded extended sections of solo choreography, and dominate the sections of spoken word as well as the physical action.

More so than any of Bausch's works, *'Sweet Mambo'* is concerned with a specifically female experience – Alice Bain has proposed that, 'from this heavenly place, the ensemble send signals from the frontline of their psyches about what it feels like to live in female skin'.[41] As the cast wanders on and off stage, the action shifts from the realm of the living to the inner workings of the unconscious. In stark contrast to the faded dance halls of *Bandoneon* and *Kontakthof*, however, *'Sweet Mambo'* exudes, even revels in, a sense of glamour and sophistication. The dinner party motif that so often ends in chaos in Bausch's works – as in the case of *Arien* or *1980*, for example – is here presented as a dream sequence. In this respect, the curtains take on a further permutation, suggesting the veil that separates our conscious and unconscious minds, or the boundary between sleep and wakefulness. A sleeping woman lying on the stage floor rouses herself by repeatedly splashing the contents of a bucket of water over her head – unsurprisingly, Bausch's favoured element finds its way back onto the stage. A wind machine blows the material into ever-changing arrangements, and when the dancers perform behind the curtains, their very physicality is called into question. They become intangible symbols, and the precision of their movements is blurred by the opacity of the fabric. At points, individuals are even cradled by other dancers through the curtains, appearing to float before our eyes, or to be swallowed up by the vast expanse of gauze.

Bausch's late works are decidedly visual productions. It is in the reduction of spoken word that she appears to rediscover the possibilities of dance technique. Emerging from the period of co-productions, Bausch's final pieces draw upon a pluralist conception of choreography, synthesising the individual vocabularies of her diverse international ensemble. Yet this syncretic tendency has been evident in her *Tanztheater* from its earliest days, as in the transatlantic modernism of her dance operas. While she does not codify a formalist approach – one cannot learn 'Bausch technique' in the same manner as that of Graham, Cunningham, or Limón – in the final years of her career, an identifiable Bauschian tendency can be more clearly discerned in the long passages of pure choreography that define these works. The undulating movements of the upper body which I identified in works such as *Orpheus* recur with increasing frequency, evoking not only the swirling qualities of her *Ausdruckstanz* predecessors, but also the precise arm and hand work of South-East Asian dance. As in classical forms of Indian dance such as Kathak and Bharatanatyam, Bausch's dancers place special emphasis on the upper body, often remaining fixed to a point on the stage. Royona Mitra explains that:

> The upper body of the kathak dancer uses the rootedness of the lower body to explore highly complex and virtuosic movements through the arms, wrists, neck and spine. The mercurial and circular nature of these extended arm movements always returns to the centre, the solar plexus, from which the movements seem to emanate, and the journeys undertaken by the arms are always traced by the dancer's shifting eye focus and head.[42]

Many of Bausch's Western predecessors utilise similar tendencies, from Duncan to Wigman and Graham. Their collective fascination with the exotic Other is well documented, though in Bausch's case, her repeated exposure to Indian dance (consider, for example, the company's international tours, the collaboration with Shivalingappa, and the 2007 Indian co-production) seems to complement an existing interest in the articulation of the upper body over balletic pointe work. While this marriage of styles is most closely associated with *Bamboo Blues*, in which aspects of Indian classical dance are overtly blended with Bausch's own aesthetic, I propose that we might read this tendency in a number of her late dance works. By this stage, she had evolved a more complex, internationalist approach which had benefitted from extensive touring and the creative development of work overseas, but perhaps most significantly, from her multinational company of dancers. By situating her late period not simply as a further evolution of the co-production model, but as a synthesis of tendencies that underpinned the duration of her career, we are able to interpret these lesser-discussed works as exemplifying her syncretic and intercultural language of dance theatre.

While *'Sweet Mambo'* is a primarily visual and largely choreographed piece, it also draws upon the concluding theme of this volume, namely the importance of legacy and remembrance. Ideas of heritage and memory are plaintively recurring themes. The dancers repeatedly remind the audience of their names, imploring us not to forget them. A woman discusses the ways in which she feels she has inherited parts of her body from her extended family. Bausch's late works espouse a sense of anxiety around ageing that is reminiscent of Beckett's Krapp – there is a desire to preserve youth and the possibilities it offers, though ultimately all parties realise this act is futile. Though the programme notes for *'Sweet Mambo'* indicate the piece is a reinterpretation of the set and subject matter of *Bamboo Blues*, I suggest instead that it acts as a companion piece or foil to *Vollmond*.[43] Both take place within intangible dreamscapes and centre on the desire for intimacy. Yet while the earlier piece celebrates the youthful physicality of Bausch's new generation of dancers, *'Sweet Mambo'* is an elegy to the ageing dancer and the importance of being remembered. Its reduced cast is comprised almost entirely of long-serving company members, several of whom no longer dance in physically challenging choreographed works such as *Sacre*. In this piece, however, they are permitted extended periods of solo stage time, each dancing in their own language, and luxuriating in the collective attention of the audience.

In the second act, the disparity between age and experience is made explicit when a dancer announces, 'the old can't do what they know how to do, but the young don't know how to do what they can do'. Viewed in the wider context of Bausch's late works, this seemingly flippant aside takes on new significance. Working with a multigenerational cast of performers presents a choreographer with a unique set of challenges, issues that would not exist in the context of a classical ballet company. Yet, where *Vollmond* may have depicted the aestheticism and physical prowess of her younger members, *'Sweet Mambo'* explores the possibilities of dance for the older body. It is not a bitter piece, however, nor does it seek to imbue the moving bodies of these performers with a sense of pathos or tragedy. Instead, in its dreamlike interior, *'Sweet Mambo'* presents a compendium of memories. Bausch's previous works are obliquely referenced, and an older generation of dancers is given the opportunity to dance once more, reliving earlier phases of their respective careers.

Significantly, Bausch's presence is less keenly felt in these final works. Though they are made through the same collaborative *Stichworte* process, there is a sense that Bausch the *monteur* has taken on a less active role in compiling the content and editing vast quantities of rehearsal material. Instead, these pieces give more voice to the dancers in her company, and allow the combination of movement, music and stage design to speak for themselves. The increasing visibility of dance in the late works suggests a change in attitude, shifting away from the confrontational and absurdist style that alienated many audiences.

The final works seek instead to broaden the reach of her *Tanztheater*, translating across borders both theatrical and geographical. Curiously, in doing so, they demonstrate a cyclical return to the language in which her first works were written – that of dance. They urge us not only to emotionally invest in Bausch's works but, most importantly, never to forget them.

*

> I'm always trying. I keep desperately trying to dance. I'm always hoping I'm going to find new ways of relating to movement. I can't go on working in the previous way. It would be like repeating something, something strange.[44]

Bausch died on 30 June 2009, only a few days after being diagnosed with cancer. Tanztheater Wuppertal was on tour in Warsaw at the time with her Turkish co-production, *Nefés*, and the dancers received the news knowing they were due to go on stage only a few hours later. A group decision was hastily reached to go ahead with the performance though, by the end of the intermission, the tragic news had filtered through to most of the audience. At the close of the performance, the cast came on stage for a single curtain call, leaving a space in the middle of the row where Bausch ought to have stood.

Towards the end of her 1998 article on Bausch's method, Cody concluded that, 'Bausch's is a theatre of traces, culminating out of and into aftermaths. The embodiment of her substance is that she does not have a "system" of notation or mise-en-scene. Her repertory will most likely die with her.'[45] There is both truth and fallacy contained within this statement. Bausch's sudden death brought a sharp end to the evolution of her *Tanztheater*, and left the future of her company in doubt. In the intervening years, however, significant changes have occurred. She is survived by a considerable catalogue of productions and a company of dancers intimately associated with the work made through the collaborative *Stichworte* method. In 2015, Tanztheater Wuppertal performed the work of external choreographers and theatre-makers for the first time in its history, and several of Bausch's pieces are now licensed for performance by other companies: in April 2016, the Bayerisches Staatsballett staged a production of Bausch's *Für die Kinder von gestern, heute und morgen (For the Children of Yesterday, Today and Tomorrow*, 2002) following a period of collaboration with several long-serving company members. In 2017, English National Ballet became the first British company to perform Bausch's *Sacre*.

Cody's hypothesis was, it seems, not entirely correct. Unlike the dissolution of the Merce Cunningham Dance Company a year after its figurehead's death, Tanztheater Wuppertal Pina Bausch lives on and continues to perform works from Bausch's extensive catalogue. As new dancers are continually recruited, a new generation of company members has emerged. The Tanztheater's youngest members – who had never met her – perform alongside those who worked with Bausch across several decades. Productions made through the *Stichworte* method are regularly reprised with new casts, and thus Bausch's repertoire remains resolutely alive. However, there appears to be no appetite to appoint an artistic director that seeks to follow blindly in Bausch's footsteps. Her hybridic approach to dramaturgy cannot be adopted like another dance technique or choreographic language. The pieces produced through her *Stichworte* method are collaborative productions that emerged from a unique working relationship between Bausch and her ensemble. To return to Cody's suggestion, then, what was lost with Bausch's death was not her repertoire, but the potential for new works to emerge bearing her signature.

Bausch's late productions, though under-examined in current literature, represent a crucial aspect of her legacy. They demonstrate that her creative approach was in the process of a further evolution, manifested in the return to dance choreography. Her return to such principles is not surprising, as it remains an essential component of Bausch's work. Her work is corporeal and embodied. The *Stichworte* method she evolved attempts to formulate a language for the inner workings of the psyche, to translate desire, intimacy and longing into a universal language. Dance itself defies borders and a singular notion of identity. It necessitates travel and imbues in its practitioners the ability to work across different styles and forms. Dance is also inherently cruel at times, capable of inflicting pain upon the body and mind, yet it offers unique opportunities for freedom of expression and connection with the wider world. Bausch, throughout her *oeuvre*, uses theatrical techniques and devices, but dance is the language in which her work begins and ends. In this regard, her final productions come close to realising the physical Esperanto she sought through her mature works and into the era of co-productions. Co-authored and performed by a thoroughly international, multigenerational ensemble, her late works espouse the universalist philosophy proposed in Bausch's own assessment of reception of her dance theatre: 'I never wanted to provoke. Actually, I only tried to speak about us.'[46] It may have taken global audiences several decades to learn the language of Bausch's *Tanztheater* yet, ironically, she was talking about us all along.

Notes

1. Elswit, 'Ten Evenings with Pina', pp. 217–18. For examples of this criticism of Bausch's creative method, see Briginshaw and Burt, *Writing Dancing Together*, and Daly, 'Tanztheater'.
2. A recent exception to this tendency is Coates' essay on Bausch's last production, 'Pina . . . Are You There?', pp. 63–8.
3. Mulrooney, *Orientalism, Orientation, and the Nomadic Work of Pina Bausch*, p. 132.
4. Delahaye, *Pina Bausch*, p. 13.

5. Hoghe and Tree, 'The Theatre of Pina Bausch', p. 63.
6. Mercy, quoted in Hoghe, *Pina Bausch*, p. 134.
7. Shanahan, quoted in Wiegand, 'Let's Tanz'.
8. Lawson, 'Pina, Queen of the Deep', in Climenhaga (ed.), *The Pina Bausch Sourcebook*, p. 217.
9. Jennings, 'Tanztheater Wuppertal Pina Bausch'.
10. Mulrooney, *Orientalism, Orientation, and the Nomadic Work of Pina Bausch*, p. 165.
11. On the specific issue of archiving, Wagenbach's edited volume (2014) provides discussion and analysis of recent challenges faced by the Pina Bausch Foundation in preserving her legacy.
12. Amarante, quoted in Fernandes, *Pina Bausch and the Wuppertal Dance Theatre*, p. 114.
13. Ibid., p. 115.
14. Bausch, originally quoted at a press conference in Rome, reprinted in Servos and Müller, *Pina Bausch – Wuppertal Dance Theater*, p. 234.
15. Copeland and Cohen (eds), *What is Dance?*, p. 232.
16. Graham, *Blood Memory*, p. 4.
17. Broadhurst, 'Pina', in Broadhurst and Machon (eds), *Identity, Performance and Technology*, p. 91.
18. Wiegand, 'Let's Tanz'.
19. Kaufmann, quoted in Brinkmann, 'Reconstruction as a Creative Process', in Wagenbach (ed.), *Inheriting Dance*, p. 86.
20. Klein and Wagenbach, 'Wild Gardens. Archiving as Translating', in Wagenbach (ed.), *Inheriting Dance*, p. 40.
21. Many of Bausch's handwritten rehearsal notes and production scripts were included in the 2016–17 'Pina Bausch and the Tanztheater' exhibition (Bonn/Berlin).
22. Abrams, 'The Contemporary Moment of Dance', p. 50.
23. Bausch, quoted in *Kontakthof with Ladies and Gentlemen over 65*.
24. Bourdieu and Wacquant, *An Invitation to Reflexive Sociology*, p. 16.
25. Bourdieu, *The Logic of Practice*, p. 56.
26. Wainwright and Turner, '"Just Crumbling to Bits"?', p. 241
27. Ibid., pp. 246–7.
28. Siegmund, 'Konzept ohne Tanz?' in Clavadetscher and Rosiny (eds), *Zeitgenössischer Tanz*, pp. 47–8.
29. Siegmund, *Abwesenheit*, p. 318.
30. Schwaiger, 'Performing One's Age', pp. 107–8.
31. Wainwright and Turner, '"Just Crumbling to Bits"?', p. 243
32. Suchy, 'Der Tanz ist aufgegangen'.
33. Meyer, *Pina Bausch*, p. 121.
34. Servos, *Pina Bausch*, p. 203.
35. Mackrell, 'Tanztheater Wuppertal – Vollmond'.
36. Price, 'The Politics of the Body', p. 322.
37. Kisselgoff, 'Pina Bausch Adds Humor to Her Palette'.
38. Heathfield in Kelleher and Ridout (eds), *Contemporary Theatres in Europe*, p. 188.
39. Förster, quoted in Daly, 'Tanztheater', p. 48.
40. Servos, *Pina Bausch*, p. 214.
41. Bain, 'Sweet Mambo'.
42. Mitra, *Akram Khan*, pp. 8–9.
43. Servos, *Pina Bausch*, p. 213.

44. Bausch, quoted in Servos and Müller, *Pina Bausch – Wuppertal Dance Theater*, p. 230.
45. Cody, 'Woman, Man, Dog, Tree', p. 129.
46. Bausch, 'What Moves Me'.

CONCLUDING THOUGHTS

In all its myriad incarnations, Bausch's *Tanztheater* eludes definition. It is a shape-shifting hybrid, a fluid practice that reflects the conditions of its changing contexts. In writing this text, I have endeavoured to provide new perspectives for reading Bausch's complex, oneiric and multivalent work. In doing so, however, I have not attempted to fashion a singular lens with which to interpret Bausch's practice, nor have I proposed a specific or 'correct' interpretation of the content of her work. Through close analysis of individual productions, I have sought to demonstrate that Bausch's conception of dance theatre cannot be neatly categorised. Rather, it is underpinned by a constant process of evolution, from its origins in bilingual modern dance practice, via the radical experimentations that sharply polarised audiences, to the opulent and celebratory late productions. Similarly, her dancers have survived transitions through different working methods and the challenges of co-creating large-scale works, adjusting to the peripatetic company schedule, and passing on roles deeply imbued with personal significance.

My charting of the development of Bausch's *oeuvre* has revealed a stylistic evolution that begins and ends in dance. The twin influences of German and American modern dance – competing forms that dominated stages of the postwar era – are clearly discernible in her early pieces. In the experimental and mature periods of her career, she devised a new method of creating work through the *Stichworte* method, eschewing established forms of choreographic practice. Throughout this period, Bausch produced some of her most well-known pieces; yet, as Sörgel has observed, her 'theatricality wasn't framed in a dance language'.[1] At the same time, her enduring fascination with migration, a tendency apparent in some of her earliest choreographies, would come to hallmark the era of global co-productions and her late works. The *Tanztheater* works that materialised from these creative investigations embody Bausch's individual movement vocabulary, an innovative form that can nonetheless be seen as formally and thematically allied with the work of such pioneering theatre-makers as Artaud, Beckett, Brecht and Wilson.

Although this amalgamation of experimental dance and theatre practice is precisely what frustrates efforts to classify her creative approach, it underpins the central proposition of my own study: in order to comprehend the complexities of Bausch's *Tanztheater*, it is vital to consider the relationship between her own practice and various facets of avant-garde theatre practice. Given that Bausch's work does not remain solely in theatrical territory, this blended approach is essential – indeed, the term 'dance theatre' is itself a portmanteau. Her productions exhibit many key commonalities with Lehmann's framing of postdramatic theatre, but, ultimately, her *Tanztheater* still exists somewhere outside this categorisation. After all, despite an apparent rejection of dance technique in the mature era of Bausch's career, in its late period her work began to move away from estrangement and absurdity towards a renewed dance vocabulary. That this phase ended so abruptly leaves the evolution of Bausch's dance theatre, perhaps appropriately, unfinished.

There are, of course, unique difficulties inherent in this kind of research framework. I have been careful to avoid a form of investigation that is too deeply connected to the near-mythologised personae of pivotal figures such as Wigman and Graham. A tendency to deify these women – including Bausch, now, herself – constitutes another factor that has had an adverse effect on objective analysis of their contributions to twentieth-century performance history. Similarly, selecting works for analysis presented a challenge, especially when considering the extensive range of choreographies Bausch produced (the full catalogue of her productions far outweighs the capacity for in-depth analysis afforded by the limits of this volume).

There are further interdisciplinary issues requiring discussion that have not been possible to examine here, the relationship between Bausch's work and cinema, for example, including her own production, *Die Klage der Kaiserin* (*The Lament of the Empress*, 1990) as well as Bausch's collagist use of music. The correlation between her *Tanztheater* and experimental choreographic forms such as Butoh demands much deeper analysis, not least due to the numerous historical and thematic links they share. Similarly, a comprehensive evaluation of Bausch's impact on immersive theatre has also yet to emerge. When, in 2015, Tim Etchells of Forced Entertainment was invited to contribute a new piece for the company to open the season's touring schedule, it marked the first occasion that the company would perform work by a director other than Bausch. The selection of Etchells as a collaborator underlines the intimate relationship between her own creative method and experimental theatre, and it is my hope that this contribution to the study of Bausch's work might catalyse further investigation into the enduring relationship between dance and theatre practice.

In the opening chapter of this volume, I discussed Nijinsky's *Sacre*, a piece that heralded the beginnings of modernism on European stages. Its legacy is intractably associated with the alleged scandal of its premiere, yet today it comprises the crucial starting point for discussions of modern dance practice. Bausch's career followed a curiously similar trajectory, first alienating (and, on occasion, enraging) audiences before reaching global prominence. Indeed, Bausch is now widely acknowledged as one of the most significant choreographers of the twentieth century, venerated and emulated by a new generation of artists. Indeed, for the present-day spectator, Bausch's work may not retain the same shock value associated with her performances of the 1970s and 1980s. Her work has reached extensive new audiences, and the influence of her *Tanztheater* is clearly visible across the landscape of contemporary performance practice. Yet, somewhat ironically, it was not Bausch's intention to fundamentally change the face of dance; as Climenhaga has observed, 'Bausch doesn't set out to stake a claim in formal revolution against existing forms of dance, she simply concentrates on how we are connected to the world and how we feel what we feel.'[2] In the end, Bausch's understated explanation of her work is one of the most powerful definitions of the *Tanztheater* form. It was, and remains, her way of 'speaking about us'.

NOTES

1. Sörgel, *Dance and the Body in Western Theatre*, p. 117.
2. Climenhaga, *Pina Bausch*, p. 63.

BIBLIOGRAPHY

Abrams, Joshua, 'The Contemporary Moment of Dance: Restaging Recent Classics', *PAJ: A Journal of Performance and Art*, vol. 30, no. 3 (September 2008), pp. 41–51.

Arens, Katherine, 'Robert Wilson: Is Postmodern Performance Possible?' *Theatre Journal*, vol. 43, no. 1 (March 1991), pp. 14–40.

Artaud, Antonin, trans. Corti, Victor, *Collected Works – Volume 4* (London: Calder and Boyars, 1974 [1964]).

Baird, Bruce, *Hijikata Tatsumi and Butoh: Dancing in a Pool of Gray Grits* (New York: Palgrave Macmillan, 2011).

Banes, Sally, *Dancing Women: Female Bodies on Stage* (London: Routledge, 1998).

Barnett, David, '"I have to change myself instead of interpreting myself": Heiner Müller as Post-Brechtian Director', *Contemporary Theatre Review*, vol. 20, no. 1 (2010), pp. 6–20.

Bathrick, David 'Robert Wilson, Heiner Müller, and the Preideological', *New German Critique*, vol. 33, no. 2 (Summer 2006), pp. 65–76.

Bausch, Pina, 'What Moves Me', commemorative lecture on receipt of the Kyoto Prize in Arts and Philosophy (2007).

Beausang, Michael, 'Myth and Tragi-comedy in Beckett's Happy Days', *Mosaic*, vol. 5, no. 1 (1971), pp. 59–77.

Beckett, Samuel, *Endgame* (London: Faber and Faber, 1964 [1957]).

——, *Waiting for Godot* (London: Faber and Faber, 2006 [1963]).

Benjamin, Walter, ed. and trans. Arendt, Hannah, *Illuminations* (New York: Schocken, 1968).

Bentivoglio, Leonetta, trans. Hörner, Unda, *Pina Bausch oder die Kunst, über Nelken zu tanzen* (Frankfurt: Suhrkamp, 2007).

Bermel, Albert, 'Ionesco: Anything but Absurd', *Twentieth Century Literature*, vol. 21, no. 4 (December 1975), pp. 411–20.

Bhabha, Homi, *The Location of Culture* (London: Routledge, 2007 [1994]).

Birringer, Johannes, 'Pina Bausch: Dancing Across Borders', *TDR: The Drama Review*, vol. 30, no 2 (Summer 1986), pp. 85–97.

——, *Theatre, Theory, Postmodernism* (Bloomington: Indiana University Press, 1991).

Bourdieu, Pierre, *The Logic of Practice* (Palo Alto: Stanford University Press, 1990).

Bourdieu, Pierre and Wacquant, Loïc J D, *An Invitation to Reflexive Sociology* (London: University of Chicago Press, 1992).

Braun, Rebecca and Marven, Lyn (eds), *Cultural Impact in the German Context: Studies in Transmission, Reception, and Influence* (Rochester, NY: Camden House, 2010).

Brecht, Bertolt, eds. Silberman, Mark, Giles, Steve and Kuhn, Tom, *Brecht on Theatre* (London: Bloomsbury Methuen Theatre, 2015).

Briginshaw, Valerie and Burt, Ramsay, *Writing Dancing Together* (Basingstoke: Palgrave Macmillan, 2009).

Broadhurst, Susan and Machon, Josephine (eds), *Identity, Performance and Technology: Practices of Empowerment, Embodiment and Technicity* (Basingstoke: Palgrave Macmillan, 2012).

Brook, Peter, *The Empty Space* (New York: Atheneum, 1968).

Brown, Ismene, 'A Place Where Life Happens', *The Telegraph* (19 January 2002), <http://www.telegraph.co.uk/culture/theatre/dance/3572066/A-place-where-life-happens.html> (last accessed 6 October 2017).

Bruckner, D. R. J. (ed.), *The New York Times Guide to the Arts of the 20th Century: 1900-1929* (Chicago: Fitzroy Dearborn, 2002).

Burt, Ramsay, *The Male Dancer: Bodies, Spectacle, Sexualities* (London: Routledge, 1995).

——, *Alien Bodies: Representations of Modernity, 'Race,' and Nation in Early Modern Dance* (London: Routledge, 1998).

Cappelle, Laura, 'Pina's Ghost', *Financial Times* (26 May 2012), <https://www.ft.com/content/0ab4274a-a40c-11e1-84b1-00144feabdc0> (last accessed 11 June 2015).

Carlson, Marvin, *The Haunted Stage: The Theatre as Memory Machine* (Ann Arbor: University of Michigan Press, 2001).

Caruth, Cathy (ed.), *Trauma: Explorations in Memory* (Baltimore: Johns Hopkins University Press, 1995).

Clavadetscher, Reto and Rosiny, Claudia (eds), *Zeitgenössischer Tanz. Körper – Konzepte – Kulturen. Eine Bestandsaufnahme* (Bielefeld: Transcript, 2007).

Climenhaga, Royd, *Pina Bausch*, London: Routledge, 2009.

—— (ed.), *The Pina Bausch Sourcebook: The Making of Tanztheater* (New York: Routledge, 2013).

Coates, Emily Carson, 'Pina ... Are You There?', *PAJ: A Journal of Performance and Art*, vol. 35, no. 2 (May 2013), pp. 63–8.

Cody, Gabrielle, 'Woman, Man, Dog, Tree: Two Decades of Intimate and Monumental Bodies in Pina Bausch's Tanztheater', *TDR: The Drama Review*, vol. 42, no. 2 (Summer 1998), pp. 115–31.

Coldiron, Margaret, *Trance and Transformation of the Actor in Japanese Noh and Balinese Masked Dance-Drama* (Lewiston, NY: E. Mellen Press, 2004).

Copeland, Roger and Cohen, Marshall (eds), *What is Dance? Readings in Theory and Criticism* (Oxford: Oxford University Press, 1983).

Copeland, Roger, *Merce Cunningham: The Modernizing of Modern Dance* (New York: Routledge, 2004).

Daly, Ann, 'Tanztheater: The Thrill of the Lynch Mob or the Rage of a Woman?' *TDR: The Drama Review*, vol. 30, no. 2 (Summer 1986), pp. 46–56.

Davies, Mererid Puw, *The Tale of Bluebeard in German Literature: From the Eighteenth Century to the Present* (Oxford: Oxford University Press, 2001).

Davis, Nathaniel, '"Not a soul in sight!": Beckett's Fourth Wall', *Journal of Modern Literature*, vol. 38, no. 2 (Winter 2015), pp. 86–102.

Delahaye, Guy, *Pina Bausch* (Kassel: Bärenreiter, 1989).

Dell'Antonio, Andrew (ed.), *Beyond Structural Listening: Postmodern Modes of Hearing* (Berkeley: University of California Press, 2004).

Eksteins, Modris, *Rites of Spring: The Great War and the Birth of the Modern Age* (London: Black Swan, 1989).

Elswit, Kate, 'Ten Evenings with Pina: Bausch's "Late" Style and the Cultural Politics of Coproduction', *Theatre Journal*, vol. 65, no. 2 (May 2013), pp. 215–33.

Endicott, Josephine Ann, *Ich bin ein anständige Frau!* (Frankfurt am Main: Suhrkamp, 1999).

Esslin, Martin, *The Theatre of the Absurd* (Harmondsworth: Penguin, 1968).

Felciano, Rita, 'Pina Bausch: The Voice from Germany', *Dance Magazine* (October 1996), pp. 68–71.

Fernandes, Ciane, *Pina Bausch and the Wuppertal Dance Theatre: The Aesthetics of Repetition and Transformation* (New York: Peter Lang, 2001).

Fiebach, Joachim, 'Resisting Simulation: Heiner Müller's Paradoxical Approach to Theater and Audiovisual Media since the 1970s', *New German Critique*, no. 73 (Winter 1998), pp. 81–94.

Finter, Helga and Griffin, Matthew, 'Antonin Artaud and the Impossible Theatre: The Legacy of the Theatre of Cruelty', *TDR: The Drama Review*, vol. 41, no. 4 (Winter 1997), pp. 15–40.

Fischer-Lichte, Erika, trans. Jain, Saskya Iris, *The Transformative Power of Performance: A New Aesthetics* (New York: Routledge, 2008).

Fraleigh, Sondra and Nakamura, Tamah, *Hijikata Tatsumi and Ohno Kazuo* (London: Routledge, 2006).

Fritsch-Vivié, Gabriele, *Mary Wigman* (Reinbek: Rowohlt Taschenbuch Verlag, 1999).

Gitelman, Claudia and Martin, Randy (eds), *The Returns of Alwin Nikolais: Bodies, Boundaries and the Dance Canon* (Middletown, CT: Wesleyan University Press, 2007).

Goldberg, Marianne, 'Artifice and Authenticity: Gender Scenarios in Pina Bausch's Dance Theatre', *Women & Performance: A Journal of Feminist Theory*, vol. 4, no. 2 (1986), pp. 104–17.

Goldfarb, Alvin, 'Theatrical Activities in Nazi Concentration Camps', *Performing Arts Journal*, vol. 1, no. 2 (Autumn 1976), pp. 3–11.

Graham, Martha, *Blood Memory* (New York: Doubleday, 1991).

Grotowski, Jerzy, *Towards a Poor Theatre* (London: Routledge, 2012 [1968]).

Harich, Wolfgang, 'Der entlaufene Dingo, das vergessene Floß', *Sinn und Form*, vol. 25, no. 1 (January 1973), pp. 189–218.

Härms, Kathy, Reuter, Lutz and Dürr, Volker (eds), *Coping With the Past: Germany and Austria After 1945* (Madison: University of Wisconsin Press, 1990).

Henrichs, Benjamin, 'Die zum Lächeln nicht Zwingbaren', *Die Zeit* (24 May 1974), <http://www.zeit.de/1974/22/die-zum-laecheln-nicht-zwingbar en> (last accessed 6 October 2017).

Hoghe, Raimund, *Bandoneon: für was kann Tango alles gut sein?* (Darmstadt: Luchterhand, 1981).

——, *Pina Bausch: Tanztheatergeschichten* (Frankfurt am Main: Suhrkamp, 1986).

Hoghe, Raimund and Tree, Stephen, 'The Theatre of Pina Bausch', *TDR: The Drama Review*, vol. 24, no. 1 (March 1980), pp. 63–74.

Holmberg, Arthur, *The Theatre of Robert Wilson* (Cambridge: Cambridge University Press, 1996).

Homans, Jennifer, *Apollo's Angels: A History of Ballet* (London: Granta, 2010).

Huyssen, Andreas, *Twilight Memories: Marking Time in a Culture of Amnesia* (London: Routledge, 1995).

Iwata, Miki, 'Records and Recollections in "Krapp's Last Tape,"' *Journal of Irish Studies*, vol. 23 (2008), pp. 34–43.

Jankowsky, Karen and Love, Carla (eds), *Other Germanies: Questioning Identity in Women's Literature and Art* (Albany, NY: State University of New York Press, 1997).

Jannarone, Kimberley, *Artaud and his Doubles* (Ann Arbor: University of Michigan Press, 2010).

Jennings, Luke, 'Obituary: Pina Bausch', *The Guardian* (1 July 2009), <https://www.theguardian.com/stage/2009/jul/01/pina-bausch-obituary-dance> (last accessed 6 October 2017).

——, 'Tanztheater Wuppertal Pina Bausch', *The Observer* (28 March 2010), <https://www.theguardian.com/stage/2010/mar/28/tanztheater-wuppertal-pina-bausch> (last accessed 6 October 2017).

Jones, Susan, *Literature, Modernism, and Dance* (Oxford: Oxford University Press, 2013).

Jordan, Stephanie, *Stravinsky Dances: Re-Visions across a Century* (Alton: Dance Books, 2007).

Kalb, Jonathan, *The Theater of Heiner Müller* (New York: Limelight Editions, 1998).

Kelleher, Joe and Ridout, Nick (eds), *Contemporary Theatres in Europe: A Critical Companion* (London: Routledge, 2006).

Kendall, Elizabeth, *Balanchine and the Lost Muse: Revolution and the Making of a Choreographer* (Oxford: Oxford University Press, 2013).

Kiebuzinska, Christine, *Revolutionaries in the Theater: Meyerhold, Brecht, and Witkiewicz* (Ann Arbor: UMI Research Press, 1988).

Kumiega, Jennifer, *The Theatre of Grotowski* (London: Methuen, 1985).

Lamont, Rosette, 'The Metaphysical Farce: Beckett and Ionesco', *The French Review*, vol. 32, no. 4 (February 1959), pp. 319–28.

Langston, Richard, *Visions of Violence: German Avant-Gardes after Fascism* (Evanston, IL: Northwestern University Press, 2008).

Leafstedt, Carl Stuart, *Inside Bluebeard's Castle: Music and Drama in Béla Bartok's Opera* (New York: Oxford University Press, 1999).

Lehmann, Hans-Thies, trans. Jürs-Munby, Karen, *Postdramatic Theatre* (New York: Routledge, 2006).

Lepecki, André (ed.), *On the Presence of the Body: Essays on Dance and Performance Theory* (Middletown, CT: Wesleyan University Press, 2004).

Lesschaeve, Jacqueline, 'Robert Wilson: réponses', *Tel Quel*, no. 71–3 (Autumn 1997), pp. 217–25.

Linsel, Anne, 'Pina Bauschs Wildgruber', *K.West* (December 2008), <http://www.kulturwest.de/buehne/detailseite/artikel/pina-bauschs-wildgruber/> (last accessed 6 October 2017).

Loney, Glenn, 'I Pick My Dancers as People', *On The Next Wave*, vol. 3, no. 1–2 (October 1985), pp. 14–19.

Mackintosh, Fiona (ed.), *The Ancient Dancer in the Modern World* (Oxford: Oxford University Press, 2010).

McMillan, Dougald and Fehsenfeld, Martha, *Beckett in the Theatre: The Author as Practical Playwright and Director* (London: Riverrun Press, 1988).

McMullan, Anna, *Performing Embodiment in Samuel Beckett's Drama* (New York: Routledge, 2010).

Manning, Susan, 'An American Perspective on Tanztheater', *TDR: The Drama Review*, vol. 30, no. 2 (Summer 1986), pp. 57–79.

——, 'German Rites: A History of Le Sacre du Printemps on the German Stage', *Dance Chronicle*, vol. 14, no. 2/3 (1991), pp. 129–58.

——, *Ecstasy and the Demon: Feminism and Nationalism in the Dances of Mary Wigman* (Berkeley: University of California Press, 1993).

——, 'Pina Bausch: 1940-2009', *TDR: The Drama Review*, vol. 54, no. 1 (Spring 2010), pp. 10–13.

Mariani, Evi, 'Dancing and Making it in the World', *Jakarta Post* (9 August 2012), <http://www.thejakartapost.com/news/2012/08/09/dancing-and-making-it-world.html> (last accessed 6 October 2017).

Marranca, Bonnie, 'The Forest as Archive: Wilson and Interculturalism', *Performing Arts Journal*, vol. 11, no. 3 (1989), pp. 36–44.

Marranca, Bonnie and Dasgupta, Gautam (eds), *Interculturalism and Performance: Writings from PAJ* (New York: PAJ Publications, 1991).

Martin, Mick, 'Theatre of Cruelty: Artaud's Impossible Double', *Nottingham French Studies*, vol. 22, no. 1 (1983), pp. 52–64.

Mercier, Vivian, 'The Uneventful Event', *The Irish Times* (18 February 1956), p. 6.

Meyer, Marion, *Pina Bausch: Tanz kann fast alles sein* (Remscheid: Bergischer Verlag, 2012).

Michaelis, Rolf, 'Tanzangst. Angsttanz', *Die Zeit* (6 June 1997), <http://www.zeit.de/1997/24/Tanzangst_Angsttanz> (last accessed 6 October 2017).

Mitra, Royona, *Akram Khan: Dancing New Interculturalism* (New York: Palgrave Macmillan, 2015).

Mitter, Shomit, *Systems of Rehearsal: Stanislavsky, Brecht, Grotowski, and Brook* (London: Routledge, 1992).

Morfee, Adrian, *Antonin Artaud's Writing Bodies* (Oxford: Clarendon, 2005).

Mori, Naoya, 'Beckett's Windows and the Windowless Self', *Samuel Beckett Today/Aujourd'hui*, vol. 14 (2004), pp. 357–70.

Mozingo, Karen, 'The Haunting of Bluebeard: While Listening to a Recording of Béla Bartók's Opera "Duke Bluebeard's Castle"', *Dance Research Journal*, vol. 37, no. 1 (Summer 2005), pp. 94–106.

Müller, Hedwig, *Mary Wigman: Leben und Werk der großen Tänzerin* (Weinheim: Quadriga Verlag, 1986).

Müller, Heiner, *Rotwelsch* (Berlin: Merve Verlag, 1982).

——, *Krieg ohne Schlacht: Leben in Zwei Diktaturen* (Cologne: Kiepenheuer and Witsch, 1994).

Mulrooney, Deirdre, *Orientalism, Orientation, and the Nomadic Work of Pina Bausch* (Frankfurt am Main: Peter Lang, 2002).

Mumford, Meg, 'Pina Bausch Choreographs *Blaubart:* A Transgressive or Regressive Act?' *German Life and Letters*, vol. 57, no. 1 (January 2004), pp. 44–57.

Murray, Simon and Keefe, John (eds), *Physical Theatres: A Critical Introduction* (London: Routledge, 2007).

Nelson, Maggie, *The Art of Cruelty: A Reckoning* (New York: W. W. Norton & Co., 2011).

Pinckney, Darryl, 'Tensions and Nostalgias: Berlin Days with Robert Wilson and Heiner Müller', *Salmagundi*, no. 144/145 (Fall 2004 – Winter 2005), pp. 145–55.

Price, David, 'The Politics of the Body: Pina Bausch's "Tanztheater"', *Theatre Journal*, vol. 42, no. 3 (October 1990), pp. 322–31.

Ramone, Jenni, *Postcolonial Theories* (Basingstoke: Palgrave Macmillan, 2011).

Regitz, Hartmut (ed.) *Tanz in Deutschland: Ballett seit 1945: eine Situationsbeschreibung* (Berlin: Quadriga, 1984).

Richards, Thomas, *At Work with Grotowski on Physical Actions* (London: Routledge, 1995).

Riding, Alan, 'Using Muscles Classical Ballet Has No Need For', *The New York Times* (15 June 1997), <http://www.nytimes.com/1997/06/15/arts/using-muscles-classical-ballet-has-no-need-for.html> (last accessed 6 October 2017).

Rutherford, Jonathan, *Identity: Community, Culture, Difference* (London: Lawrence & Wishart, 1990).

Said, Edward, *Orientalism* (New York: Pantheon Books, 1978).

Sawyer, Elizabeth, 'Antony Tudor and English Theater', *Dance Chronicle*, vol. 34, no. 2 (2011), pp. 217–36.

Schechner, Richard, *Performance Studies: An Introduction* (second edition) (New York: Routledge, 2006).

Schlicher, Susanne, *TanzTheater: Traditionen und Freiheiten Pina Bausch, Gerhard Bohner, Reinhild Hoffmann, Hans Kresnik, Susanne Linke* (Reinbek: Rowohlt-Taschenbuch-Verlag, 1987).

Schmidt, Jochen, *Tanztheater in Deutschland* (Frankfurt am Main: Propyläen, 1992).

——, 'Ballet after the fall from Grace', *Ballett International/Tanz Aktuell*, vol. 19, no. 8 (August 1996), pp. 20–5.

Schulze-Reuber, Rika, *Das Tanztheater Pina Bausch: Spiegel der Gesellschaft* (Frankfurt am Main: Fischer, 2005).

Schwaiger, Liz, 'Performing One's Age: Cultural Constructions of Aging and Embodiment in Western Theatrical Dancers', *Dance Research Journal*, vol. 37, no. 1 (Summer 2005) pp. 107–20.

Schwarzer, Alice, 'Ein Stück für Pina Bausch', *Emma* (January 2010) <http://www.emma.de/node/264664> (last accessed 6 October 2017).

Servos, Norbert, trans. Morris, Stephen, *Pina Bausch: Dance Theatre* (Munich: K. Kieser, 2007).

Servos, Norbert and Müller, Hedwig, *Pina Bausch – Wuppertal Dance Theater, or, the Art of Training a Goldfish: Excursions into Dance* (Köln: Ballett-Bühnen-Verlag, 1984).

Severini, Carlo, trans. Fonkoue, Ramon and Cheng, Joyce Suechun, 'Primitivist Empathy', *Art in Translation*, vol. 4, no. 1 (2012), pp. 99–130.

Siegmund, Gerald, *Abwesenheit: Eine performative Ästhetik des Tanzes: William Forsythe, Jérôme Bel, Xavier le Roy, Meg Stuart* (Bielefeld: Transcript, 2006).

Soares, Janet Mansfield, *Louis Horst: Musician in a Dancer's World* (Durham, NC: Duke University Press, 1992).

Sokolova, Lydia, ed. Buckle, Richard, *Dancing for Diaghilev: The Memoirs of Lydia Sokolova* (London: Murray, 1960).

Sorell, Walter, *Mary Wigman: Ein Vermächtnis* (Wilhelmshaven: F. Noetzel, 1986).

Sörgel, Sabine, *Dance and the Body in Western Theatre: 1948 to the Present* (New York: Palgrave Macmillan, 2015).

Stamp Miller, Ann, *The Cultural Politics of the German Democratic Republic: The Voices of Wolf Biermann, Christa Wolf, and Heiner Müller* (Boca Raton: BrownWalker Press, 2004).

Tallon, Mary Elizabeth, 'Appia's Theatre at Hellerau', *Theatre Journal*, vol. 36, no. 4 (December 1984), pp. 495–504.

Taxidou, Olga, *Modernism and Performance: Jarry to Brecht* (Basingstoke: Palgrave Macmillan, 2007).

Toepfer, Karl, *Empire of Ecstasy: Nudity and Movement in German Body Culture 1910–1935* (Berkeley: University of California Press, 1997).

Tsushima, Michiko, '"Memory is the Belly of the Mind": Augustine's Concept of Memory in Beckett', *Samuel Beckett Today / Aujourd'hui*, vol. 19 (2008), pp. 123–32.

Van Praagh, Peggy, 'Working with Antony Tudor', *Dance Research: The Journal of the Society for Dance Research*, vol. 2, no. 2 (Summer 1984), pp. 56–67.

Vork, Robert, 'The Things No One Can Say: The Unspeakable Act in Artaud's *Les Cenci*', *Modern Drama*, vol. 56, no. 3 (Fall 2013), pp. 306–26.

Wagenbach, Marc (ed.) *Inheriting Dance: An Invitation from Pina* (Bielefeld: Transcript, 2014).

Wainwright, Steven and Turner, Bryan, '"Just Crumbling to Bits"? An Exploration of the Body, Ageing, Injury and Career in Classical Ballet Dancers', *Sociology*, vol. 40, no. 2 (April 2006), pp. 237–55.

Walther, Susanne, *The Dance of Death: Kurt Jooss and the Weimar Years* (Chur: Harwood Academic Publishers, 1994).

Weir, Lucy, 'Abject Modernism: Interpreting the Postwar Male Body in the Works of Tatsumi Hijikata, Günter Brus and Rudolf Schwarzkogler', *Tate Papers*, no. 23 (Spring, 2015), <http://www.tate.org.uk/research/publications/tate-papers/23/abject-modernism-the-male-body-in-the-work-of-tatsumi-hijikata-gunter-brus-and-rudolf-schwarzkogler> (last accessed 6 October 2017).

Weiss, Katherine, 'Beckett's "Happy Days": Rewinding and Revolving Histories', *South Atlantic Review*, vol. 75, no. 4 (Fall 2010), pp. 37–50.

Wiegand, Chris, 'The Sound of Pina Bausch', *The Guardian* (24 August 2014), <https://www.theguardian.com/stage/2014/aug/24/pina-bausch-music-sweet-mambo-tanztheater-wuppertal> (last accessed 6 October 2017).

——, 'Let's Tanz: Pina Bausch's Wuppertal Dancers on Her Unearthed 80s Creations', *The Guardian* (7 April 2015), <https://www.theguardian.com/stage/2015/apr/07/pina-bausch-wuppertal-dancers-ahnen-gebirge-sadlers-wells> (last accessed 6 October 2017).

Witkiewicz, Stanisław, ed. and trans. Gerould, David, *Country House* (London: Routledge, 2004).

Whitelaw, Billie, *Billie Whitelaw ... Who He?* (London: Hodder and Stoughton, 1995).

REVIEWS

Bain, Alice, 'Sweet Mambo – an exquisite love letter to Pina Bausch' *The Observer* (24 August 2014), <https://www.theguardian.com/stage/2014/aug/24/edinburgh-festival-2014-review-sweet-mambo-pina-bausch> (last accessed 6 October 2017).

Brunel, Lise 'Pina Bausch chez Shakespeare: Macbeth ou l'absurdité du monde', *Les Saisons nouvelles de la danse*, no. 214 (June 1990), pp. 12–13.

Cheng, Germaine, 'Carnations on Shaky Ground', *The Straits Times* (15 October 2016), <http://www.straitstimes.com/lifestyle/arts/carnations-on-shaky-ground> (last accessed 6 October 2017).

Croce, Arlene, Jowitt, Deborah, Kisselgoff, Anna, Bernheimer, Martin and Kriegsman, Alan, 'Pina Bausch in America', *Ballett International/Tanz Aktuell*, vol. 7, no. 11 (November 1984), pp. 14–18.

Donkin, Ellen and Blair, Rhonda, 'The Seven Deadly Sins', *Women &*

Performance: A Journal of Feminist Theory, vol. 3, no. 1 (1985), pp. 116–17.

Ebrahimian, Babak, 'Mascura Fogo', *Theatre Journal*, vol. 54, no. 4 (December 2002), pp. 653–4.

Kahn, Judy, 'The Paul Sansardo Dance Company: Saratoga Performing Arts Center, August 13, 1972', *Dance Magazine* (October 1972), p. 86.

Kisselgoff, Anna, 'Pina Bausch Adds Humor to Her Palette', *The New York Times* (17 July 1988), <http://www.nytimes.com/1988/07/17/arts/dance-view-pina-bausch-adds-humor-to-her-palette.html> (last accessed 6 October 2017).

——, 'Sun, Surf and Sexuality in a Pina Bausch Romp', *The New York Times* (8 November 2001), <http://www.nytimes.com/2001/11/08/arts/dance-review-sun-surf-and-sexuality-in-a-pina-bausch-romp.html> (last accessed 6 October 2017).

Koegler, Horst, 'Germany [reviews]', *Dance and Dancers* (June 1974), pp. 52–4.

——, 'Germany: Season's Round Up', *Dance and Dancers* (November 1975), pp. 35–6.

Macauley, Alastair, 'Meat and Veg', *The Times Literary Supplement* (4 March 2005), p. 16.

——, 'Squeezing All the Love out of a Love Story: Pina Bausch's "Orpheus and Eurydice" from Paris Opera Ballet', *The New York Times* (22 July 2012), <http://www.nytimes.com/2012/07/23/arts/dance/pina-bauschs-orpheus-and-eurydice-from-paris-opera-ballet.html> (last accessed 6 October 2017).

Mackrell, Judith, 'Tanztheater Wuppertal – Vollmond', *The Guardian* (26 February 2013), <https://www.theguardian.com/stage/2013/feb/26/tanztheater-wuppertal-vollmond-review> (last accessed 6 October 2017).

Perlmutter, Donna, 'Reviews: *Café Müller*', *Dance Magazine*, vol. 58, no. 9 (1984), pp. 34–5.

Schlagenwerth, Michaela, 'Nicht eins, nicht zwei sein können: Pina Bausch gastiert mit *Frülingsopfer* und *Café Müller* in Berlin', *Berliner Zeitung* (25 September 1999), <http://www.berliner-zeitung.de/pina-bausch-gastiert-mit--fruehlingsopfer--und--caf%C3%A9-mueller--in-berlin-nicht-eins--nicht-zwei-sein-koennen-16523608> (last accessed 6 October 2017).

Schmidt, Jochen, 'Return to Wuppertal, Eleven Years Later . . . Pina Bausch's "He Takes Her by the Hand"', *Ballett International/Tanz Aktuell*, vol. 12, no. 6 (June 1989), p. 44.

Servos, Norbert, 'Und dann hat Pina gesagt . . . Pina Bauschs "Walzer" beim Holland Festival', *Ballett International/Tanz Aktuell*, vol. 5, no. 8/9 (August/September 1982), pp. 18–21.

Siegel, Marcia, 'Carabosse in a Cocktail Dress', *The Hudson Review*, vol. 39, no. 1 (Spring 1986), pp. 108–12.

——, 'Re-Radicalizing Graham', *The Hudson Review*, vol. 48, no. 1 (Spring 1995), pp. 101–7.

Suchy, Melanie, 'Der Tanz ist aufgegangen', *Die Zeit* (18 May 2006), <http://www.zeit.de/2006/21/P_Bausch_neu_xml> (last accessed 6 October 2017).

UNPUBLISHED SOURCES

Sturm, Robert, 'Illustrated talk on the work of Pina Bausch', University of Glasgow (24 March 2011).

Wigman, Mary, 'Aus Hellerau', Akademie der Künste, Berlin, Mary Wigman-Archiv, no. 529.

FILMOGRAPHY

Archival footage (courtesy of the Tanztheater Wuppertal Pina Bausch archive)

1980: Ein Stück von Pina Bausch, Schauspielhaus Wuppertal, 19 October 2001.

Arien, location unknown, 2 November 1982.

Auf dem Gebirge hat man ein Geschrei gehört, Opernhaus Wuppertal, 16 December 1995.

Blaubart, Schauspielhaus Wuppertal, 31 August 1986.

Kontakthof, Venice, 16 June 1985.

Nelken, Schauspielhaus Wuppertal, 4 October 2008.

Viktor, Wuppertal, 10 December 1994.

Walzer, location unknown, date unknown.

PUBLISHED FOOTAGE

Café Müller – Tanztheater Wuppertal, directed by Rach, Herbert (Paris: L'Arche, 2010).

Coffee with Pina, directed by Yanor, Lee (Bonn: Goethe-Institut, 2004).

Dancing Dreams, directed by Hoffmann, Rainer (New York: First Run Features, 2010).

European Tanztheater: An Overview of its Past and Present, directed by Bergsohn, Harold (Pennington: Dance Horizons Video, 1997).

Orpheus and Eurydice, directed by Bataillon, Vincent (Paris: Bel Air, 2009).

Pina Bausch, directed by Linsel, Anne (Cologne: WDR, 2006).

Pina, directed by Wenders, Wim (London: Artificial Eye, 2011).

The Rite of Spring – Tanztheater Wuppertal, directed by Weyrich, Pit (Mainz: ZDF, 1978).

Sacre, directed by Weyrich, Pit (Mainz: ZDF, 1978).

Sacre: Probe (Paris: L'Arche Éditeur, 2013).

Un jour Pina a demandé ... directed by Akerman (London: A2 RM/Arts, 1999).

Walzer (Paris: L'Arche Éditeur, 2012).

INDEX